Perspectives on Behavioural Interventions in Palliative and End-of-Life Care

The challenges faced by individuals and families at the end of life are still incredibly diverse, and many behavioural interventions and clinical approaches have been developed to address this great diversity of experiences in the face of dying and death, helping providers to care for their clients. *Perspectives on Behavioural Interventions in Palliative and End-of-Life Care* is an accessible resource that collates and explores interventions that can be used to address a wide range of behavioural, psychological, social and spiritual issues that arise when people are facing advanced chronic or life-limiting illness.

With perspectives from experienced clinicians, providers, and caregivers from around the world, this book offers a strong foundation in contemporary evidence-based practice alongside seasoned practice insights from the field. Its chapters explore:

- Interventions to enhance communication and decision making
- The management of physical and mental health symptoms
- Meaning-Centred Psychotherapy for cancer patients
- Dignity Therapy
- Interventions embracing cultural diversity and intersectionality.

Together with *Perspectives on Palliative and End-of-Life Care: Disease, Social and Cultural Context*, the book provides a foundation for collaborative international and interprofessional work by providing state-of science information on behavioural interventions addressing mental health and wellness. It is of interest to academics, researchers and postgraduates in the fields of mental health, medicine, psychology and social work, and is essential reading for healthcare providers and trainees from psychosocial and palliative medicine, social work and nursing.

Rebecca S. Allen is Professor of Psychology at the Alabama Research Institute on Aging and the Department of Psychology, the University of Alabama, USA.

Brian D. Carpenter is Professor of Psychological & Brain Sciences, Washington University, St. Louis, USA.

Morgan K. Eichorst is a clinical psychologist working within the Veterans Affairs Medical Center, USA.

Aging and Mental Health Research
Series Editor: Martin Orrell

In the 21st century, the world's aging population is growing more rapidly than ever before. This is driving the international research agenda to help older people live better for longer and to find the causes and cures for chronic diseases such as dementia. This series provides a forum for the rapidly expanding field by investigating the relationship between the aging process and mental health. It compares and contrasts scientific and service developments across a range of settings, including the mental changes associated with normal and abnormal or pathological aging, as well as the psychological and psychiatric problems of the aging population. The series encourages an integrated approach between biopsychosocial models and etiological factors to promote better strategies, therapies and services for older people. Creating a strong alliance between the theoretical, experimental and applied sciences, the series provides an original and dynamic focus, integrating the normal and abnormal aspects of mental health in aging so that theoretical issues can be set in the context of important new practical developments in this field.

In this series

Cognitive Stimulation Therapy for Dementia
History, Evolution and Internationalism
Edited by Lauren A. Yates, Jen Yates, Martin Orrell,
Aimee Spector, and Bob Woods

Perspectives on Behavioural Interventions
in Palliative and End-of-Life Care
Edited by Rebecca S. Allen, Brian D. Carpenter and
Morgan K. Eichorst

Perspectives on Palliative and End-of-Life Care
Disease, Social and Cultural Context
Edited by Rebecca S. Allen, Brian D. Carpenter and
Morgan K. Eichorst

For more information about the series, please visit www.routledge.com/Aging-and-Mental-Health-Research/book-series/AMHR.

Perspectives on Behavioural Interventions in Palliative and End-of-Life Care

Edited by Rebecca S. Allen,
Brian D. Carpenter and
Morgan K. Eichorst

Routledge
Taylor & Francis Group

LONDON AND NEW YORK

First published 2018
by Routledge
2 Park Square, Milton Park, Abingdon, Oxon OX14 4RN

and by Routledge
711 Third Avenue, New York, NY 10017

Routledge is an imprint of the Taylor & Francis Group, an informa business

British Library Cataloguing-in-Publication Data
A catalogue record for this book is available from the British Library

Library of Congress Cataloging-in-Publication Data
Names: Allen, Rebecca S., editor. | Carpenter, Brian D., editor. |
    Eichorst, Morgan K., editor.
Title: Perspectives on behavioural interventions in palliative and
    end-of-life care / edited by Rebecca S. Allen, Brian D. Carpenter
    and Morgan K. Eichorst.
Description: Abingdon, Oxon ; New York, NY : Routledge, 2018. |
    Includes bibliographical references.
Identifiers: LCCN 2018003043 | ISBN 9780415791526 (hbk) |
    ISBN 9781315212265 (ebk)
Subjects: LCSH: Terminal care—Psychological aspects. |
    Terminally ill—Psychology. | Palliative treatment.
Classification: LCC R726.8 P4716 2018 | DDC 616.02/9—dc23
LC record available at https://lccn.loc.gov/2018003043

ISBN: 978-0-4157-9152-6 (hbk)
ISBN: 978-1-315-21226-5 (ebk)

Typeset in Bembo
by Apex CoVantage, LLC

Contents

Contributors

Rebecca S. Allen (Ph.D., ABPP) is Professor of Psychology at the Alabama Research Institute on Aging and the Department of Psychology at the University of Alabama, USA. Her research and clinical interests are: 1) interventions to reduce the stress of individuals, family, and professional caregivers within the context of advanced chronic or terminal illness; 2) the cultural dynamics (race/ethnicity; rural/urban) of healthcare decision making; and 3) clinical training issues, particularly ethics, LGBTQ+ issues, and acceptance and commitment therapy. She has published on translation of end-of-life/dignity interventions, diversity in advance care planning, clinical training, behavioral interventions in long-term care, and mental health among aging prisoners. Dr. Allen is a member of the American Board of Geropsychology, a member of the APA Working Group on End-of-Life Issues and Care, a Fellow of the Gerontological Society of America and the APA, and is Editor for the Americas of *Aging and Mental Health.*

Gary Annable is a Research Officer in the Research Institute in Oncology and Hematology located at CancerCare Manitoba in Winnipeg, Canada.

William Breitbart (MD) is Chairman, the Jimmie C. Holland Chair in Psychiatric Oncology, Department of Psychiatry & Behavioral Sciences, Memorial Sloan Kettering Cancer Center, New York, USA. He is the recipient of Lifetime Achievement Awards from the International Psycho-oncology Society, the Academy of Psychosomatic Medicine, the American Psychosocial Oncology Society, and the American Cancer Society. Dr. Breitbart's research efforts focus on psychiatric aspects of cancer and palliative care. His most recent efforts focus on Meaning-Centered Psychotherapy for cancer patients. He has had continuous NIH RO1 funding of investigator-initiated research since 1989. Dr. Breitbart was PI of the Network Project, NCI R25 grant (1992–1998), which trained clinicians in cancer pain management and psycho-oncology. He is currently PI of R25 CA190169, which is training a national cohort of cancer care clinicians in Meaning-Centered Psychotherapy. He has over 400 peer reviewed publications, chapters, and review papers, and 12 textbooks, including: *Psycho-oncology − 1st,*

2nd, and 3rd Editions; the treatment manuals for *Meaning-Centered Group Psychotherapy in Advanced Cancer Patients*, and *Individual Meaning-Centered Psychotherapy for Patients with Advanced Cancer;* and *Meaning-Centered Psychotherapy in the Cancer Setting* from Oxford University Press. Dr. Breitbart is Editor-in-Chief of Cambridge University Press's palliative care journal entitled *Palliative & Supportive Care*.

Keisha D. Carden (MA) is a fourth-year graduate student in Clinical Geropsychology at the University of Alabama, USA, working under the mentorship of Dr. Rebecca S. Allen. Her primary research interests include: family caregiving for older adults (with and without cognitive impairment/ Alzheimer's disease and dementia); resilience; existential/death anxiety; intergenerational relationships; and outcomes and treatment mechanisms of non-pharmacological interventions that incorporate aspects of positive affect maximization, empathy, meaning in life optimization, and mindfulness.

Brian D. Carpenter (Ph.D.) is Professor of Psychological & Brain Sciences, Washington University, St. Louis, USA. His research, clinical, and teaching interests focus on family relationships later in life, particularly at the end of life, with an emphasis on effective collaboration and communication among patients, their care partners, and healthcare providers.

Harvey Max Chochinov (MD) is a Distinguished Professor of Psychiatry at the University of Manitoba and a Senior Scientist at the Research Institute in Oncology and Hematology at CancerCare Manitoba, Canada. He held the only Canada Research Chair in Palliative Care from 2002–2017, and was named an Officer of the Order of Canada in 2015. His most recent book, *Dignity Therapy: Final Words for Final Days*, is published by Oxford University Press and was the 2012 winner of the American Publishers' Association Prose Award for Clinical Medicine.

Hillary R. Dorman (BA) is a second-year graduate student in Clinical Geropsychology at the University of Alabama, USA, working under the mentorship of Dr. Rebecca S. Allen. Hillary's primary research interest focuses upon the promotion of late life resilience utilizing a biopsychosocial and ecological framework. She is also interested in end-of-life care, underscoring the importance of choice, autonomy, and communication.

Morgan K. Eichorst (Ph.D.) is a clinical psychologist working within the Veterans Affairs Medical Center, USA.

Toni L. Glover's (Ph.D.) program of research focuses on aging, pain, and palliative care. Her goal is to provide older adults that suffer with chronic or serious illness, especially those who are the most vulnerable, with comprehensive, high-quality, person-centered care that is consistent with their goals and values and honors their dignity. Dr. Glover mentors students in palliative and end-of-life nursing care.

Ann L. Horgas (RN, Ph.D.) is an Associate Professor and Chair of the Biobehavioral Nursing Science Department in the College of Nursing at the University of Florida, USA. Dr. Horgas is an internationally recognized expert in the field of gerontological nursing, focusing on pain, dementia, and palliative care. She is a Fellow of the Gerontological Society of America and the American Academy of Nursing.

Melissa Masterson (MA) is a doctoral candidate at Fordham University, USA, in the Clinical Psychology program. She is a student research affiliate at Memorial Sloan Kettering Cancer Center. She has served as an interventionist on several randomized controlled trials of Meaning-Centered Psychotherapy for both cancer patients and other populations (i.e., bereaved parents).

Lee H. Matthews (Ph.D., ABPP, ABAP) is a Consulting Psychologist for the Akula Foundation, New Orleans, USA. He is a licensed neuropsychologist. He is Board Certified in Clinical Psychology and in Assessment Psychology. He has been involved with the Foundation for 10 years. He previously served as Director, Grief Resource Center, a program founded following Hurricanes Katrina and Rita in 2006 to provide outpatient services for the community and professional education on clinical treatment for depression, anxiety disorder, PTSD and other emotional difficulties. He has served as Chair, Louisiana State Board of Examiners of Psychologists. He was named 2014 Distinguished Psychologist of the Year by the Louisiana Psychological Association. Since 2000 he has co-authored six book chapters on graduate training, undergraduate training and psychotherapy; and six journal articles on personality assessment and licensing, neuropsychology, professional life after a natural disaster, and adolescence psychology. He is co-owner of a private practice, Psychological Resources, PC, with his wife, Dr. Janet R. Matthews. He is on Clinical Faculty at two university medical centers, and consultant to five area hospitals or treatment centers.

Susan McClement (RN, Ph.D.) is a Professor in the College of Nursing at the University of Manitoba in Winnipeg, Canada. Her program of research includes studies about the psychosocial dimensions of cancer-anorexia-cachexia, ethics in end-of-life care, and expert care of the dying in acute and long-term care settings.

Meghan McDarby (BS) completed her undergraduate training at Cornell University Department of Human Development and is currently a graduate student in the Department of Psychological and Brain Sciences at Washington University in St. Louis, USA. Her research focuses on family relationships at the end of life, methods to enhance the advanced care planning experience, and improving communication between providers and patients regarding palliative care services.

Kaleb Murry (BS) is a doctoral student in Clinical Psychology at the University of Alabama, USA, where he specializes in the study of geropsychology.

His specific research interests include evaluating the efficacy of LGBTQ diversity training initiatives within clinical training programs, community-based participatory research, and mental health disparities among LGBTQ and ethnic minority populations.

Barry Rosenfeld (Ph.D.) is Professor and Chair of the Department of Psychology at Fordham University, USA. He has published widely on a range of topics that encompass health and legal psychology, including an award-winning book on physician assisted suicide. For the past 25 years, he has maintained an active collaboration with colleagues at the Memorial Sloan Kettering Cancer Center, where he has been principal investigator or co-PI of numerous federally funded research studies addressing desire for hastened death, medical treatment decision-making, the assessment of psychological functioning at the end of life, and the effectiveness of interventions to alleviate existential despair.

Kristy Shoji (Ph.D.) obtained her doctorate degree in Clinical Psychology with an emphasis in geropsychology from the University of Alabama-Tuscaloosa, USA. She then completed a geropsychology internship and fellowship at the South Texas Veterans Health Care System. Dr. Shoji is currently a staff geropsychologist at the South Texas VA working with the palliative care consult team and the hospice unit of the community living center.

Genevieve Thompson (RN, Ph.D.) is an Associate Professor in the College of Nursing at the University of Manitoba in Winnipeg, Canada. Dr. Thompson's program of research aims to improve the care of persons living and dying in long-term care settings. Dr. Thompson is a CIHR New Investigator (2013–2018), was the recipient of the Canadian Association for Nursing Research – Outstanding New Investigator Award in 2012, and was awarded the Excellence in Professional Nursing Award (Nursing Research) from the College of Registered Nurses of Manitoba in 2011.

Chapter 1

The international context of behavioural palliative and end-of-life care

Biopsychosocial and lifespan perspectives

Rebecca S. Allen, Brian D. Carpenter, and Morgan K. Eichorst

Palliative care is defined by the World Health Organization (WHO) as meeting the physical, psychosocial, and religious/spiritual needs of patients with life-limiting, terminal, or advanced chronic or progressive illness, as well as the needs of their families and caregivers, through an interprofessional team (World Health Organization, 2002). Although the WHO definition clearly delineates psychosocial needs as squarely within the purview of palliative care, certain professions and their treatment approaches (e.g., psychology) have been largely absent in most palliative care settings (Haley, Larson, Kasl-Godley, Neimeyer, & Kwilosz, 2003; Kasl-Godley, King, & Quill, 2014). Similarly, the 2014 Institute of Medicine (IOM) report on Dying in America defined palliative care as "relief from pain and other symptoms, that supports quality of life, and that supports patients with serious advanced illness and their families". The IOM definition does not specifically mention psychosocial needs and largely omits reference to the potential role of psychologists. The emphasis on supporting quality of life among patients and families, however, focuses greater attention on *behavioural* health issues and needs that may be addressed by psychologists and other behavioural health professionals (e.g., social workers) within the palliative care setting.

The question may be asked, "What is meant by psychosocial needs or behavioral health issues?" Recent systematic reviews (Candy, Jones, Drake, Leurent, & King, 2009; Keall, Clayton, & Butow, 2014; Singer et al., 2016) identify critical gaps in evidence and practice pertaining to behavioural health strategies that may be used to address psychosocial issues within palliative and end-of-life care, including: 1) the need for greater understanding of the role of palliative care among the public and professionals; 2) the need for focus on underserved and under-resourced, potentially high-risk populations; 3) improved communication between patients and family care providers regarding values and treatment preferences; and 4) the value of home services provided either in person or via telemedicine and telehealth. Therefore, behavioural mental health and wellness interventions within the context of palliative and end-of-life care may be defined as directly addressing psychosocial issues that arise and may reflect conflicts of cognition, emotion, and communication both within the individual and within the interpersonal and environmental care context.

This chapter reviews the history of hospice and the palliative care movement and describes theoretical models relevant to behavioural intervention delivery. We describe complexities of conducting intervention research with individuals and families near the end of life. Given the international perspective of this book, we emphasize diversity and intersectionality among individuals and families across practice settings and the course of palliative and end-of-life care. Finally, this introductory chapter ends with an overview of content within this book.

History of the hospice and the palliative care movement

The hospice movement is based on a holistic view of human nature and the fundamental idea that not only physical but also psychological, social, spiritual, and existential suffering may impede a satisfactory quality of life for the dying individual and his/her family. The modern hospice concept was developed by Cicely Saunders, who worked as a social worker, nurse, and, later, a physician in the United Kingdom. Early in her career as a nurse and social worker, Saunders identified several areas for improvement of the treatment of dying patients, such as telling patients about the terminality of their condition; better pain relief; attention to spiritual, emotional, and social needs; and the right to die peacefully (Clark, 1998, 1999). In 1963, prior to the establishment of the first hospice, Saunders traveled to the United States to discuss her ideas about hospice care and soon encountered Florence Wald, who was then the Dean of the Yale School of Nursing (Siebold, 1992). Wald later aided in the founding of the first United States hospice. Around this same time in the U.S., the psychiatrist Elisabeth Kübler-Ross published her book *On Death and Dying* (1969), with interviews of dying patients. This book had international influence and helped to shape people's attitudes about transitions to death (Milicevic, 2002). Saunders, Kübler-Ross, and Wald contributed to the development of the modern hospice movement in the United States, Canada, and Europe. The hospice movement spread apace in Westernized cultures (e.g., Australia) but then lagged behind in other countries and cultures (e.g., Asia, Africa).

During the 21st century, the term palliative care has emerged as a distinct, complementary model of care in comparison with hospice (Kelly & Morrison, 2015). Palliative care encompasses all phases of advanced chronic illness and may be initiated at the time of diagnosis and provided concurrently with other disease-related or curative treatments. In many countries worldwide, the palliative care movement has experienced exponential growth. A barrier to systematic and high-quality provision of palliative care remains a lack of understanding by providers as well as the general public about what this treatment model involves. Currently, many providers consider palliative care synonymous with hospice, and community-dwelling adults are unfamiliar with the term.

Unfortunately, direct attention to mental and behavioural health within palliative and hospice care systems has lagged behind its recognition and alleviation of physical, and perhaps even spiritual, symptoms. This seems to be true despite the holistic nature of palliative care, and despite the pervasive psychosocial needs of individuals and families near the end of life. Reasons for this include misperceptions of the potential role of disciplines such as psychology, challenges in reimbursement of all team members, and the nonconcurrent timing regarding delineation of competencies within each profession (Haley et al., 2003). For example, psychology has lagged behind medicine, nursing, and social work in establishing educational curricula and clinical competencies necessary for work in palliative and end-of-life care. In order to address the lack of clinical competencies for psychologists, Kasl-Godley and colleagues (Kasl-Godley et al., 2014) describe the work of psychologists practicing in primary care settings wherein palliative care may be provided. These authors provide case illustration to enrich their discussion of needed competencies for work in palliative care. These competencies include but are not limited to knowledge of: 1) the biological aspects of illness and the dying process, 2) normal versus abnormal grief and bereavement, 3) communication and advance care planning, 4) assessment, 5) intervention, 6) family treatment, and 7) work in multidisciplinary, interdisciplinary, and transdisciplinary treatment teams. These competencies are, of course, shared by other behavioural and mental health professionals. However, psychologists also may bring unique theoretical knowledge, expertise in program evaluation, and other research skills into intervention design and delivery across wide ranging disease and treatment contexts. Foundational knowledge in the biopsychosocial model, as well as developmental and stress and coping theories, may guide treatment and facilitate the functioning of and communication within interprofessional teams.

The biopsychosocial-spiritual model

In his 2002 article using methods of philosophical anthropology to describe a biopsychosocial-spiritual model of care at the end of life, Sulmasy stated:

> Having cracked the genetic code has not led us to understand who human beings are, what suffering and death mean, what may stand as a source of hope, what we mean by death with dignity, or what we may learn from dying persons.

(p. 25)

The cornerstone of this model is the premise that individuals are innately spiritual, as many individuals search for transcendent meaning, perhaps particularly near the end of life. Sulmasy elaborates upon Engel's (1977) original biopsychosocial model by adding spirituality and explaining the importance of additional propositions. First, Sulmasy posits that all individuals exist as beings in relationship; sickness therefore is a disruption of right relationships within and outside of the individual. These relationships exist in interpersonal, social, and transcendent contexts. Second, Sulmasy suggests that healing involves the whole person and restores that which may be restored even when this does not restore perfect wholeness or health. Sulmasy proposes assessing four domains as necessary in the measurement of healing, including religiosity, spiritual/religious coping, spiritual well-being, and spiritual need. The logic of this expanded model fits well in the consideration of psychosocial and behavioural interventions within the context of palliative and end-of-life care. During this period of life, mental health and wellness frequently entail grappling with existential distress, sadness, anxiety, or depression within oneself or within one's interpersonal and spiritual relationships. Hence, in addition to addressing biological needs for the relief of suffering in palliative and end-of-life care, psychosocial and spiritual needs require direct attention and possible intervention for healing.

As suggested by Sulmasy's expansion of the biopsychosocial model, many interventions targeting behavioural and mental health and wellness near the end of life incorporate elements of meaning-seeking or spirituality into their treatment approach. Knowledge of such interventions is a core competency for behavioural health specialists in palliative and end-of-life care (Kasl-Godley et al., 2014). For example, in this volume, the chapter by Masterson, Rosenfeld, and Breitbart (Chapter 4) describes Meaning-Centered Psychotherapy for Cancer Patients and references Victor Frankl's Logotherapy and the search for meaning (Frankl, 1955/1986; 1969/1988) as seminal to their treatment approach. Additionally, the chapter by Annable, Chochinov, and colleagues on Dignity Therapy (Chapter 5) describes the importance of dignity within the experience of palliative care and approaching death, both for individuals and for their interpersonal support systems. These and other palliative care interventions to address behavioural and mental health and wellness near the end of life incorporate principles of lifespan developmental or stress and coping theories into treatment planning and therapeutic goals.

Lifespan and stress and coping theories

Our own intervention work with community-dwelling palliative care dyads (Allen, Hilgeman, Ege, Shuster, & Burgio, 2008; Allen, 2009; Allen et al., 2014, 2016) applies socioemotional selectivity theory (Carstensen, Fung, & Charles, 2003; Carstensen, Isaacowitz, & Charles, 1999) and the strength and vulnerability integration model (Charles, 2010) to conceptualize why individuals and self-defined family systems are motivated to engage in meaning-making in the service of emotion regulation near the end of life. These theories posit that a foreshortened perspective on time left to live shifts an individual's motivation toward regulating emotions and engaging in meaningful activities. Stress and coping theories also have considered the importance of meaning-making and suggested how these activities sustain the coping process. For example, Folkman's (1997) revised stress and coping model expands early theory (Lazarus & Folkman, 1984) and describes how the coping process is maintained in the face of unresolved or unresolvable outcomes that may initially be addressed through problem-focused coping strategies. Folkman posits that meaning-based coping consists of revising goals, engaging in positive events, and considering religious and spiritual beliefs. Thus, our intervention approach, like others (e.g., Chapters 4 and 5) uses reminiscence and engagement in dyadic creative activity or legacy making as a therapeutic tool (Allen et al., 2014) (see Figure 1.1.). Through focusing individuals' attention on lifetime accomplishments and challenges, relationships, and values, behavioural interventions containing these elements facilitate meaning reconstruction and reduce existential distress. Clearly, individuals of different ages or developmental "stages" may approach the end of their lives with differing levels of acceptance and proclivities for positive or negative emotional reactions. Practitioners must approach this work with a sense of curiosity and humility, respecting individual variability embedded within cultural contexts.

Global and cultural diversity and intersectionality in palliative and end-of-life care

Although our prior work has incorporated non-Hispanic White and African American palliative care patients and a self-defined family member from both urban and rural communities in the southeastern United States, many behavioural interventions, including our own, have not adequately addressed issues of diversity and intersectionality (see Chapter 6). With regard to race and ethnicity, it is well known that individuals of varying cultures approach palliative and end-of-life care from different perspectives, emphasizing different

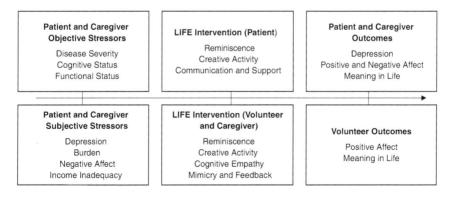

Figure 1.1 LIFE Intervention model

values (Kwak & Haley, 2005). With regard to geographic diversity, culture in rural areas is more conservative than in urban ones, valuing self-reliance and religiosity while potentially maintaining a distrust of the medical community (Bushy, 2000). This is particularly true in the southeastern United States, stemming in part from the egregious suffering resulting from 40 years of the Tuskegee Syphilis Study, during which rural African American men were denied a known effective treatment for syphilis in order to examine the long-term effects of untreated disease (Ball, Lawson, & Alim, 2013). Likewise, there is likely wide variability in different regions of the world regarding the experience of serious illness and, therefore, what might make for effective psychosocial care at the end of life. Globally, more research is needed to explore the translation of current interventions into culturally appropriate delivery models and settings.

In considering diversity, it is notable that very little information exists with regard to palliative and end-of-life care needs of individuals self-identifying as members of the LGBTQ community, an issue addressed in Chapter 6 of this volume. Another recent book (Acquaviva, 2017) covers communication, attitudes and access to care, shared decision-making and family dynamics, care planning and coordination, ethical and legal issues, psychosocial and spiritual issues, and ways to facilitate institutional inclusiveness for individuals who self-identify within this group and their allies. In certain countries internationally, self-identifying within the LGBTQ community still caries significant personal safety risk directly relevant to biopsychosocial-spiritual palliative and end-of-life care.

The intersection of ethnicity, gender identity, socioeconomic status, and geographic place of residence may expose individuals with greater combinations of low social status identities to significantly more stigma and discrimination. Ghavami, Katsiaficas, and Rogers (2016) describe the need for developmental theories and methods that account for intersectional identities and that examine their relation to lifespan outcomes across life domains. These authors clearly and cogently argue that a focus on only one social status or domain of identity hinders the development and delivery of culturally appropriate and clinically effective behavioural and psychosocial interventions across the lifespan. In this volume, the editors and authors have attempted to include consideration of cultural diversity and ethical care delivery in every chapter, with particular attention given to intersectionality of identities across the adult lifespan.

In palliative and end-of-life behavioural and psychosocial care, fostering a sense of intersectionality and positive marginality (Mayo, 1982; Unger, 2000) may be therapeutically effective in healing. Positive marginality exists when the individual embraces marginal identities and positions himself or herself as an activist by making their outsider status explicit and known to others. Unger's essay focuses on less observable forms of marginality based on group membership, including social class, religion, sexual orientation, concealable physical disabilities, and chronic illness. Although these identities and social statuses may be a source of stigma, prejudice, and discrimination, they are not usually evident to an observer. Hence, revelation of these marginal identities rests in the power of the individual. Individuals with one or more marginal identities may, by virtue of holding such identities, possess values and worldviews that are more inclusive and focused on resilience. Unger notes that positive marginality requires "the acknowledgement that previously neglected aspects of one's life story are personally and professionally legitimate" (p. 177). This life story approach certainly fits many behavioural and psychosocial interventions in palliative and end-of-life care.

How might inclusive behavioural palliative care be fostered? The use of community-based participatory research (CBPR) and establishment of true science-community partnerships (Israel, Schulz, Parker, & Becker, 1998; Israel et al., 2010) are a necessary first step in addressing diversity and intersectionality in behavioural interventions during palliative and end-of-life care. This approach has been successful in public health interventions for children and at-risk youth using the concept of creating nurturing environments that promote health (Biglan, Flay, Embry, & Sandler, 2012). It is our premise that perhaps these elements may inform translation of behavioural interventions in palliative care. As described by Biglan and colleagues (2012) nurturing environments include those that: 1) minimize biologically and psychologically toxic events; 2) teach, promote, and reinforce self-regulatory behaviors; 3) monitor and limit problematic behaviors; and 4) foster psychological flexibility – mindfulness about one's feelings, thoughts and actions in the service of one's values. Although our focus is global, patient-centered delivery of palliative and end-of-life care must necessarily rely upon local norms and values and incorporate community members as partners in intervention delivery. Even with a CBPR approach that attempts to harness the power of local communities in the provision of palliative and end-of-life care, provision of effective, therapeutic, and ethical behavioural and psychosocial care near the end of life is complex. Community engagement and ethical issues are covered in our second volume, *Perspectives on Palliative and End-of-Life Care: Disease, Social and Cultural Context*. As is clearly evident across the chapters included in this volume, conducting intervention research within this context is even more daunting.

Complexities of conducting research and practice with individuals and families in palliative and end-of-life care

The choice of a behavioural intervention within palliative and end-of-life care, and the extent to which such intervention will embrace intersectionality, will depend on the setting of care (including gatekeepers and geographic characteristics), disease trajectory, capacity for informed consent, and reimbursement and policy issues (Bush, Allen, & Molinari, 2017; Kasl-Godley et al., 2014). With regard to setting, privacy and confidentiality of sessions may be compromised in double occupancy inpatient settings in hospital or long-term care and even within single occupancy rooms due to the nearby presence of healthcare staff. Within community home-based settings, the presence of other family members and friends may preclude the individual's ability to share existential distress or other mental health and wellness issues openly and freely. Staff and family care partners may also limit access to the person receiving palliative and end-of-life care, possibly due to their own stress and worries regarding the proximity of that person's death. Due to fatigue and disease trajectory or prognosis, traditional psychotherapeutic treatments following a typical 50-minute outpatient model may not be feasible (Kasl-Godley et al., 2014). Moreover, varying cognitive status due to illness may limit the person's ability to provide and maintain informed consent for behavioural and psychosocial treatment. Finally, reimbursement for behavioural and psychosocial palliative and end-of-life care varies globally. Within the United States, interprofessional palliative care provision that embraces behavioural and psychosocial care is the norm within the Veterans Affairs medical system but is rarely available in community healthcare settings.

With regard to conducting research needed to identify efficacious behavioural interventions and validate appropriate assessment instruments, issues of individual consent capacity, stress on the family system, and attrition due to health decline and death pose challenges. Due to physical and emotional symptoms, interventions and assessments may need to occur over short periods of time in any one session, and these sessions may need to occur within or across days or weeks, depending on the illness trajectory and setting. At any given contact, the individual or family may lack the cognitive or emotional capacity to participate in the research. As just one example of the influence of health decline and illness context on intervention research in palliative care, our randomized controlled trial to test the effectiveness of community volunteers in the delivery of a reminiscence and creative activity intervention began with 256 patient referrals, 76 dyads assessed for eligibility, 45 randomized, 28 dyadic completers with pre-post data, and 23 dyads at the three-month follow-up (Allen et al., 2014).

Scope of the book

The overarching goal of this text is to offer an accessible resource for scientists, practitioners, and trainees with relevant information on behavioural and psychosocial mental health and wellness interventions in palliative and end-of-life care. Hence, this book contains five chapters addressing interventions to enhance communication and decision-making (Chapter 2), management of physical and mental health symptoms broadly (Chapter 3), Meaning-Centered Psychotherapy for cancer patients (Chapter 4), Dignity Therapy (Chapter 5), and interventions embracing cultural diversity and intersectionality (Chapter 6). Our second volume, *Perspectives on Palliative and End-of-Life Care: Disease, Social and Cultural Context*, covers behavioural interventions within specific populations. This includes those living and dying globally with HIV/AIDS, individuals with serious mental illness, individuals with dementia, ethics, bereavement, and policy issues.

Across the two books, the editors recruited 11 writing groups of authors who were asked to include in their work certain material in every chapter. Thus, each chapter includes: 1) a review of behavioural interventions, 2) an evaluation of the strength of the evidence base of intervention and topic-based research, 3) identification of gaps within the knowledge base, 4) coverage of cultural and diversity issues, 5) consideration of ethical issues, 6) practice implications, and 7) at least one case example with questions illustrating salient issues. Of necessity, chapter content and emphasis varies by topic in each book. In every chapter, an attempt has been made to address palliative and end-of-life care globally, but each chapter is written by an authorship team from a specific national or regional perspective. While authors are primarily from the United States, Europe, and Canada, perspectives from Africa and Australia are included in certain chapters.

The global growth in palliative care necessitates a renewed focus on behavioural and psychosocial issues. Definitions of palliative care provided by WHO and the IOM within the United States have not traditionally emphasized the potential role of psychologists and other behavioural healthcare providers in addressing these issues in clinical and scientific realms. Our hope is that these books will provide a foundation for collaborative international and interprofessional work by providing state-of-science information on behavioural interventions addressing mental health and wellness in palliative and end-of-life care.

References

Acquaviva, K. D. (2017). *LGBTQ-Inclusive Hospice and Palliative Care*. New York, NY: Harrington Park Press.

Allen, R. S. (2009). The legacy project intervention to enhance meaningful family interactions: Case examples. *Clinical Gerontologist, 32*(2), 164–176.

Allen, R. S., Harris, G. M., Burgio, L. D., Azuero, C. B., Miller, L. A., Shin, H., . . . Parmelee, P. (2014). Can senior volunteers deliver reminiscence and creative activity interventions? Results of the legacy intervention family enactment randomized controlled trial. *Journal of Pain and Symptom Management, 48*(4), 590–601.

Allen, R. S., Hilgeman, M. M., Ege, M. A., Shuster, J. L., Jr., & Burgio, L. D. (2008). Legacy activities as interventions approaching the end of life. *Journal of Palliative Medicine, 11*(7), 1029–1038.

Allen, R. S., Azuero, C. B., Csikai, E. L., Parmelee, P. A., Shin, H. J., Kvale, E., . . . Burgio, L. D. (2016). "It was very rewarding for me . . .": Senior volunteers' experiences with implementing a reminiscence and creative activity intervention. *The Gerontologist, 56*(2), 357–367.

Ball, K., Lawson, W., & Alim, M. D. (2013). Medical mistrust, conspiracy beliefs and HIV related behavior among African Americans. *Journal of Psychology and Behavioral Science, 1*(1), 1–7.

Biglan, A., Flay, B. R., Embry, D. D., & Sandler, I. N. (2012). The critical role of nurturing environments for promoting human well-being. *The American Psychologist, 67*(4), 257–271.

Bush, S. S., Allen, R. S., & Molinari, V. (2017). *Ethical Practice in Geropsychology.* Washington, DC: American Psychological Association.

Bushy, A. (2000). *Orientation Into Nursing in a Rural Community.* Thousand Oaks, CA: Sage.

Candy, B., Jones, L., Drake, R., Leurent, B., & King, M. (2009). Interventions for supporting informal caregivers of patients in the terminal phase of a disease. *Cochrane Database Systematic Review, 6.*

Carstensen, L. L., Fung, H. H., & Charles, S. T. (2003). Socioemotional selectivity theory and the regulation of emotions in the second half of life. *Motivation and Emotion, 27*(2), 103–123.

Carstensen, L. L., Isaacowitz, D. M., & Charles, S. T. (1999). Taking time seriously: A theory of socioemotional selectivity theory. *American Psychologist, 54*(3), 165–181.

Charles, S. T. (2010). Strength and vulnerability integration: A model of emotional well-being across adulthood. *Psychological Bulletin, 136*(3), 1068–1091.

Clark, D. (1998). Originating a movement: Cicely Saunders and the development of St. Christopher's Hospice, 1957–1967. *Mortality, 3,* 43–63.

Clark, D. (1999). "Total pain", disciplinary power and the body in the work of Cicely Saunders, 1958–1967. *Social Science & Medicine, 49,* 727–736.

Engel, G. L. (1977). The need for a new medical model: A challenge for biomedicine. *Science, 196*(4286), 129–136.

Folkman, S. (1997). Positive psychological states and coping with severe stress. *Social Sciences and Medicine, 45,* 1207–1221.

Frankl, V. E. (1962). *Man's Search for Meaning: An Introduction to Logotherapy, Death-camp to existentialism,* New York: Simon & Schuster

Frankl, V. F. (1969/1988). *The Will to Meaning: Foundations and Applications of Logotherapy,* Expanded Edition. New York, NY: Penguin Books.

Ghavami, N., Katsiaficas, D., & Rogers, L. O. (2016). Toward an intersectional approach in developmental science: The roles of race, gender, sexual orientation, and immigrant status. *Advances in Child Development and Behavior, 50*(1), 31–73.

Haley, W. E., Larson, D., Kasl-Godley, J., Neimeyer, R., & Kwilosz, D. (2003). Roles for psychologists in end of life care: Emerging models of practice. *Professional Psychology Research and Practice, 34,* 626–633.

Institute of Medicine. (2014). *Dying in America: Improving Quality and Honoring Preferences Near the End of Life.* Washington, DC: The National Academies Press.

Israel, B. A., Coombe, C. M., Cheezum, R. R., Schulz, A. J., McGranaghan, R. J., Lichtenstein, R., . . . Burris, A. (2010). Community-based participatory research: A capacity-building approach for policy advocacy aimed at eliminating health disparities. *American Journal of Public Health, 100*(11), 2094–2102. doi:10.2105/AJPH.2009.170506

Israel, B. A., Schulz, A. J., Parker, E. A., & Becker, A. B. (1998). Review of community-based research: Assessing partnership approaches to improve public health. *Annual Review of Public Health, 19,* 173–202.

Kasl-Godley, J. E., King, D. A., & Quill, T. A. (2014). Opportunities for psychologists in palliative care: Working with patients and families across the disease continuum. *American Psychologist, 69*(4), 364–376.

Keall, R. M., Clayton, J. M., & Butow, P. N. (2014). Therapeutic life review in palliative care: A systematic review of quantitative evaluations. *Journal of Pain and Symptom Management, 49*(4), 747–761.

Kelly, A. S., & Morrison, R. S. (2015). Palliative care for the seriously ill. *New England Journal of Medicine, 373*(8), 747–755.

Kübler-Ross, E. (1969). *On Death and Dying.* New York, NY: Scribner.

Kwak, J., & Haley, W. E. (2005). Current research findings on end-of-life decision making among racially or ethnically diverse groups. *The Gerontologist, 45*(1), 634–641.

Lazarus, R. S., & Folkman, S. (1984). *Stress, Appraisal, and Coping.* New York, NY: Springer.

Mayo, C. (1982). Training for positive marginality. In L. Bickman (Ed.), *Applied Social Psychology Annual* (Vol. 3, pp. 57–73). Beverly Hills, CA: Sage.

Milicevic, N. (2002). The hospice movement: History and current worldwide situation. *Archives of Oncology, 10,* 29–32.

Siebold, C. (1992). *The Hospice Movement: Easing Death's Pains.* New York, NY: Maxwell Macmillan International.

Singer, A. E., Goebel, J. R., Kim, Y. S., Dy, S. M., Ahluwalia, S. C., Clifford, M., . . . Goldberg, J. (2016). Populations and interventions for palliative and end-of-life care: A systematic review. *Journal of Palliative Medicine, 19*(9), 995–1008. doi:10.1089/jpm.2015.0367.

Sulmasy, D. P. (2002). A biopsychosocial-spiritual model for the care of patients at the end of life. *The Gerontologist, 42*(Spec. no III), 24–33.

Unger, R. W. (2000). Outsiders inside: Positive marginality and social change. *Journal of Social Issues, 56*(1), 163–179.

World Health Organization. (2002). *The World Health Report 2002: Reducing Risks, Promoting Healthy Life.* World Health Organization. Retrieved from www.barnesandnoble.com/w/world-health-report-2002-world-health-organization/1119231978?ean=9789241562072

Chapter 2

Interventions to enhance communication and decision-making in the context of serious illness

Brian D. Carpenter and Meghan McDarby

Introduction

The focus of this chapter is on two fundamental elements of healthcare inter-actions: communication and decision-making. Communication is at the very core of most healthcare encounters. Patients tell their provider about symptoms and the impact on their lives; providers, in turn, listen, share their conclusions, and suggest treatments. Patients, providers, and very often other family members and care partners, exchange information, share stories, and offer support. That brief description makes communication sound simple, but, for several reasons, it is anything but that. To begin with, the information that is exchanged in a healthcare situation can be technically complex, voluminous, and sometimes ambiguous. Sources of information may contradict each other, narratives may change over time, and the basic processes of saying what is intended clearly and hearing what was intended accurately are themselves complicated. Moreover, particularly in the case of serious illness, communication often happens in situations of great emotional distress, when people are facing, literally, matters of life and death, making comprehension of care options and deliberate decision-making even more challenging.

As with communication, decision-making responsibilities fall on patients, caregivers, and providers alike. For patients, decision-making may precede actual illness by years, when people undertake the process of advance care planning by completing advance directives that express their future care preferences. Other decisions happen as illness unfolds, as providers present treatment and care options and as patients weigh the benefits and costs of different paths. Again, as with communication, these decisions are made within the context of technically complex medical information that may or may not lead to one obvious preferred option, and decisions often must be made rapidly, without ample time for reflection, and in a psychological state colored by pain, fear, hopelessness, or sadness (Lerner, Li, Valdesolo, & Kassam, 2015; Lowenstein & Lerner, 2003; Raghunathan & Pham, 1999).

In this chapter, we review the literature on interventions and tools designed to improve communication and decision-making in the context of serious and sometimes life-limiting illness. We focus on interventions that target patients, family members, and providers, in some cases individually, and in others collectively. We also wish to emphasize that the boundary between communication interventions and decision-making interventions is not distinct: some communication interventions have the ultimate goal of helping people make decisions, and some decision-making interventions rely on effective communication. Across purposes, our goal is to explicate interventions that have demonstrated (or hold the promise of demonstrating) a capacity to improve the experience of living with serious illness, for both patients and care partners.

Communication

Effective communication is the foundation of high-quality, person-centered healthcare (Arnold et al., 2009; Davis, Schoenbaum, & Audet, 2005; Epner & Baile, 2014; Gamondi, Larkin, & Payne, 2013; Stewart et al., 2000). In the United States, communication skills are prominent in the professional competencies outlined for physicians (Accreditation Council for Graduate Medical Education, 2016), nurses (American Association of Colleges of Nursing, 2013), social workers (National Association of Social Workers, 2004), psychologists (American Psychological Association, 2011), and interprofessional healthcare teams (Interprofessional Education Collaborative, 2011). Several organizations around the world are also focused on collaborative communication as an essential ingredient in person-centered healthcare, including the International Association for Communication in Healthcare (www.each.eu), the American Academy on Communication in Healthcare (www.aachonline.org), and the International Research Centre for Communication in Healthcare (www.ircch.org). These communication skills, as highlighted by their prominent focus in the aforementioned organizations, are important not only for patients but also for the people in their social network who support them, though opportunities for people to learn these skills are less organized and systematic than they are for professionals.

What are the communication skills that patients, care partners, and providers need? Table 2.1 is our attempt to summarize key elements. Some skills are common across individuals, whereas others are distinct to a particular role. All fall into two broad categories: giving (information, support) and receiving (listening, comprehending). Within those categories, communication can focus on goals that are informational (e.g., sharing a diagnostic impression, educating about a disease, conveying treatment information) or relational (e.g., expressing empathy, mediating conflict) (Schram, Hougham, Meltzer, & Ruhnke, 2016).

Of course, communication is always a transaction: one party gives, the other party receives and responds, the first party receives and responds in turn, and so on. An overarching skill, therefore, is being able to undertake a *mutual* conversation in which individuals understand and appreciate the needs, goals, perspective, strengths, and limitations of the other person (or people) involved in the

Table 2.1 Key communication activities in healthcare situations

Patients and care partners		Providers	
Giving	Receiving	Giving	Receiving
• Providing information about illness symptoms (onset, frequency, duration, intensity, quality, etc.) • Relaying treatment response and side effects • Expressing goals of care, stance toward information needs and decisional involvement, philosophy about treatments, quality vs. quantity of life, etc. • Asking important questions	• Comprehending and accepting assessment results and diagnoses • Understanding treatment recommendations, their risks and benefits • Comprehending when curative treatments are no longer expected to be beneficial • Offering emotional support	• Providing feedback on test/assessment results • Sharing diagnostic and prognostic information in understandable ways • Describing treatment options, their risks and benefits • Motivating treatment compliance • Offering emotional support and hope • Being present and attentive during conversations	• Synthesizing descriptions of symptoms • Understanding impact of illness on function and quality of life • Appreciating patient/family perspective on goals of care, values, and preferences

conversation. Effective communication is, by definition, social, and having some degree of empathy for the person in the other chair, on the other side of the room, on the other end of the telephone or e-mail, may be the most important competency of all (consider, for example, the concept of "therapeutic presence" identified by Chochinov and colleagues (2013) in their model of components of effective communication). Below we describe interventions intended to facilitate communication, organized by the intervention target, though acknowledging that training one person will surely have an effect on the others.

Interventions targeting communication between patients/caregivers and providers

Question prompt lists (QPLs)

As a group, QPLs are designed to empower patients as they seek information about disease and treatment, express their questions and concerns, and collaborate on decision-making with their healthcare providers. QPLs typically include a set of brief, written questions or topics (sometimes generated by patients, sometimes selected from a pre-established list) that can be taken to appointments as reminders, or prompts, for areas of discussion. QPLs usually cover medical topics, but some also address practical, psychosocial, and spiritual concerns. A recent review completed by Sansoni, Grootemaat, and Duncan (2015) concluded that, although evidence is preliminary, QPLs do increase the frequency with which patients ask questions and the amount of information given by providers. These effects are particularly robust when the QPL is shared with the provider, who then uses the QPL as a checklist of topics to cover; the impact is less consistent when the QPL, or a copy of it, is not shown to the provider. In addition, QPLs appear to be used most consistently when patients develop or receive them shortly before their appointment (1–2 days), rather than weeks in advance. The review concluded that results are equivocal regarding whether QPLs increase patient knowledge, alter anxiety, increase patient satisfaction, or increase consultation length (which has obvious cost implications). Sansoni and colleagues also point out several methodological limitations of the research to date, including questionable validity of measures and the relatively narrow range of patients with whom the tools have been evaluated (i.e., primarily people with cancer, limited racial/ethnic heterogeneity).

Among the many examples in the literature, we highlight two in particular. The QPL developed by Clayton and colleagues (2007) is notable because it encourages questions about prognosis and end-of-life care and includes resources for both patients and caregivers. Comprehensive in its scope, the tool can be segmented, with items pulled out that are specific to a patient's particular stage in the illness trajectory. QPLs from this research team are available online at http://sydney.edu.au/science/psychology/cemped/com_question_prompt.shtml. The QPL developed by Hebert, Schulz, Copeland, and Arnold (2009) was designed for family members. Questions address a range of medical (e.g., "What are the common side effects of my loved one's medications?") and psychosocial (e.g., "What do I do if my loved one seems depressed?") issues, including topics related to the very end of life.

Appointment coaching

Often used in combination with a QPL, appointment coaching, as its name suggests, involves teaching patients and care partners how to be active agents during healthcare encounters, asking questions and getting the information they need. Coaching typically focuses on empowering patients and care partners to ask questions, guide conversations, and make decisions. In addition to a QPL, other resources that may be provided during coaching include educational booklets, charts, and videos (see Sansoni et al., 2015). Coaches may be laypeople or healthcare professionals, most often nurses or social workers, although there is not clear evidence that one type of coach is more effective than another (Alders, Smits, Brand, & van Dulmen, 2017).

As an example of a typical coaching intervention, we highlight work by Doorenbos, Levy, Curtis, and Dougherty (2016) conducted with heart failure patients. Their multicomponent intervention included a pre-appointment telephone consultation with a nurse coach, who 1) discussed perceived barriers and facilitators to communication, education about heart failure treatments, and patient preferences for communication around end-of-life topics; 2) helped the patient develop a "patient-activation outline" (much like a QPL), which was eventually shared with both patient and provider; and 3) conducted role playing and skills enhancement exercises with the patient to enhance communication self-efficacy. Patients who received this information initiated more goals-of-care conversations with their provider and had more high-quality conversations, without concomitant increases in depression or anxiety.

A recent literature review of patient coaching interventions in specialist consultations examined evidence in 17 high-quality studies of 13 unique interventions (Alders et al., 2017). Across these studies, findings were inconsistent, though the most rigorous studies demonstrated the most positive effects: patients who receive coaching demonstrate greater participation and greater control over the conversation, with effects persisting 1–12 months following coaching. The authors of the review contend that the low quality of much of the research and its heterogeneity may be responsible for the variability in outcomes, as researchers vary in how they define coaching, who they target with the intervention (patient, provider, or both), the dose of coaching offered, and the outcomes measured. Another limitation is that these studies have not recruited samples that reflect sociodemographic diversity, restricting the generalizability of results.

The **Stanford Letter Writing Project**, a kind of secondary coaching intervention, aims to help people generate information to be shared and discussed with their healthcare provider during an appointment. Care preferences are articulated in the form of a three-page "letter" addressed to "My Doctor." In the letter, which can be completed via a fillable PDF or online, individuals state what activities are most meaningful to them, preferences regarding the disclosure of bad news and medical decision-making, preferred proxy decision-makers, end-of-life treatment wishes, preferences regarding sedation for pain, and guidance if family opinion on care differs from the individual's. Versions of the letter are available in eight languages, and the associated website also includes an app wherein the individual's responses are formatted into an advance directive that can be printed and signed. According to information on the project website (https://med.stanford.edu/letter.html), at the time of this writing, results from a feasibility study are under review, and two additional research projects are comparing letters to traditional advance directives in a sample of bone marrow transplant patients.

Other novel interventions

Several other creative interventions defy categorization but make use of inventive methods to enhance communication. For example, implemented in the context of pediatric palliative care, Chin et al. (2014) described the use of 12 miniature chairs to facilitate conversations with children about significant events in their life, including their own serious illness. The authors present three brief case studies that describe the benefits of this approach, although no objective evaluation data are provided. Several researchers have used case examples with patients as a jumping-off point for conversations about patients' own health situations and care preferences (see a review by Michael, O'Callaghan, & Clayton, 2016). Hypothetical scenarios are presented, and patients are invited to weigh in on how someone else might respond or what they themselves would do if in a similar situation. Presumably, the third-person nature of these case examples facilitates discussion about goals of care with a degree of psychological distance: patients discuss the care situation of others but are not expected to refer specifically to themselves. Personal experiences and perspectives can be introduced by the patient when they feel ready. At the same time, limitations of this technique include the possibility that patients will not identify with their fictional counterparts or will focus on only one facet of the case to the exclusion of other important elements. Skilled facilitation is obviously required for this technique to be effective, and formal evaluations have not been completed.

Two online resources distributed by the National Cancer Institute, one designed for patients and family members, the other for healthcare professionals, include a summary of key issues in cancer care communication (PDQ® Supportive and Palliative Care Editorial Board, 2015). The patient/family version reviews the role of family members, the role of patients, effective communication with the healthcare team, and current clinical trials. The version for healthcare professionals reviews aspects of competent communication. To our knowledge, the effectiveness of these resources has not been evaluated, but they are very thorough and easily accessible.

> Bernacki and colleagues (2015) developed a **Serious Illness Care Program** (SICP) that includes several components designed to improve communication among patients, family members, and providers. Components of the program were designed to train clinicians to use a structured guide for advanced [sic] care planning discussion with patients, 'trigger' clinicians to have conversations, prepare patients and families for the conversation, and document outcomes of the discussion in a structured format in the electronic medical record.
>
> (p. 1)

A seven-item Serious Illness Conversation Guide for clinicians prompts them to address patient understanding of their illness, information sharing preferences, goals, fears, valued functional abilities, opinions regarding quality versus quantity of life, and perceptions about how much family knows patient wishes. A Family Communication Guide is also available to help patients talk with caregivers about their values and preferences, and patients also receive a QPL to take to their next appointment. At the time of this writing, the initial trial to evaluate the SICP is still underway.

The **SPIRIT** intervention (Sharing Patient Illness Representations to Increase Trust) relies on the patient's understanding of illness to inform conversations about EOL treatment options that ultimately facilitate EOL decision-making (Song & Ward, 2015). Patients meet with their preferred surrogate decision-maker and a trained interventionist for two sessions in order to describe their conceptualization of the illness, explore their goals of care and values related to life-sustaining treatments, and consider a variety of care treatment options. The interventionist supports communication between the patient and surrogate to reach a mutual understanding of the patient's preferences. These preferences are relayed to the patient's care team by the interventionist, and ideas about how to communicate these care preferences to other integral family members are explored. To date, this intervention has been examined only in the context of end-stage renal disease. However, the SPIRIT intervention appears to increase dyadic congruence about goals of care and to reduce patient decisional conflict (Song et al., 2016). In addition, a strength of this intervention is that it was developed 1) to be sensitive to spiritual and religious perspectives on illness among African Americans, and 2) to employ language easily understandable to people with less education. Indeed, it is one of the few interventions reviewed so far that has been developed with the recognition that cultural and other forms of diversity may influence communication.

Interventions targeting communication competencies of providers

Resources for providers cluster into two types, 1) tools that can be used directly during conversations, and 2) educational interventions and curricula offered to providers to enhance their communication skills. See Table 2.2 for a summary of select interventions focusing on provider education, intervention tools that may be used in conversations are reviewed in the text.

Conversational scripts and templates

As a group, these tools include a structured or semistructured list of topics or prompts that providers can follow during their conversations with patients. The structured format is intended to reduce the cognitive load for providers and ensure that important topics are not overlooked. Perhaps the most widely used tool in this category is the **SPIKES** protocol (Buckman, 2005). This template guides providers through a set of broad conversational goals – Setting, Perception, Invitation, Knowledge, Empathy, and Summary – when delivering bad news. Originally developed for oncologists to help them discuss diagnosis and prognosis, SPIKES has been found to enhance informational and relational aspects of bad news communication and has since been adapted for

Table 2.2 Communication interventions, format, audience, and evaluation results

Curriculum title (if available) and citation	Format and objectives	Audience	Summary of evaluation
Workshops and Training			
Flint, Meyer, Hossain, and Klein (2015)	• 3-hr workshop • Didactic session about discussing GOC, emotional responses, and empathy • Discussion about serious illness with recently bereaved parents • Role play exercise with parents	Pediatric residents (n = 42)	• Increased confidence discussing goals of care, managing emotions, and expressing empathy • Confirmed value of role playing exercise and intention to integrate skills into future practice
"Difficult Discussions" Erickson, Blackhall, Brashers, and Varhegyi (2015)	• 90-min workshop • Didactics on EOL communication and family meetings • Simulated family meeting with standardized patient/family	3rd-year nursing and medical students (n = 215)	• Higher ratings of perceived importance of teamwork in healthcare in both groups • Higher ratings of importance of physician-nurse collaboration among nurses • Variable changes in both groups for communication self-efficacy
Sanchez-Reilly, Wittenberg-Lyles, and Villagran (2007)	• 8-hr curriculum • Didactics on hospice and palliative care, geriatric medicine, pain and symptom management, SPIKES protocol, and importance of an interdisciplinary team approach • Supervised geriatric and hospice consultation • Final reflections on personal and emotional reactions to the curriculum	4th-year medical students (n = 25)	• Significant improvement in knowledge, but no other significant changes in communication willingness, comfort, or confidence • Students were asked about messaging strategies for delivering bad news, but most did not suggest the techniques emphasized in the SPIKES protocol

(Continued)

Table 2.2 (Continued)

Curriculum title (if available) and citation	Format and objectives	Audience	Summary of evaluation
Hagiwara, Ross, Lee, and Sanchez-Reilly (2016)	• Mandatory course in palliative care • 60-min online course on conducting a family meeting • 1-hr small-group opportunity to role play family meeting	4th-year medical students (n = 674)	• Students attained at least 70% on checklist of important behaviors when observed in a hypothetical meeting with two standardized family members
"we DECide" Ampe, Smets, Declercq, and Van Audenhove (2017)	• Two, 4-hr workshops to enhance shared decision-making skills and conversations on advance care planning • Homework assignment to talk with a resident about care preferences in context of routine care	Nursing home staff in dementia care units (n = 90)	• Review of recorded conversations at time of admission and during one crisis situation. After training, advance care planning conversations were no more frequent
"ACA" Slort, Blankenstein, Schweitzer, Deliens, and van der Horst (2013)	• 6-hr training program on communication with palliative care patients • Components included videotaped interactions with simulated patient, oral feedback on the videotapes, instructions on a conversation checklist, and role playing	General practitioners (n = 118)	• Based on analysis of videotaped interactions between providers and simulated patients, training had no effect on number of current and anticipated issues that providers discussed in consultations, percentage of consultations in which they discussed issues, quality of communication, or knowledge about medical aspects of palliative care
"Physician Communication Training Program" Rucker & Browning (2015)	• Training modules presented in 15–20 min sessions • Program content on conducting family conferences, discussing advance directives, giving bad news,	Medical students, residents, and attending physicians (n = not reported)	• Qualitative feedback from participants was positive regarding their understanding of how to conduct a family meeting and how to give bad news

Study	Description	Participants	Results
Curtis et al. (2015)	explaining brain death, and addressing withdrawal of life support and other ethical issues • Role playing based on scripts from actual family meetings • 2-day training that included didactics and role playing to help nurses and social workers become communication facilitators for both family and providers in the ICU • Content included evidence in the conduct of clinician–family communication in the ICU, implications of attachment style for communication, and mediation strategies	Nurses and social workers (n = 168)	• Compared to control group, families who had facilitators working with them reported fewer symptoms of depression (but not anxiety) after 6 months (but not 3 months) • Also found reductions in ICU and hospital length of stay
"Comskil" Bylund et al. (2011)	• Nine 3-hr teaching modules focused on 26 communication skills • Components include didactics and videotaped role playing with simulated patients	Oncology fellows (n = 515)	• Evaluation of pre/post communication behaviors in standardized patients and recorded consultations with actual patients (including feedback from patients) • Results document increases in communication self-efficacy and implementation of skills taught
"COM-ON-p" Goelz et al. (2011)	• Pre-assessment with actor patients • 1.5-day workshop • Individual coaching session ~2 weeks after workshop • Post-assessment with actors • Focus is on the transition to palliative care.	Oncologists (n = 41)	• Compared to control group, program participants demonstrated improved communication with patients and were better at encouraging participation of family members

(Continued)

Table 2.2 (Continued)

Curriculum title (if available) and citation	Format and objectives	Audience	Summary of evaluation
"OncoTalk" Back et al. (2007)	• 4-day residential workshop with didactic skills overview, skills practice sessions in small groups with simulated patients, and reflective discussions • Taught "cognitive road maps" for giving bad news and discussing transitions of care	Medical oncology fellows (n = 115)	• Ratings of two standardized patient encounters before and after training revealed significant improvements in verbal and nonverbal communication skills
"Geritalk" Kelley et al. (2012) Gelfman et al. (2014)	• 2-day workshop designed to improve communication skills with patients with serious illness and their families • Course features include large-group didactic presentations, small-group communication skills practice with simulated patients, and future skills practice commitment	Geriatrics and palliative medicine fellows (n = 18)	• Evaluations documented high learner satisfaction, improved sense of preparation for communication challenges, and self-reported frequent use of course skills • Most recent evaluation documented improvements on a communication checklist used during observation of actual family meetings pre/post training
"NephroTalk" Cohen et al. (2016)	• Full-day communication skills workshop focused on delivering bad news and defining goals of care • Components include didactics, discussion, and practice with simulated patients	First-year nephrology fellows (n = 26)	• Improvements in self-reported pre- and post-course changes in skills, and self-reported changes in communication behaviors after three months

Self-Study Training Modules

"Breaking Bad News" Gorniewicz, Floyd, Krishnan, Bishop, Tudiver, and Lang (2016)	• Five 60-min, self-paced training modules available on CD or online • Address breaking bad news, living through treatment, palliative and end-of-life care, spirituality, and family • Include videos from actual cancer patients discussing challenging communication situations	Medical students and residents ($n = 66$)	• Based on ratings of two (breast and colon cancer scenarios) objective structured clinical examinations, students who received the training performed significantly better than students in control group
"SCOPE" Skinner, Pollack, Farrell, Olsen, Jeffreys, and Tulsky (2009)	• Interactive training program available on CD designed to improve providers' awareness of patient negative emotions and build confidence and skills to address patient concerns • Include didactic information, video clips, and audio clips of recordings of the provider's encounters with patients	Oncologists ($n = 48$)	• Positive ratings of helpfulness of information, self-rated effectiveness of training, and perceived use of skills presented
"COMFORT" Wittenberg-Lyles, Goldsmith, Ferrell, and Burchett (2014)	• Four 50–60-min online modules that included didactic information, video clips of a hospice team interacting with actual caregivers, and roundtable analysis by three providers • Modules focused on communication, health literacy, cultural theory, families, and teams	Available to all staff within one healthcare system; most participants were nurses and physicians ($n = 177$)	• Self-reported ratings of confidence in communication were high after the program, although comparisons with pre-program ratings were not conducted • Descriptive data presented on what participants found most useful

other patient populations and clinical contexts such as emergency medicine (Park, Gupta, Mandani, Haubner, & Peckler, 2010), intensive care (Buono-core, Wiegand, Hollyday, & Buonocore, 2015), mental health (Milton & Mullan, 2016), dentistry (Curtin & McConnell, 2012), and optometry (Spafford, Schryer, & Creutz, 2008).

White and Fromme (2012) developed two structured conversation "road maps" for use early in admission and throughout an inpatient stay to help clinicians discuss goals of care. The **SPAM** (Surrogate, Preferences, Assume Full Code, More Discussion) is designed to assess resuscitation preferences, in particular at the beginning of routine admission. Meanwhile, the **UFO-UFO** (Understand, Fill in Gaps, Outcomes, Understand, Feasible Outcomes) is to be used with patients who have a poor or uncertain prognosis in order to elucidate preferences regarding the balance between quality of life and functional status. The authors believe that this tool is particularly useful when families are requesting that "everything" be done and that request runs counter to patient values. To our knowledge, however, these tools have not been evaluated empirically.

A similar strategy underlies the **SAGE** and **THYME** conversation guides (Griffiths, Wilson, Ewing, Connolly, & Grande, 2015), developed for use by home-care oncology nurses in the UK. These prompts elicit patient concerns ("Can I ask what you are concerned about?") and encourage nurses to use empathetic conversational techniques ("You have a lot on your mind."). Several thousand providers in the UK have been trained to use these resources, and evaluations suggest that they increase nurses' knowledge and confidence (Connolly et al., 2014). Finally, as mentioned earlier, the **Serious Illness Conversation Guide** developed by Bernacki and colleagues (2015) also guides providers through a series of topics to ensure comprehensive assessment of patient values and preferences.

A recent and comprehensive review by Singer and colleagues (2016) identified 23 tools that have been designed to enhance the effectiveness of family meetings in the context of palliative and intensive care. These include family meeting planners, meeting guides, points of strategy for family meetings, decision aids, checklists, and documentation templates. Of the 16 articles in the review, only four formally evaluated the tools in a clinical environment, and outcomes were inconsistent regarding whether use of the tools influenced length of stay or aggressiveness of care.

Training curricula and workshops

There are many educational interventions for providers that take the form of either specialized workshops that address communication specifically in the context of palliative care or serious illness or communication topics embedded in more broad training programs. Some are delivered by experienced providers, and others are self-study programs. Evaluation of these interventions has been highly variable in their quality and depth. Some programs test students using simulated patients or other behavioral samples, and evaluations indicate positive effects (e.g., Gorniewicz et al., 2016; Hagiwara, Ross, Lee, & Sanchez-Reilly, 2016); others examine changes in practice in care settings, and evaluations have found small or nonexistent effects (e.g., Ampe, Smets, Declercq, & Van Audenhove, 2017; Sanchez-Reilly, Wittenberg-Lyles, & Villagran, 2007; Slort, Blankenstein, Schweitzer, Deliens, & van der Horst, 2013).

Interventions targeting communication within families

As a group, these communication interventions emerge from a public health orientation toward palliative care and target large segments of the general public to promote the reflection and conversation on end-of-life wishes and the completion of advance care planning documents. The most comprehensive and systematic program is **The Conversation Project** (TCP), an initiative in the United States that provides training and educational materials on advance care planning. TCP consists of an extensive website (http://theconversationproject. org) with resources for organizations, groups, and individuals about how to have conversations about end-of-life care preferences. The goal of the materials is to help people overcome the psychological and practical barriers to end-of-life conversations. The signature resource, a Conversation Starter Kit, contains information about the importance of advance care planning and a set of guided questions individuals can use to reflect on and articulate their care preferences, along with tips about how to share preferences with family members and other key care partners. Translations are available in several languages, and a tailored version is available for care partners of people with Alzheimer's disease and other dementias. The TCP website includes a set of suggested tools for evaluation, including surveys regarding actions participants have taken after completing the program and community-level metrics for measuring the impact of the program more broadly (e.g., prevalence of advance directive and health proxy completion in the population). Despite its widespread dissemination in the United States, to our knowledge, however, no empirical findings regarding the program's effectiveness have been published to date in peer-reviewed outlets.

Hoping for a similarly broad reach, **Death Over Dinner** is a website (deathoverdinner.org) that includes resources for individuals who want to host a meal with family and friends and talk about end-of-life care. Hosts receive a customized invitation that can be sent to their guests, along with links to articles, podcasts, and videos. Hosts also receive a set of discussion prompts they can use throughout the gathering to facilitate conversation. As with TCP, no empirical evaluation of the program has been published. Utilizing a slightly more structured approach, **My Gift of Grace** is a playing card–based game that prompts participants to answer 20 questions about death, dying, and end-of-life care. In a recent evaluation undertaken with 86 community dwelling volunteers, outcomes measured immediately after playing the game and three months later included completing a living will, completing a health-care proxy, discussing end-of-life wishes with loved ones, and discussing quality versus quantity of life with loved ones (Van Scoy, Green, Reading, Scott, Chuang, & Levi, 2016). Seventy-eight percent had engaged in at least one care planning activity within three months, and, based on the transtheoretical model of behavior change (Fried, Bullock, Iannone, & O'Leary, 2009), 73% had progressed in stage of readiness to pursue advance care planning. This initial evaluation included a small ($n = 68$), homogeneous (94% White) sample, so information about generalizability is limited.

Another card-based tool, **Go Wish** (Menkin, 2007), is also designed to promote conversations about end-of-life care. Originally developed for assisted living residents with limited language skills, the tool consists of 35 cards, each printed with a life or care value (e.g., "To be free from pain") and one "wild card." Participants sort the cards into three piles based on whether the value is very important, somewhat important, or not important to them. The cards in the "very important" pile are ranked, and the top ten can be shared with providers. The process of sorting the cards is used to stimulate discussion on end-of-life care goals. Evaluations of the tool have been conducted with medical, rehabilitation, and transitional care inpatients in a Veterans hospital (Lankarani-Fard et al., 2010), cancer patients (Delgado-Guay et al., 2016), and older adults with cognitive impairment (Siefman, Brummel-Smith, Baker, & Edgerton, 2013). Results suggest that the tool is acceptable to users and promotes discussion, but more distal effects have not been evaluated. The veteran sample ($n = 33$) and cancer sample ($n = 100$) were from urban settings and approximately one third of both samples included racially diverse individuals. The dementia sample ($n = 31$) was also urban (and Canadian), though no information was provided about racial identity.

Another newly developed program currently under evaluation is **FAmily CEntered (FACE)** advance care planning (Kimmel, Wang, Scott, Briggs, & Lyon, 2015). This two-session intervention was designed for people with HIV/AIDS and includes dyads consisting of a patient and a surrogate decision-maker. In the first session, an interventionist completes an interview about care values and preferences and facilitates a conversation about goals and experiences that underlie treatment preferences. In the second session, the interventionist helps the dyad complete an advance directive. The developers of this program note several of its strengths over current standards of care, including its emphasis on shared decision-making, integration of an evidence-based HIV/AIDS specific curriculum, and grounding in theory related to self-regulation and illness representations. As with several other interventions reviewed in this chapter, evaluation of the program is still underway at the time of this writing, although a previous version designed for adolescents with HIV and their family members had positive results on rates of advance directive completion (Lyon et al., 2010).

Another dyadic intervention, this one for patients with cancer, uses Chochinov's Dignity Therapy as a framework to enhance communication in couples

(Mowll et al., 2015). The investigators manualized an interview based on the meaning-affirming principles of Dignity Therapy. A psychosocial oncologist (e.g., clinical psychologist, social worker, psychiatrist) administers an interview with a patient and then with a care partner, who estimates how they think the patient is feeling. The provider then reviews the combined interview results with the couple, summarizing areas of agreement and disagreement and facilitates reflection and further discussion. In a pilot study with nine dyads, participants reported that the program helped couples identify differences in perspective and come to a mutual understanding of the challenges each was facing.

Decision-making

Similar to the goal of enhancing communication, efforts to support patient decision-making are at the forefront of the healthcare agenda (Arnold et al., 2009). All individuals will make decisions eventually about the care they want to receive at the end of life. Some will make these decisions quite early, potentially even years before the onset of a serious or life-limiting illness. Others who do not plan in advance will nonetheless be confronted with difficult choices when serious threats to health and well-being arrive. Decisions about end-of-life care can be framed in ways that are very broad ("Who will you choose to be your surrogate decision-maker?") or very specific ("Do you want to have a tube placed in your stomach through which you'll receive food?"). In addition, when considered in advance, decisions may be hypothetical ("Would you want to have chemotherapy if you develop breast cancer in your late 80s?") or very real when people must make immediate decisions ("Do you want more morphine to control your pain now, even though it might make you less alert and able to talk with your family?"). Some individuals will want to (or have to) make these decisions independently, but others will seek input from family members, close companions, and healthcare providers. Yet even when individuals do contemplate their healthcare preferences in advance, many still fail to document those preferences. Two-thirds of all adults and 40% of adults over 60 have not taken necessary steps to document preferences for EOL care and treatment (Benson & Aldrich, 2012).

In many ways, it should not come as a surprise that a vast number of individuals have not documented preferences for end-of-life care, given the challenges that accompany the process of making such serious decisions (Kwak, Ko, & Kramer, 2014; Woo, Matal, & Stern, 2006). Factors such as time pressure (Brom et al., 2015; Young, Goodie, Hall, & Wu, 2012), fluctuating emotions (Lerner, Li, Valdesolo, & Kassam, 2015), and family/interpersonal conflict (Schickedanz et al., 2009) may create barriers to quality decision-making and decrease an individual's feeling of readiness to address future healthcare choices. Fear of thinking about declining health states or "lack of readiness" in and of itself may be a barrier to ACP (Fried, Bullock, Iannone, & O'Leary, 2009).

Cognitive impairment, fatigue, and frailty further complicate matters (Dening, Jones, & Sampson, 2012; Mitchell, Kiely, & Hamel, 2004). Moreover, external factors related to the structure of healthcare systems are impediments (Norton & Talerico, 2000). Regardless of the source, these challenges inevitably and exponentially obfuscate care-planning issues as the end of life approaches.

The reality of misinformed or postponed decision-making translates into stress for healthcare providers (Escher, Perrier, Rudaz, Dayer, & Perneger, 2015), dissatisfaction among patients and family members (Detering, Hancock, Reade, & Silvester, 2010; Gries, Curtis, Wall, & Engelberg, 2008), and prolongation of low-quality life (Teno, Gruneir, Schwartz, Nanda, & Welte, 2007). Therefore, researchers have developed interventions to facilitate the process. With their emphasis on patient-centered care and shared decision-making, these interventions aim to bolster autonomy (Elwyn et al., 2012) by encouraging people to weigh EOL care options, often with the input of family, providers, or both (Cohen, 2017).

What is a decision aid?

A decision aid is "a tool used to inform patients about available treatments, along with potential benefits, risks and costs, during clinical encounters" (Mayo Clinic Center for Innovation, 2016). They provide patients and care partners (e.g., co-decision-makers) with the information required to make person-centered decisions about healthcare. The International Patient Decision Aids Standards (IPDAS) Collaboration recognizes sound decision aids as those that provide detailed information about treatment options, use plain language, are not biased in their presentation of information, incorporate processes of development and revision, and are efficacious in their attempts to encourage individuals to make decisions that are both informed and centered around their values (Elwyn et al., 2006; IPDAS Collaboration, 2005). Well-developed decision aids also foster the patient's understanding of health outcomes, explicate the personal value of benefits and harms of various care options, ensure that the patient (and care partner) feels supported in decision-making, assist the patient in moving through the steps of making a healthcare decision, and facilitate the patient's engagement in deciding about future healthcare (Stacey et al., 2014).

Decision aids can encourage deliberation about a wide range of topics related to immediate and future care, including general explication of treatment alternatives, information about cost for different treatment options, and detailed steps about both making a care decision and communicating that choice to others (Stacey et al., 2014). Care planning that is facilitated by decision aids is more successful at promoting informed decision-making (and careful deliberation about decisions) among patients, families, and providers (Butler, Ratner, McCreedy, Shippee, & Kane, 2014; Stacey et al., 2014). Decision aids may not only decrease patients' feelings of passiveness and decisional conflict but also increase the probability that the patient will make value-congruent decisions

(Hanson et al., 2011; Munro, Stacey, Lewis, & Bansback, 2016). Well-designed decision aids for EOL may result in greater preparedness among patients and decreased responsibility for providers to guide decisions singlehandedly. More importantly, they communicate patient treatment preferences when those preferences have otherwise not been documented.

Decision aid interventions for patients

Among the decision aids useful in advance care planning that have been rigorously evaluated, many focus exclusively on helping patients weigh care options and determine treatment preferences. These decision aids take on a variety of formats (e.g., online, print, a combination) and employ many different strategies.

Several decision aids simultaneously engage the patient in advance care planning and organize preferences into a succinct written summary that can be distributed to the patient's healthcare provider, care team, and family. **Making Your Wishes Known** is a computer-based decision aid designed to help with ACP and decision-making (Green & Levi, 2009). It incorporates both an educational component and a decision-making tool that translates patient preferences into a printable document. Making Your Wishes Known relies on Multi-Attribute Utility Theory (Torrance, Boyle, & Horwood, 1982), a framework of decision analysis wherein an individual weighs alternatives in terms of positives and negatives. Information is presented at an eighth-grade reading level in a series of six sections targeting different steps in the ACP preparation process (e.g., exploring your values, choosing a spokesperson, your medical wishes). The program relies on diverse multimedia, including both audio and videos. Furthermore, actors playing the role of decision-makers in video vignettes and photos in the program appear to be racially diverse and span a range of ages (note: this program was not yet available for public use at the time of publication; thus, these interpretations are based on screenshot images of the program from the primary publication). Pilot testing of this program suggests that different groups of people (college students and cancer patients) were satisfied with the decision aid, did not find its length burdensome, and did not experience increased anxiety or hopelessness after completion (Green & Levi, 2009). Additional pilot testing with chronic obstructive pulmonary disease and heart failure patients suggests that the program also increases patient knowledge about advance care planning (Van Scoy, Green, Dimmock, et al., 2016).

Another similar decision tool, **PREPARE for Your Care**, relies on a behavior change framework to initiate advance care planning and documentation of treatment preferences (Sudore et al., 2014). This website directs users through five modules, and, at its close, generates a summary of care preferences and a tailored action plan of "next steps." Instruction is provided on how to communicate wishes successfully and how to ask questions in the healthcare setting. Users are encouraged to share this information and talk with key care partners, including healthcare professionals. The program is written at a fifth-grade reading level, includes voice-overs of text and closed captioning of videos, and is meticulously designed to be culturally inclusive. For example, video vignettes include actors playing individuals 1) from diverse racial and ethnic backgrounds, 2) with unique family circumstances (e.g., one individual plans to designate a neighbor as her surrogate decision-maker), and 3) with a variety of values that inform care planning (e.g., religion). Furthermore, the individuals depicted in the vignettes span a range of ages and thus represent a continuum of older adulthood. Versions are available in English and Spanish. In pilot testing, using the program was not associated with advance care planning actions taken, but it did encourage people at different stages of the process to think about the ways in which they should approach EOL care decision-making and documentation of preferences (Sudore et al., 2014). Additional randomized controlled trials of the website are currently underway to test its efficacy.

Other decision aids rely on a mixed-media approach to EOL care education and advance care planning. **Looking Ahead: Choices for Medical Care When You're Seriously Ill** is a decision aid that combines an informational booklet and DVD (Matlock et al., 2011), typically distributed in conjunction with a palliative care consultation. In the only evaluation of this tool to date (Matlock et al., 2011), users of **Looking Ahead** reported a greater sense of motivation to complete ACP and less concern around posing questions to their healthcare providers compared to a control group that received only a palliative care consultation. However, among the qualitative findings, there were no significant differences between groups in terms of decision conflict and knowledge about the decision-making process. Furthermore, many of the patients in the study were late in the illness trajectory, and some participants indicated that the intervention was insufficiently timely to have an effect on the EOL decision-making process (Matlock et al., 2011).

Other decision aids help individuals define future healthcare preferences by asking them to imagine health states and by presenting visual representations of terminal health conditions. For example, after watching a video about care in advanced dementia, more participants chose comfort care as a preferred EOL care approach and fewer reported interest in life-prolonging care (Deep, Hunter, Murphy, & Volandes, 2010; Volandes, Ariza, Abbo, & Paasche-Orlow, 2008). Participants reported that the video facilitated a deeper understanding of the disease and provided a lens into the difficulties of the disease as experienced by the patient and the caregiver.

In a comparison of two interventions, participants were assigned either to listen to a description of the process of CPR or to watch a video of CPR being performed on a mannequin and intravenous medications being administered to a real intubated patient. Participants in the video condition reported a greater willingness to forgo CPR, as well as more knowledge about the process of CPR in general (Volandes et al., 2013). Interestingly, when patient characteristics were included in the model as predictors, assignment to the video condition and higher health literacy were the only significant predictors of resuscitation preference (i.e., deciding against CPR), providing preliminary evidence that differences in age, race, and ethnic group may dissolve in similarly targeted approaches to education about invasive interventions.

El-Jawahri and colleagues (2010) designed a similar study in which participants (patients with malignant glioma) were randomly assigned to hear a verbal description of goals of care options or to hear the verbal description and see a video of different end-of-life medical care treatment options (e.g., CPR). Although there was not sufficient racial or ethnic diversity in the sample to make meaningful comparisons between groups, results indicate that, overall, participants in the verbal description and video condition generally preferred comfort care and declined CPR. Similar results from other studies suggest that when individuals are presented with pictures or supporting images, including statistics about the percentage of the population affected by certain conditions, they report feeling more informed about how to make healthcare decisions (Shakir, 2014). These studies suggest that audiovisual depictions of certain healthcare states, as well as other visual representations of probabilities, may promote more informed decision-making. However, further investigation is required to elucidate the long-term decision-making ramifications of these interventions with diverse groups. Because unique patient characteristics such as levels of health literacy influence the effects of such interventions (Volandes et al., 2013), focused evaluation of phrasing and presentation of information is essential.

Although some individuals make decisions about healthcare and EOL by themselves, patients frequently make these decisions with the help of partners, family members, close friends, and/or legally appointed healthcare representatives who may be responsible for executing their EOL care preferences. Among these collaborative decision aids, however, few appear to increase completion of ADs and documentation of preferences. For example, one intervention included meetings with a trained social worker to facilitate the patient's understanding of the nature of surrogate decision-making and their ability to complete a **My Preferences** booklet (Bravo et al., 2016). Participants in the intervention group discussed a vignette to understand the complicated nature of surrogate decision-making, discussed preferences with their elected surrogate decision-maker, and worked through a booklet to document their final preferences. Participants in a control group received a health education program to promote a healthy lifestyle (e.g., information about medication and vaccines). Although this intervention was successful at promoting the patient's documentation of care preferences, it was not effective at helping the proxy better understand those preferences (Bravo et al., 2016). Furthermore, the racial and ethnic homogeneity of the sample limits its generalizability to other groups.

Decision aid interventions for patients and providers

Relatively few decision aids have been developed for use between patients and providers together, although some initial limited evidence appears promising.

The **Respecting Patient Choices** intervention program provides facilitated advance care planning by a nurse or other health professional (Detering et al., 2010). Patients are encouraged to document their preferences, appoint a proxy, and include family members in their decision-making process after the facilitator provides a forum for the patient to reflect on values and care goals. Compared to a control group receiving care as usual, the care goals and wishes of patients in the intervention group were more likely to be known and followed by providers at the EOL. Family members of patients in the intervention group also had less anxiety and stress at the patient's EOL. Despite robust sample sizes ($n = 154$ in the intervention group, $n = 155$ in the control group), no information was provided about participant race and ethnicity. Thus it is unclear whether these findings would generalize to diverse individuals.

Other decision aids incorporate discussions with allied health professionals, such as psychologists and social workers, in order to increase the completion of advance directives. In a randomized controlled trial by Stein and colleagues (2013), participants in the intervention group had a semistructured discussion with a psychologist about their EOL care preferences and reviewed a pamphlet, "Living with Advanced Cancer," with the psychologist. Although participants in both the control and intervention group had higher rates of do-not-resuscitate (DNR) order completion, participants in the intervention group had placed DNR orders significantly earlier. However, the authors acknowledge that they did not randomize a group to receive only the decision aid without the discussion with the psychologist, making it impossible to tease out which portion of the intervention may have resulted in the significant effect (Stein et al., 2013). Similar to the homogeneous samples in other studies reviewed here, participants in this study were recruited exclusively in Australia, and individuals reflected minimal racial and ethnic diversity.

Another tool, **Making Your Wishes Known**, enables patients to articulate their care preferences and share that information with their providers. In one evaluation of this aid, patients approved of physicians' hypothetical treatment decisions that had been informed by review of the patient's preferences documented in Making Your Wishes Known (Levi, Heverley, & Green, 2011). This tool also has been used to educate future physicians about how to help patients make EOL care decisions and document care preferences. The study team randomized one group of medical students to use a standardized advance care planning packet and a second group to use the Making Your Wishes Known online decision aid. Student physicians rated the online decision aid as more useful for understanding patients' choices and more helpful for directing care goals conversations and explaining care options. They also stated that it helped them learn more about the process. Moreover, the patients themselves were more satisfied with the medical student performance in this condition. Despite the positive findings of this evaluation, its limited sample size and minimal racial/ethnic diversity underscore the importance of assessing efficacy in broader samples.

Decision aids also have been applied to group conversations. A recent intervention developed by Lum and colleagues (2016) involved a group discussion guided by prompts from **The Conversation Project** and the **PREPARE for Your Care** decision aid. Almost all participants agreed that participating in the conversation group was more informative than having an individual conversation about advance care planning with their physician. Thus, combining a communication intervention and a decision aid intervention may have additive effects.

The tools and interventions reviewed above are designed to be used with a range of people, in a variety of settings. In the section that follows, we present a case example that imagines how these interventions might be applied. Specifically, we consider how a question prompt list (QPL) as a tool to enhance communication, and the *Making Your Wishes Known* decision aid (Green & Levi, 2009) as a method to enhance decision-making, might be used with an older, cognitively impaired woman. Simultaneously, we depict the ways in which family dynamics and interactions with healthcare providers might intersect with utilization of these interventions.

Case example

Mrs. Spencer is a 75-year-old, African American woman who lives alone in a senior housing apartment complex in an urban metropolis. She completed high school and worked as a secretary at a law firm for 50 years, just retiring last year. Mrs. Spencer has two children, Sara (age 56) from her first marriage, and Edward (age 59), a stepson from her second marriage. Sara lives in a suburb 30 minutes away from Mrs. Spencer's apartment; she takes her mother grocery shopping from time to time, accompanies her to most medical appointments, and cleans her house every other week. Mrs. Spencer enjoys spending time with Sara's children, and she drives to Sara's house every Sunday for supper.

Mrs. Spencer walks with a few neighbors on some mornings, attends church weekly, and plays euchre with friends in her apartment complex twice a week. Her medical conditions include osteoarthritis, mild hypertension, and a history of cataracts. She takes medication for her high blood pressure, occasional anti-inflammatories for arthritis pain, and a multivitamin.

Last Sunday, Mrs. Spencer called Sara on her way to her daughter's home because she was confused: although she had traveled the same route to Sara's house for nearly two decades, she was lost. Sara could sense the panic in her mother's voice, but once Sara had explained the route to her house, the confusion subsided, and Mrs. Spencer laughed it off, explaining to her daughter, "I guess I just didn't get my usual second cup of coffee."

In the months that followed, however, Sara grew more concerned, as her mother had noticeable problems with her memory, occasional mild disorientation, and periods of agitation when she became more insistent and demanding, behavior very uncharacteristic for Mrs. Spencer. Mrs. Spencer's stepson, Edward, also observed changes in her behavior when he visited from out of town over the holidays. During a conversation at the dinner table, the two siblings convinced Mrs. Spencer to visit a geriatrician for an evaluation.

At her first appointment, Mrs. Spencer was accompanied by Sara. The geriatrician interviewed both Mrs. Spencer and Sara, inquiring about what both of them had been noticing. The physician also conducted a brief neurological exam and ordered blood work and an MRI. At the close of that appointment, the geriatrician shared an initial impression that Mrs. Spencer was in the early stages of dementia, but that a more definitive conclusion would be provided once the test results were back. A second appointment was scheduled two weeks later, at which the geriatrician planned to confirm the initial diagnostic impression and discuss a treatment plan. Several days before that appointment, the geriatrician sent Mrs. Spencer and Sara a question prompt list (QPL). The geriatrician encouraged Mrs. Spencer and Sara to review the questions on the QPL, add new questions they hoped to ask, and bring the form to the second appointment. Sara made a point of having lunch with her mother the weekend before her appointment, and she reviewed the QPL with her. They highlighted several questions on the QPL that seemed relevant:

- "What is the name for the medical condition you think I have? Are there any other names people use for this condition?"
- "What treatments do you recommend I take for my medical condition? How do you think they will help me? What are the risks of taking those treatments?"
- "What changes do you think I should be making in my life because of my medical condition?"

Sara said she also wanted to ask the physician, "How will this condition affect my mother in the future? What can we expect?" and "How do I know if my mother is safe to drive?"

At the next appointment, the geriatrician told Mrs. Spencer and Sara that, altogether, the evaluation and test results suggested that Mrs. Spencer was in the early stages of dementia, and the most likely cause was Alzheimer's disease. After having a moment to let this news sink in, Mrs. Spencer and Sara turned to their QPL and worked their way through their questions. Mrs. Spencer said that the diagnosis was unexpected, because her physical health was so good, and her daughter agreed. The geriatrician and nurse discussed the possible course of the disease, pharmacological treatment options, details about a driving evaluation, health promotion suggestions, and they provided a list of community resources.

Mrs. Spencer returned to her geriatrician a year later, this time accompanied by both Sara and Edward. During the intervening year, Mrs. Spencer's cognition had continued to decline. Sara started to help her write checks and balance her bank statements and, following a minor accident, Mrs. Spencer was driving only during the day, and only around her neighborhood. In addition, she had one fall that resulted in a fractured wrist. After discussing Mrs. Spencer's current status, the geriatrician suggested that Mrs. Spencer have a driving evaluation and a home safety assessment. Finally, the geriatrician asked several questions neither Mrs. Spencer nor her children knew how to answer: "Have you filled out an advance directive? Have you designated a health care proxy?" It was clear to the geriatrician that no one had talked with the family yet about end-of-life plans, and the geriatrician suggested they undertake advance care planning.

At first, Mrs. Spencer resisted, saying, "I'm still healthy and I've got plenty of time before I need to think about these things." The geriatrician responded that *everyone* should think about their healthcare preferences, even Mrs. Spencer's children, and maybe all three of them could work on this together. They agreed, but were unsure how to start. The geriatrician recommended that they look at the *Making Your Wishes Known* decision aid, a computer program that would guide them through many of the decisions that would be important for Mrs. Spencer to consider given her diagnosis of dementia and the healthcare choices she might face in the future.

The next week, Mrs. Spencer logged onto the *Making Your Wishes Known* website. Almost immediately, she understood the urgency of selecting a healthcare advocate but had trouble deciding which family member to appoint. Mrs. Spencer eventually decided that Sara would be her surrogate decision-maker and power of attorney, but that if something happened to Sara, Edward would be in charge. All three realized they would need to review Mrs. Spencer's preferences together. Mrs. Spencer's preferences were synthesized into an advance directive that she printed for her family and her healthcare providers.

Mrs. Spencer met with Sara and Edward to discuss the decisions she had outlined in *Making Your Wishes Known*. She provided each of them with a copy of the AD and described two places in her home where she planned to keep copies for herself. The three had a productive conversation about her wishes, and Sara and Edward decided to use the program to develop their own ADs. Later that week, Mrs. Spencer brought a copy of the final AD to her primary care physician, and Sara mailed a copy to her geriatrician.

Questions

1   How should Mrs. Spencer's geriatrician use the QPL during her second appointment with the Spencer's to get the most out of the tool?

2   Given Mrs. Spencer's cognitive decline, what might we think about the reliability and validity of her response to questions in *Making Your Wishes Known*?

3   If Mrs. Spencer and Sara had completed the decision aid together, how can we clarify that the preferences reflected in Mrs. Spencer's advance directive reflect Mrs. Spencer's healthcare preferences and not Sara's preferences *for* Mrs. Spencer?

4   If Mrs. Spencer, like many older adults, does not see her medical providers for several months or even years between visits, what steps should be taken to make sure that the advance directive reflects Mrs. Spencer's *current* preferences?

Practice implications and conclusions

When communication and decision-making tools are used in practice, several considerations are relevant to their implementation.

Health literacy and numeracy

An overarching goal of many of the interventions reviewed in this chapter is to help patients and family members understand health information so they can articulate their preferences and make informed decisions. Yet patients are diverse in their familiarity with health information and ability to comprehend what can be complex technical details. Indeed, people with low levels of health literacy may be especially reluctant to engage providers in conversations related to advance care planning, or if they do participate in these conversations, they still feel that they lack the knowledge to contribute meaningfully to decisions (Cohen, 2017). Therefore, providers shoulder the responsibility to evaluate when (and what) interventions are likely to be helpful to a patient, aware that for some people a tool may result in more confusion than elucidation. For example, in some studies of QPLs, individuals with low health literacy have difficulty understanding the questions they are supposed to ask their provider (Muscat et al., 2016), meaning the tool that was supposed to help may actually hinder communication. Literature reviews indicate that decision aids rarely employ approaches to address the needs of low health literate users, in spite of the fact that disparate levels of health literacy are well documented between and within subpopulations worldwide (Paasche-Orlow, Parker, Gazmararian, Nielson-Bohlman, & Rudd, 2005; Rikard, Thompson, McKinney, & Beauchamp, 2016), and low health literacy is related to poorer decision-making outcomes (McCaffery et al., 2013). This reality underscores the need to address the effect of divergent health literacy skills on receptiveness to interventions that aim to enhance the quality of end-of-life care planning. In sum, providers should review any decision aids they plan to implement and ensure they are appropriate for all the individuals with whom they plan to use them.

Context of interventions

Although some evidence suggests that communication and decision-making interventions are effective, there is remarkably little empirical research on how location, timing, and other contextual factors affect their impact. For example, to our knowledge, no studies have compared the usefulness of these interventions in healthy, community-based research samples to the effectiveness of the same interventions with actual patients whose preferences for end-of-life care are especially time sensitive. Similarities or differences in efficacy between these two populations might answer questions about optimal setting and timing (e.g., Do decision aids result in higher completion rates of advance directives when they are presented to individuals in the community who are not already in the midst of a complex medical decision? Do communication interventions encourage more patient-centered conversations when they are introduced immediately prior to an upcoming medical appointment?). Studies also have not yet examined the most effective timing for the introduction of these tools among individuals with life-limiting illnesses. For example, immediately after the disclosure of the diagnosis of a serious illness, when people are still processing the simple fact that they have a disease, a QPL may compound information overload and might be more effective at a follow-up conversation, after news of the illness has sunk in. Likewise, an advance care planning decision aid may yield different results at different points in the illness trajectory. Finally, we know little about who is the ideal person to administer these tools, providers or family members.

To this end, it is also possible that the interaction of context and group identity may affect openness to and successful implementation of these interventions. For example, individuals from different racial, ethnic, religious, and cultural backgrounds may be more or less affected by an intervention depending on contextual factors that include timing, setting, person, and mindset. Given that certain groups are less trusting of healthcare providers and encounters in healthcare settings (see below), greater emphasis should be placed in future research on exploring both group- and individual-level interactions likely to influence the efficacy of these interventions.

Cultural and diversity issues

Disparate treatment in healthcare settings, differential rates of healthcare utilization, and varying attitudes about medical treatments between individuals from different cultural, ethnic, and religious backgrounds are well documented in the literature (National Center for Health Statistics, 2016; Shavers, Bakos, & Sheppard, 2010; Soto, Martin, & Gong, 2013). Unsurprisingly, these disparities extend to treatment at end of life (Choi et al., 2015; Garrido, Harrington, & Prigerson, 2014; Harrison, Adrion, Ritchie, Sudore, & Smith, 2016). Providers should be aware of well-documented differences among groups in terms of care preferences and utilization, and must simultaneously recognize that individuals may or may not conform to the norms of any group of which they are a member. That is to say, genuine patient-centered care takes into account *possible* differences based on group membership but does not *assume* values and preferences based on group membership. Adopting a stance of nonjudgmental curiosity, akin to the accepting *therapeutic presence* recommended by Chochinov and colleagues (2013) would enhance the use of any of the tools or interventions reviewed in this chapter.

In the realm of end-of-life care, differences in treatment preferences may reflect cultural and religious variability in the interpretation of healthcare options (Boucher, 2016; Bullock, 2011). Focus groups with individuals from different cultural and ethnic backgrounds have documented diverse attitudes about the way in which the end of life should unfold and preferences about care at the end of life. As just one example, Arab American individuals are generally reluctant to disclose bad news, which may affect understanding of health conditions and subsequent levels of preparation for different healthcare outcomes (Duffy, Jackson, Schim, Ronis, & Fowler, 2006). Likewise, minority groups may rely more heavily on a family support system when making health-care decisions – and may also involve spiritual leaders in deliberations – so communication and decisions aids that maximize multiparty involvement may be most helpful (Hawley & Morris, 2017). Furthermore, the content of discussions about serious illness, as well as the willingness of individuals to tolerate these conversations, may differ between groups. As a result, providers must be aware of differential preparation for advance care planning and different ways in which conversations about planning may play out. As we have mentioned throughout the chapter, empirical research designed to develop and evaluate communication and decision aids in diverse groups lags well behind the need.

Equity and access

Communication and decision-making tools are most useful when they are accessible and are effective across sociodemographic groups (Coylewright et al., 2014). We found some tools that had been translated into languages other than English, were designed for use by people with a range of reading skills, and whose authors made a point to make them available for free on the internet. However, that was not the case for most tools. Moreover, we found few mentions in the literature of tools that could be used by people with cognitive or intellectual deficits, sensory impairments, or other limitations. Decision aids that are easily accessed and available to the general public remain few and far between. Many are intended for use by healthcare systems exclusively and available only for institutional purchase, and others that are available to individuals still involve a fee. Adopting a social justice perspective toward palliative care and end-of-life interventions means advocating for equitably designed and generalizable interventions and access for all.

A final note on efficacy and effectiveness

Many of the interventions reviewed in this chapter have an intuitive appeal: they aim to improve communication and decision-making with strategies that are straightforward and have good face validity. (How could giving patients a list of questions to ask their provider *not* be useful?) Yet readers should keep in mind that many of the interventions have not been evaluated in a systematic, methodologically rigorous way.

Evaluations that focus on important but narrow outcomes, such as acceptability to users or patient satisfaction, provide no information about the impact on outcomes that might be more meaningful, such as changes in clinical care. Indeed, understanding the effects of these programs is complicated by the fact that the outcomes that matter most (i.e., facility with difficult conversations at the end of life, compliance with care preferences) may not occur for years after participation, during which time many other factors could influence those very same outcomes. Interventions may produce attitudinal changes in the short term, and may prompt some actions (e.g., completion of an advance directive), but their ultimate value remains equivocal. Therefore, using one of these tools or interventions demands an awareness of the research conducted with them to date and their potential limitations. Of course, a lack of research should also be considered an incentive to ambitious scholars to fill these gaps in the empirical literature.

References

Accreditation Council for Graduate Medical Education. (2016 July 1). *ACGME Common Program Requirements*. Retrieved from www.acgme.org/Portals/0/PFAssets/Program Requirements/CPRs_07012016.pdf

Alders, I., Smits, C., Brand, P., & van Dulmen, S. (2017). Does patient coaching make a difference in patient-physician communication during specialist consultations? A systematic review. *Patient Education and Counseling, 100*, 882–896. doi:10.1016/j.pec.2016.12.029

American Association of Colleges of Nursing. (2013). *Competencies and Curricular Expectations for Clinical Nurse Leader Education and Practice*. Retrieved from www.aacn.nche.edu/cnl/CNL-Competencies-October-2013.pdf

American Psychological Association. (2011). *Revised Competency Benchmarks in Professional Psychology*. Retrieved from http://apa.org/ed/graduate/competency.aspx

Ampe, S., Sevenants, A., Smets, T., Declercq, A., & van Audenhove, C. (2017). Advance care planning for nursing home residents with dementia: Influence of "we DECide" on policy and practice. *Patient Education and Counseling, 100*, 139–146.

Arnold, R., Billings, J. A., Block, S. D., Goldstein, N., Morrison, L. J., Okon, T., . . . Scott, J. O. (2009). *Hospice and Palliative Medicine Core Competencies. Version 2.3*. Chicago, IL: American Academy of Hospice and Palliative Medicine.

Back, A. L., Arnold, R. M., Baile, W. F., Fryer-Edwards, K. A., Alexander, S. C., Barley, G. E., . . . Tulsky, J. A. (2007). Efficacy of a communication skills training for giving bad news and discussing transitions to palliative care. *Archives of Internal Medicine, 167*, 453–460.

Benson, W. F., & Aldrich, N. (2012). *Advance Care Planning: Ensuring Your Wishes Are Known and Honored If You Are Unable to Speak for Yourself, Critical Issue Brief, Centers for Disease Control and Prevention*. Retrieved from www.cdc.gov/aging

Bernacki, R., Hutchings, M., Vick, J., Smith, G., Paladino, J., Lipsitz, S., . . . Block, S. D. (2015). Development of the serious illness care program: A randomised controlled trial of a palliative care communication intervention. *BMJ Open, 5*, e009032. doi:10.1136/bmjopen-2015–009032

Boucher, N. A. (2016). Direct engagement with communities and interprofessional learning to factor culture into end-of-life health care delivery. *American Journal of Public Health, 106*(6), 996–1001.

Bravo, G., Trottier, L., Arcand, M., Boire-Lavigne, A., Blanchette, D., Dubois, M., Guay, M., . . . Bellemare, S. (2016). Promoting advance care planning among community-based older adults: A randomized controlled trial. *Patient Education and Counseling, 99*, 1785–1795.

Brom, L., de Snoo-Trimp, J. C., Onwuteaka, B. D., Widdershoven, G. A. M., Stiggelbout, A. M., & Pasman, H. R. W. (2015). Challenges in shared decision making in advanced cancer care: A qualitative longitudinal observational and interview study. *Health Expectations, 20*, 69–84.

Buckman, R. (2005). Breaking bad news: The S-P-I-K-E-S strategy. *Community Oncology*, *2*, 138–142.

Bullock, K. (2011). The influence of culture on end-of-life decision making. *Journal of Social Work in End-of-Life and Palliative Care*, *7*, 83–98.

Buonocore, D., Wiegand, D. L., Hollyday, S. L., & Buonocore, D. (2015). Breaking bad news and discussing goals of care in the intensive care unit. *AACN Advanced Critical Care*, *26*, 131–141.

Butler, M., Ratner, E., McCreedy, E., Shippee, N., & Kane, R. L. (2014). *Decision Aids for Advance Care Planning. Technical Brief No. 16*. (Prepared by the Minnesota Evidence-based Practice Center under Contract No. 290–2012–00016-I.) AHRQ Publication No. 14-EHC039-EF. Rockville, MD: Agency for Healthcare Research and Quality. Retrieved from www.effectivehealthcare.ahrq.gov/reports/final.cfm

Bylund, C. L., Brown, R. F., Bialer, P. A., Levin, T. T., Lubrano di Ciccone, B., & Kisssane, D. W. (2011). Developing and implementing an advanced communication training program in oncology at a comprehensive cancer center. *Journal of Cancer Education*, *26*, 604–611.

Chin, L. E., Loong, L. C., Ngen, C. C., Beng, T. S., Shireen, C., Kuan, W. S., & Shaw, R. (2014). Pediatric palliative care: Using miniature chairs to facilitate communication. *American Journal of Hospice & Palliative Medicine*, *31*, 833–835. doi:10.1177/1049909113509001

Chochinov, H. M., McClement, S. E. Hack, T. F., McKeen, N. A., Rach, A. M., Gagnon, P., . . . Taylor-Brown, J. (2013). Health care provider communication: An empirical model of therapeutic effectiveness. *Cancer*, *119*, 1706–1713. doi:10.1002/cncr.27949

Choi, H. A., Fernandez, A., Jeon, S., Schmidt, J. M., Connolly, E. S., Mayer, S. A., . . . Lee, K. (2015). Ethnic disparities in end-of-life care after subarachnoid hemorrhage. *Neurocritical Care*, *22*, 423–428.

Clayton, J. M., Butow, P. N., Tattersall, M. H. N., Devine, R. J., Simpson, J. M., Aggarwal, G., . . . Noel, M. A. (2007). Randomized controlled trial of a prompt list to help advanced cancer patients and their caregivers to ask questions about prognosis and end-of-life care. *Journal of Clinical Oncology*, *25*, 715–723. doi:10.1200/JCO.2006.06.7827

Cohen, M. D. (2017). Engaging patients in understanding and using evidence to inform shared decision making. *Patient Education and Counseling*, *100*, 2–3.

Cohen, R. A., Jackson, V. A., Norwich, D., Schell, J. O., Schaefer, K., Ship, A. N., & Sullivan, A. M. (2016). Nephrology fellows' communication skills course: An educational quality improvement report. *American Journal of Kidney Diseases*, *68*, 208–211.

Connolly, M., Thomas, J., Orford, J., Schofield, N., Whiteside, S., Morris, J., & Heaven, C. (2014). The impact of the SAGE & THYME foundation level workshop on factors influencing communication skills in health care professionals. *Journal of Continuing Education in Health Professions*, *34*, 37–46.

Coylewright, M., Branda, M., Inselman, J. W., Shah, N., Hess, E., LeBlanc, A., . . . Ting, H. H. (2014). Impact of sociodemographic patient characteristics on the efficacy of decision aids. *Circulation: Cardiovascular Quality and Outcomes*, *7*, 360–367.

Curtin, S., & McConnell, M. (2012). Teaching dental students how to deliver bad news: S-P-I-K-E-S model. *Journal of Dental Education*, *76*, 360–365.

Curtis, J. R., Back, A. L., Ford, D. W., Downey, L., Shannon, S. E., Doorenbos, A. Z., . . . Engelberg, R. A. (2015). Randomized trial of communication facilitators to reduce family distress and intensity of end-of-life care. *American Journal of Respiratory and Critical Care Medicine*, *193*, 154–162.

Davis, K., Schoenbaum, S. C., & Audet, A. (2005). A 2020 vision of patient-centered primary care. *Journal of General Internal Medicine*, *20*, 953–957.

Deep, K. S., Hunter, A., Murphy, K., & Volandes, A. (2010). "It helps me see with my heart": How video informs patients' rationale for decisions about future care in advanced dementia. *Patient Education and Counseling, 81*, 229–234.

Delgado-Guay, M. O., Rodriguez-Nunez, A., De la Cruz, V., Frisbee-Hume, S., Williams, J., Wu, J., . . . Bruera, E. (2016). Advanced cancer patients' reported wishes at the end of life: A randomized controlled trial. *Supportive Care in Cancer, 24,* 4273–4281. doi:10.1007/s00520-016-3260-9

Dening, K. H., Jones, L., & Sampson, E. L. (2012). Preferences for end of life care: A nominal group study of people with dementia and their family careers. *Palliative Medicine, 27,* 409–417.

Detering, K. M., Hancock, A. D., Reade, M. C., & Silvester, W. (2010). The impact of advance care planning on end of life care in elderly patients: Randomised controlled trial. *BMJ, 340,* 1345.

Doorenbos, A. Z., Levy, W. C., Curtis, J. R., & Dougherty, C. M. (2016). An intervention to enhance goals-of-care communication between heart failure patients and heart failure providers. *Journal of Pain and Symptom Management, 52,* 353–360.

Duffy, S. A., Jackson, F. C., Schim, S. M., Ronis, D. L., & Fowler, K. E. (2006). Racial/ethnic preferences, sex preferences, and perceived discrimination related to end-of-life care. *Journal of the American Geriatrics Society, 54,* 150–157.

El-Jawahri, A., Podgurski, L. M., Eichler, A. F., Plotkin, S. R., Temel, J. S., Mitchell, S. L., . . . Volandes, A. E. (2010). Use of video to facilitate end-of-life discussions with patients with cancer: A randomized controlled trial. *Journal of Clinical Oncology, 28,* 305–310.

Elwyn, G., Frosch, D., Thomson, R., Joseph-Williams, N., Lloyd, A., Kinnersley, P., . . . Barry, M. (2012). Shared decision making: A model for clinical practice. *Journal of General Internal Medicine, 27,* 1361–1367.

Elwyn, G., O'Connor, A., Stacey, D., Volk, R., Edwards, A., Coulter, A., . . . Whelan, T. (2006). Developing a quality criteria framework for patient decision aids: Online international Delphi consensus process. *BMJ, 333,* 417. doi:10.1136/bmj.38926.629329.AE

Epner, D. E., & Baile, W. F. (2014). Difficult conversations: Teaching medical oncology trainees communication skills one hour at a time. *Academic Medicine, 89*(4), 578–584.

Erickson, J. M., Blackhall, L., Brashers, V., & Varhegyi, N. (2015). An interprofessional workshop for students to improve communication and collaboration skills in end-of-life care. *American Journal of Hospice & Palliative Medicine, 32,* 876–880. doi:10.1177/1049909114549954

Escher, M., Perrier, A., Rudaz, S., Dayer, P., & Perneger, T. V. (2015). Doctors' decisions when faced with contradictory patient advance directives and health care proxy opinion: A randomized vignette-based study. *Journal of Pain and Symptom Management, 49,* 637–645.

Flint, H., Meyer, M., Hossain, M., & Klein, M. (2015). Discussing serious news: Teaching communication skills through role play with bereaved parents. *American Journal of Hospice & Palliative Care.* doi:10.1177/1049909115617140

Fried, T. R., Bullock, K., Iannone, L., & O'Leary, J. R. (2009). Understanding advance care planning as a process of health behavior change. *Journal of the American Geriatrics Society, 57,* 1547–1555.

Gamondi, C., Larkin, P., & Payne, S. (2013). Core competencies in palliative care: An EAPC white paper on palliative care education – part 2. *European Journal of Palliative Care, 20,* 140–145.

Garrido, M. M., Harrington, S. T., & Prigerson, H. G. (2014). End of life treatment preferences: A key to reducing ethnic/racial disparities in advance care planning? *Cancer, 120*(24), 3981–3986.

Gelfman, L. P., Lindenberger, E., Fernandez, H., Goldberg, G. R., Lim, B. B., Litrivis, E., . . . Kelley, A. S. (2014). The effectiveness of the Geritalk communication skills course: A real time assessment of skill acquisition and deliberate practice. *Journal of Pain and Symptom Management, 48,* 738–744.

Goelz, T., Wuensch, A., Stubenrauch, S., Ihorst, G., de Figueiredo, M., Bertz, H., . . . Fritzsche, K. (2011). Specific training program improves oncologists' palliative care communication skills in a randomized controlled trial. *Journal of Clinical Oncology, 29,* 3402–3407.

Gorniewicz, J., Floyd, M., Krishnan, K., Bishop, T. W., Tudiver, F., & Lang, F. (2016). Breaking bad news to patients with cancer: A randomized control trial of a brief communication skills training module incorporating the stories and preferences of actual patients. *Patient Education and Counseling.* doi:http://dx.doi.org/10.1016/j.pec.2016.11.008

Green, M. J., & Levi, B. H. (2009). Development of an interactive computer program for advance care planning. *Health Expectations, 12,* 60–69.

Gries, C. J., Curtis, J. R., Wall, R. J., & Engelberg, R. A. (2008). Family member satisfaction with end-of-life decision-making in the intensive care unit. *CHEST, 133,* 704–712.

Griffiths, J., Ewing, G., Wilson, C., Connolly, M., & Grande, C. (2015). Breaking bad news about transitions to dying: A qualitative exploration of the role of the district nurse. *Palliative Medicine, 29,* 138–146.

Hagiwara, Y., Ross, J., Lee, S., & Sanchez-Reilly, S. (2016). Tough conversations: Development of a curriculum for medical students to lead family meetings. *American Journal of Hospice & Palliative Care.* doi:10.1177/1049909116669783

Hanson, L. C., Carey, T. S., Caprio, A. J., Lee, T. J., Ersek, M., Garrett, J., . . . Mitchell, S. (2011). Improving decision making for feeding options in advanced dementia: A randomized, controlled trial. *Journal of the American Geriatrics Society, 59,* 2009–2016.

Harrison, K. L., Adrion, E. R., Ritchie, C. S., Sudore, R. L., & Smith, A. K. (2016). Low completion and disparities in advance care planning activities among older Medicare beneficiaries. *JAMA Internal Medicine, 176*(12), 1872–1875.

Hawley, S. T., & Morris, A. M. (2017). Cultural challenges to engaging patients in shared decision making. *Patient Education and Counseling, 100,* 18–24.

Hebert, R. S., Schulz, R., Copeland, V. C., & Arnold, R. M. (2009). Pilot testing of a question prompt sheet to encourage family caregivers of cancer patients and physicians to discuss end-of-life issues. *American Journal of Hospice & Palliative Medicine, 26,* 24–32.

International Patient Decision Aid Standards Collaboration. (2005). *IPDAS 2005: Criteria for Judging the Quality of Patient Decision Aids.* Retrieved from http://ipdas.ohri.ca/IPDAS_checklist.pdf

Interprofessional Education Collaborative Expert Panel. (2011). *Core Competencies for Interprofessional Collaborative Practice: Report of an Expert Panel.* Washington, DC: Interprofessional Education Collaborative.

Kelley, A. S., Back, A. L., Arnold, R. M., Goldberg, G. R., Lim, B. B., Litrivis, E., . . . O'Neill, L. B. (2012). Geritalk: Communication skills training for geriatric and palliative medicine fellows. *Journal of the American Geriatrics Society, 60,* 332–337.

Kimmel, A. L., Wang, J., Scott, R. K., Briggs, L., & Lyon, M. E. (2015). FAmily CEntered (FACE) advance care planning: Study design and methods for a patient-centered communication and decision-making intervention for patients with HIV/AIDS and their surrogate decision-makers. *Contemporary Clinical Trials, 43,* 172–178.

Kwak, J., Ko, E., & Kramer, B. (2014). Facilitating advance care planning with ethnically diverse groups of frail, low-income elders in the USA: Perspectives of care managers on challenges and recommendations. *Health and Social Care, 22,* 169–177.

Lankarani-Fard, A., Knapp, H., Lorenz, K. A., Golden, J. F., Taylor, A., Feld, J. E., . . . Asch, S. M. (2010). Feasibility of discussing end-of-life care goals with inpatients using a structured, conversational approach: The Go Wish card game. *Journal of Pain and Symptom Management*, 39, 637–643. doi:10.1016/j.jpainsymman.2009.08.011

Lerner, J. S., Li, Y., Valdesolo, P., & Kassam, K. S. (2015). Emotion and decision making. *Annual Review of Psychology*, 66, 799–823.

Levi, B. H., Heverley, S. R., & Green, M. J. (2011). Accuracy of a decision aid for advance care planning: Simulated end-of-life decision making. *Journal of Clinical Ethics*, 22, 223–238.

Lowenstein, G., & Lerner, J. S. (2003). The role of affect in decision making. In R. J. Davidson, K. R. Scherer, & H. H. Goldsmith (Eds.), *Handbook of Affective Sciences* (pp. 619–642). Oxford: Oxford University Press.

Lum, H. D., Jones, J., Matlock, D. D., Glasgow, R. E., Lobo, I., Levy, C. R., . . . Kutner, J. S. (2016). Advance care planning meets group medical visits: The feasibility of promoting conversations. *Annals of Family Medicine*, 14(2), 125–132.

Lyon, M. E., Garvie, P. A., Briggs, L., He, J., Malow, R., D'Angelo, L. J., & McCarter, R. (2010). Is it safe? Talking to teens with HIV/AIDS about death and dying: A 3-month evaluation of Family Centered advance care (FACE) planning – anxiety, depression, quality of life. *HIV/AIDS – Research and Palliative Care*, 2, 27–37.

Matlock, D. D., Keech, T. A. E., McKenzie, M. B., Bronsert, M. R., Nowels, C. T., & Kutner, J. S. (2011). Feasibility and acceptability of a decision aid designed for people facing advanced or terminal illness: A pilot randomized trial. *Health Expectations*, 17, 49–59.

Mayo Clinic Center for Innovation. (2016). *Decision Aids. Mayo Foundation for Medical Education and Research*. Retrieved from http://centerforinnovation.mayo.edu/decision-aids/

McCaffery, K. J., Holmes-Rovner, M., Smith, S. K., Rovner, D., Nutbeam, D., Clayman, M. L., . . . Sheridan, S. L. (2013). Addressing health literacy in patient decision aids. *BMC Medical Informatics and Decision Making*, 13, S10.

Menkin, E. S. (2007). Go Wish: A tool for end-of-life care conversations. *Journal of Palliative Medicine*, 10, 297–303. doi:10.1089/jpm.2006.9983

Michael, N., O'Callaghan, C., & Clayton, J. M. (2016). Exploring the utility of the vignette technique in promoting advance care planning discussions with cancer patients and caregivers. *Patient Education and Counseling*, 99, 1406–1412.

Milton, A. C., & Mullan, B. (2016). Views and experience of communication when receiving a serious mental health diagnosis: Satisfaction levels, communication preferences, and acceptability of the SPIKES protocol. *Journal of Mental Health*. Retrieved from http://dx.doi.org/10.1080/09638237.2016.1207225

Mitchell, S. L., Kiely, D. K., & Hamel, M. B. (2004). Dying with advanced dementia in the nursing home. *Archives of Internal Medicine*, 164, 321–326.

Mowll, J., Lobb, E. A., Lane, L., Lacey, J., Chochinov, H. M., Kelly, B., . . . Kearsley, J. H. (2015). A preliminary study to develop an intervention to facilitate communication between couples in advanced cancer. *Palliative and Supportive Care*, 13, 1381–1390.

Munro, S., Stacey, D., Lewis, K. B., & Bansback, N. (2016). Choosing screening and treatment options congruent with values: Do decision aids help? Sub-analysis of a systematic review. *Patient Education and Counseling*, 99, 491–500.

Muscat, D. M., Shepherd, H. L., Morony, S., Smith, S. K., Dhillon, H. M., Trevena, L., . . . McCaffery, K. (2016). Can adults with low health literacy understand shared decision making questions? A qualitative investigation. *Patient Education & Counseling*, 99(11), 1796–1802.

National Center for Health Statistics. (2016). *Health, United States, 2015. Special Feature on Racial and Ethnic Health Disparities.* Hyattsville, MD: National Center for Health Statistics.

National Association of Social Workers. (2004). *NASW Standards for Palliative and End of Life Care.* Retrieved from www.socialworkers.org/practice/bereavement/standards/standards 0504New.pdf

Norton, S. A., & Talerico, K. A. (2000). Facilitating end-of-life decision-making strategies for communicating and assessing. *Journal of Gerontological Nursing, 26,* 6–13.

Paasche-Orlow, M. K., Parker, R. M., Gazmararian, J. A., Nielson-Bohlman, J. T., & Rudd, R. R. (2005). The prevalence of limited health literacy. *Journal of General Internal Medicine, 20,* 175–184.

Park, I., Gupta, A., Mandani, K., Haubner, L., & Peckler, B. (2010). Breaking bad news education for emergency medicine residents: A novel training module using simulation with the SPIKES protocol. *Journal of Emergencies, Trauma, and Shock, 3,* 385–388.

PDQ® Supportive and Palliative Care Editorial Board. *PDQ Communication in Cancer Care.* Bethesda, MD: National Cancer Institute. Updated July 16, 2015. Retrieved from www. cancer.gov/about-cancer/coping/adjusting-to-cancer/communication-hp-pdq. Accessed 1/2/2017. [PMID: 26389370]

Raghunathan, R., & Pham, M. T. (1999). All negative moods are not equal: Motivational influences of anxiety and sadness on decision making. *Organizational Behavior and Human Decision Processes, 79,* 56–77.

Rikard, R. V., Thompson, M. S., McKinney, J., & Beauchamp, A. (2016). Examining health literacy disparities in the United States: A third look at the national assessment of adult literacy (NAAL). *BMC Public Health, 16,* 975.

Rucker, B., & Browning, D. M. (2015). Practicing end-of-life conversations: Physician communication training program in palliative care. *Journal of Social Work in End-of-Life & Palliative Care, 11,* 132–146.

Sanchez-Reilly, S., Wittenberg-Lyles, E. M., & Villagran, M. M. (2007). Using a pilot curriculum in geriatric palliative care to improve communication skills among medical students. *American Journal of Hospice & Palliative Medicine, 24,* 131–136.

Sansoni, J. E., Grootemaat, P., & Duncan, C. (2015). Question prompt lists in health consultations: A review. *Patient Education and Counseling, 98,* 1454–1464.

Schickedanz, A. D., Schillinger, D., Landefeld, C. S., Knight, S. J., Williams, B. A., & Sudore, R. L. (2009). A clinical framework for improving the advance care planning process: Start with patients' self identified barriers. *Journal of the American Geriatrics Society, 57,* 31–39.

Schram, A. W., Hougham, G. W., Meltzer, D. O., & Ruhnke, G. W. (2016). A systematic review of communication-based competencies essential for patient and family satisfaction. *American Journal of Hospice & Palliative Medicine.* doi:10.1177/1049909116667071

Shakir, H. (2014). "Seeing is believing": Imaging modalities aid in decision making in end-of-life care. *Journal of Palliative Medicine, 17,* 863.

Shavers, V. L., Bakos, A., & Sheppard, V. B. (2010). Race, ethnicity, and pain among the U.S. adult population. *Journal of Health Care for the Poor and Underserved, 21,* 177–220.

Siefman, M., Brummel-Smith, K., Baker, S., & Edgerton, L. (2013). Consistency of choices of end-of-life wishes using the "Go Wish" cards: A comparison of elders with intact cognition and mild cognitive impairment. *Journal of the American Geriatrics Society, 61,* S120.

Singer, A. E., Ash, T., Ochotorena, C., Lorenz, K. A., Chong, K., Shreve, S. T., & Ahulwalia, S. C. (2016). A systematic review of family meeting tools in palliative and intensive care settings. *American Journal of Hospice & Palliative Care, 33,* 797–806. doi:10.1177/1049909115594353

Skinner, C. S., Pollack, K. I., Farrell, D., Olsen, M. K., Jeffreys, A. S., & Tulsky, J. A. (2009). Use of and reactions to a tailored CD-ROM designed to enhance oncologist-patient communication: The SCOPE trial intervention. *Patient Education and Counseling, 77*, 90–96.

Slort, W., Blankenstein, A. H., Schweitzer, B. P. M., Knol, D. L., Deliens, L., Aaronson, N. K., & van der Horst, H. E. (2013). Effectiveness of the ACA (Availability, Current issues, and Anticipation) training programme on GP-patient communication in palliative care: A controlled trial. *BMC Family Practice, 14*, 93.

Song, M., & Ward, S. E. (2015). Making visible a theory-guided advance care planning intervention. *Journal of Nursing Scholarship, 47*, 389–346.

Song, M., Ward, S. E., Lin, F., Hamilton, J. B., Hanson, L. C., Hladik, G. A., & Fine, J. P. (2016). Racial differences in outcomes of an advance care planning intervention for dialysis patients and their surrogates. *Journal of Palliative Medicine, 19*, 134–142.

Soto, G. J., Martin, G. S., & Gong, M. N. (2013). Healthcare disparities in critical illness. *Critical Care Medicine, 41*, 2784–2793.

Spafford, M. M., Schryer, C. F., & Creutz, S. (2008). Delivering bad news: Applying the SPIKES protocol to the practice of optometry. *Optometric Education, 34*, 13–21.

Stacey, D., Legare, F., Col, N. F., Bennett, C. L., Barry, M. J., Eden, K. B., . . . Wu, J. H. C. (2014). Decision aids for people facing health treatment or screening decisions. *Cochrane Database of Systematic Reviews 2014*, (1), Art. No.: CD001431. doi:10.1002/14651858. CD001431.pub4.

Stein, R. A., Sharpe, L., Bell, M. L., Boyle, F. M., Dunn, S. M., & Clarke, S. J. (2013). Randomized controlled trial of a structured intervention to facilitate end-of-life decision making in patients with advanced cancer. *Journal of Clinical Oncology, 31*, 3403–3410.

Stewart, M., Brown, J. B., Donner, A., McWhinney, I. R., Oates, J., Weston, W. W., & Jordan, J. (2000). The impact of patient-centered care on outcomes. *The Journal of Family Practice, 49*(9), 795–804.

Sudore, R. L., Knight, S. J., McMahan, R. D., Feuz, M., Farrell, D., Miao, R., & Barnes, D. E. (2014). A novel website to prepare diverse older adults for decision making and advance care planning: A pilot study. *Journal of Pain and Symptom Management, 47*, 674–686.

Teno, J. M., Gruneir, A., Schwartz, Z., Nanda, A., & Welte, T. (2007). Association between advance directives and quality of end-of-life care: A national study. *Journal of the American Geriatrics Society, 55*, 189–194.

Torrance, G. W., Boyle, M. H., & Horwood, S. P. (1982). Application of multi-attribute utility theory to measure social preferences for health states. *Annals of Operation Research, 30*, 1043–1069.

Van Scoy, L. J., Green, M. J., Dimmock, A. E. F., Bascom, R., Boehmer, J. P., Hensel, J. K., . . . Levi, B. H. (2016). High satisfaction and low decisional conflict with advance care planning among chronically ill patients with advanced chronic obstructive pulmonary disease or heart failure using an online decision aid: A pilot study. *Chronic Illness, 12*, 227–235.

Van Scoy, L. J., Green, M. J., Reading, J. M., Scott, A. M., Chuang, C. H., & Levi, B. H. (2016). Can playing an end-of-life conversation game motivate people to engage in advance care planning? *American Journal of Hospice & Palliative Care.* doi:10.1177/1049909116656353

Volandes, A. E., Ariza, M., Abbo, E. D., & Paasche-Orlow, M. (2008). Overcoming educational barriers for advance care planning in Latinos with video images. *Journal of Palliative Medicine, 11*, 700–706.

Volandes, A. E., Paasche-Orlow, M. K., Mitchell, S. L., El-Jawahri, A., Davis, A. D., Barry, M. J., . . . Temel, J. S. (2013). Randomized controlled trial of a video decision support tool for cardiopulmonary resuscitation decision making in advanced cancer. *Journal of Clinical Oncology, 31*, 380–386.

White, J., & Fromme, E. K. (2012). "In the beginning . . .": Tools for talking about resuscitation and goals of care early in the admission. *American Journal of Hospice & Palliative Care, 30*, 676–682. doi:10.1177/1049909112468609

Wittenberg-Lyles, E., Goldsmith, J., Ferrell, B., & Burchett, M. (2014). Assessment of an interprofessional online curriculum for palliative care communication training. *Journal of Palliative Medicine, 17*, 400–406.

Woo, J. A., Matal, G., & Stern, T. A. (2006). Clinical challenges to the delivery of end-of-life care. *The Primary Care Companion to the Journal of Clinical Psychiatry, 8*, 367–372.

Young, D. L., Goodie, A. S., Hall, D. B., & Wu, E. (2012). Decision making under time pressure, modeled in a prospect theory framework. *Organizational Behavior and Human Decision Processes, 118*, 179–188.

Chapter 3

Behavioural management of physical and psychological symptoms in palliative care

Kristy Shoji, Toni L. Glover, and Ann L. Horgas

Behavioural management of physical and psychological symptoms in palliative care

Individuals facing serious or life-limiting illness often have physical and psychological symptoms that are both difficult to treat effectively and lead to increased burden on the individual, their care partners, and healthcare providers (Burke et al., 2017; Saria et al., 2017; Tang et al., 2016). Palliative care is for patients of all ages facing a serious or life-limiting illness and can be offered concurrently with curative treatment. Palliative care focuses on providing relief from the symptoms and stress of serious illness (Institute of Medicine, 2015). In contrast, hospice care is a type of palliative care for people at the end of life when curative treatment is no longer feasible. There is a large body of literature addressing best practices in terms of pharmacological interventions for people receiving palliative care (e.g., Fine & Kestenbaum, 2016). However, less is known about behavioural methods to treat such symptoms, although the growing body of literature suggests that they are often beneficial as adjuvant or stand-alone treatment modalities. Behavioural methods of both physical and mental health symptom management in palliative care are the focus of this chapter. Common physical symptoms (e.g., pain, dyspnea, nausea) and psychological symptoms (e.g., depression, anxiety) are discussed, followed by a description of various behavioural methods of addressing them and the empirical evidence supporting their effectiveness in people receiving palliative care. Finally, a case summary allows readers to evaluate one scenario highlighting the potential implications of behavioural symptom management in palliative care.

Common target symptoms in palliative care

There are several symptoms commonly experienced by people facing a serious or life-limiting illness that are burdensome to patients and families and challenging for providers. Symptom experiences differ according to the specific medical condition, disease severity, comorbidities, and point in the illness trajectory, but pain, breathlessness, and fatigue are prevalent in the majority of individuals across the palliative care spectrum (Wilkie & Ezenwa, 2012). A recent secondary data analysis of home hospice patients in the last seven days of life found that 80% had moderate to severe symptoms, including loss of appetite, fatigue, drowsiness, dyspnea (difficulty breathing), anxiety, depression, nausea, myoclonus (muscle contractions), hallucinations, and pain. In examining data from the longitudinal Dutch End of Life in Dementia study, Hendriks and colleagues (2015) reported that pain was common in palliative care populations and increased in prevalence from 47–68% to 78% of long-term care residents in the last week of life (Hendriks, Smalbrugge, Galindo-Garre, Hertogh, & van der Steen, 2015). In addition, agitation was the most common behavioural symptom during the course of dementia but decreased in the last week of life, possibly due to increased pharmacological management of symptoms in the last week of life. Shortness of breath was less common, but prevalence increased in the last week of life such that half of all residents experienced dyspnea. Importantly, while more common symptoms, such as pain, are likely to be treated, less common symptoms are less well relieved, highlighting the need for improved symptom management across the array of symptoms (Smedbäch et al., 2017). These symptoms are prevalent across the progression of different diseases and are not limited to those in hospice or at the end of life. For instance, Solano and colleagues reported that more than 50% of patients with cancer, acquired immunodeficiency syndrome, chronic obstructive pulmonary disease, heart disease and renal disease had symptoms of pain, breathlessness, and fatigue (Solano, Gomes, & Higginson, 2006).

Providers should also keep in mind the subjective nature of many of the symptoms experienced during the course of serious illness, such as pain (Horgas, Grall, & Yoon, 2016) and dyspnea (Tice, 2006), and that the assessment of these symptoms can be further complicated by both individual and provider factors (Horgas, 2017a). For example, the religious/spiritual and cultural background of an individual may influence their symptom presentation or subjective experience, their view of seeking help for those symptoms, from whom it is appropriate to seek care (e.g., doctors, spiritual leaders, etc.), and the role their family members are expected to play in decisions regarding their care. At the provider level, personal biases, including implicit biases (Fitzgerald & Hurst, 2017) and level of familiarity with a particular cultural background or other factors of individual difference, may further complicate the process. Regardless of the symptom being treated, providers should be knowledgeable about both pharmacologic and nonpharmacologic interventions to alleviate those symptoms and the evidence base for various interventions to inform their clinical practice.

Challenges of symptom management in palliative care

Managing symptoms in palliative populations can be a challenging process. In addition to the diversity in symptom experience at the end of life as described above, many symptoms are difficult to relieve completely. Thus, symptom management emerges as an issue that should be prioritized in palliative care, with the simultaneous recognition that symptoms may not be entirely eliminated. It is important to understand an individual's goals with regard to symptom management from both a symptom relief perspective (e.g., pain intensity goal on a 0–10 scale) and a functional perspective (e.g., sleep comfortably, perform certain activities, remain alert). Individualized plans of care should be developed that maximize the potential of achieving an individual's goals. Treatment plans must consider individual's sociocultural background, as these factors may influence treatment goals, beliefs about pain and other symptoms, and acceptability of different treatment approaches (Busolo & Woodgate, 2015).

A multimodal approach to symptom management that includes pharmacological and nonpharmacological therapies is often recommended (Horgas, 2017b). This approach certainly applies to pain management, and analgesic medications are an integral component of pain management in those receiving palliative care (Horgas et al., 2017b; Marcum, Duncan, & Makris, 2016). However, the benefits of pharmacologic therapies to manage pain and other symptoms must be carefully weighed against the potential side effects, such as sedation, increased fall risk, or constipation, particularly in older adults. These side effects may not only be serious but also undermine quality of life. Recently, the World Health Organization (WHO) endorsed a list of essential medications for palliative care (available at www.who.int/selection_medicines/com mittees/expert/19/applications/PalliativeCare_8_A_R.pdf). Despite increased consensus regarding best practices for the use of medications for the alleviation of symptoms in palliative medicine, Currow and colleagues (2016) highlight the fact that medications are optimally effective for a minority of people, while the majority experience limited symptom relief, no symptom relief, or even adverse effects (Currow, Abernethy, Fallon, & Portenoy, 2016). In addition to the limitations related to alleviating common symptoms, the recommended medications on the WHO list are not accessible to all individuals. For example, particularly poor access has been noted in nondeveloped countries (Mojapelo, Usher, & Mills, 2016) and inner cities (Green, Shaw, & Harris, 2016), highlighting the importance of not only working to improve access to pharmacological interventions, but also exploring and encouraging the use of behavioural management strategies that may be particularly helpful in areas with restricted access to medications. Disparities in access to both types of care are also evident in rural communities. The 2013 National Healthcare Disparities Report found that, while healthcare quality improved over time in the United States, access to healthcare got worse; specifically, African Americans and Hispanics received worse healthcare than Non-Hispanic Whites for approximately 40% of quality measures, and low-income individuals received worse healthcare than high-income individuals for approximately 60% of quality measures (National Healthcare Disparities Report, 2013). The above mentioned access issues may be further compounded by the lack of behavioural health providers in certain areas where recruitment is more difficult (e.g., rural areas, inner cities). Given the above limitations with regard to pharmacologic management of symptoms, the remainder of this chapter will focus on behavioural strategies, with an emphasis on the evidence for each method, symptoms for which they may be appropriate, and a discussion of the limitations and further research still needed into their use in palliative care.

Behavioural management of symptoms

Behavioural strategies for management of physical and psychological symptoms in palliative care span a broad range of techniques from direct physical symptom relief to more cognitively based strategies that help individuals cope with symptoms. Some treatment approaches are more medically based, such as acupuncture, while others require attention to environmental factors, such as the Snoezelen method or environmental control.

Acupuncture

Acupuncture is a medical practice, often considered part of complementary medicine, that involves stimulation of various points of the body (i.e., acupoints) by inserting a thin, sterile needle into the skin. Acupuncture is generally considered an adjuvant treatment but is safe, effective, and has the most consistent evidence supporting its effectiveness in pain management relative to other symptoms (Horgas et al., 2016). In addition, the combination of acupuncture and Transcutaneous Electrical Nerve Stimulation (TENS) units has been shown to be particularly effective for pain control (Abdulla et al., 2013). In a study by Suzuki et al. (2012), acupuncture improved dyspnea, 6-minute walk distance, oxygen saturation, and quality of life for people with chronic obstructive pulmonary disease (COPD). Acupuncture has also been shown to improve the experience of fatigue, nausea/vomiting, and dental pain in palliative care populations (Mansky & Wallerstedt, 2006). Of note, this behavioural management option must be performed by a trained, experienced practitioner (Mansky & Wallerstedt, 2006).

Massage/aromatherapy massage

Massage involves rubbing or kneading muscles and/or joints in the body. Aromatherapy is a form of complementary medicine that involves the use of essential oils and aromatic plant compounds to improve an individual's health and/or mood. Used individually, massage has been shown to be an effective adjuvant treatment for pain, but the frequency and duration of massage needed for maximum effectiveness has not been established (Mansky & Wallerstedt, 2006). Lafferty and colleagues (2006) report in a review article that six out of nine studies of oncology patients found a positive association between massage and pain reduction, both immediately after massage and less often for longer durations. In addition to alleviating pain, massage has also been shown to reduce symptoms of anxiety and depression in individuals facing a life-limiting illness (Falkensteiner, Mantovan, Müller, & Them, 2011; Lafferty, Downey, McCarty, Standish, & Patrick, 2006). This technique also shows promise as a tool for caregivers to relieve symptoms in their care recipients. When caregivers provided 20 minutes of oncology massage three to four times per week for eight weeks to individuals receiving palliative care, decreases in pain, stress, anxiety, and fatigue were reported (Kozak et al., 2013). Massage has also been associated with improvements in other outcomes, such as nausea, fatigue, sleep, emotional distress, relaxation, and quality of life (Lafferty et al., 2006). Of note, the comfort level of the care partners with providing massage to individuals with life-limiting illness is an important consideration and may vary depending on the relationship between care partner and the individual receiving palliative care.

Massage used in conjunction with aromatherapy has been found to alleviate mood and pain symptoms in people receiving palliative care (Chang, 2008; Serfaty et al., 2012). Although individual studies support the use of massage to relieve symptoms, a recent Cochrane Review of 19 studies reported an overall lack of evidence that massage, with or without aromatherapy, was clinically effective in relieving pain, anxiety/depression, symptom distress or in improving quality of life (Shin et al., 2016). This result is surprising given the breadth of settings and variety of individuals for whom massage has been implemented with success, raising questions about the generalizability of the results of this particular review. Although the authors searched a broad range of databases (the Cochrane Central Register of Controlled Trials [CENTRAL, 2015, Issue 7], MEDLINE [Ovid], EMBASE [Ovid], PsycINFO [Ovid], CINAHL [EBSCO], PubMed Cancer Subset, SADCCT, and the World Health Organization ICTRP), the studies were narrow in several respects: 1) individuals agreed to participate in a randomized controlled trial; 2) massage was required to include tissue manipulation using a carrier oil, which excluded therapeutic touch, acupressure, and reflexology; and 3) aromatherapy was defined as the use of a blended carrier oil with essential oils and had to be administered with massage, excluding inhalations and humidification methods. In addition, these studies were often limited by small sample sizes (e.g., Kyle, 2006), design and measurement issues such as bias or blinding concerns (e.g., Shin et al., 2016), or were confounded by the fact that patients are engaging in multiple treatments for the target symptom (e.g., Gilligan, 2005). Finally, researchers have suggested that aromatic massage may be most useful for short-term alleviation of anxiety or other mood symptoms, while psychotherapy, such as cognitive behavioural therapy (CBT), which modifies thoughts and behaviours, may be more likely to result in long-term improvements (Wilkinson et al., 2007).

Therapeutic touch

Therapeutic touch is a form of energy therapy, also known as "laying on of hands," where the practitioner (often, but not limited to, nursing staff) places his or her hands on or near an individual's body with the intention to relax, relieve pain, or promote healing. There is limited evidence to support the use of therapeutic touch to reduce anxiety in people receiving palliative care (Mansky & Wallerstedt, 2006). However, a recent article (Senderovich et al., 2016) found a therapeutic touch program introduced to a geriatric palliative care unit was feasible, safe, and well tolerated, with improved relaxation and/or sleep in patients. At the same time, other studies have found no significant effect on fatigue or quality of life in people who experienced therapeutic touch (Fitz-Henry et al., 2014). These equivocal results highlight the need for additional research, preferably with objective outcome measures, to assess the effectiveness of this intervention in palliative care.

Environmental control

Environmental control refers to ways to modify the environment to promote positive physical and mental health outcomes. This approach can include sound, temperature, furniture, decoration, and lighting adjustments. Lawton's Environmental Press/Ecological Theory of Aging (Lawton & Nahemow, 1973) posits that the interaction between an individual's capacities and the demands and/or opportunities in their environment plays an important role in whether there is optimal fit or misfit of person and environment. Calm, consistent, safe environments with natural lighting during the day, reduced noise and stimulation at night, access to assistive devices (e.g., hearing aids, glasses), and orienting materials (e.g., clocks, newspapers) are important aspects of effective management of individuals with delirium (Hosker & Bennett, 2016). In addition, loved ones can be encouraged to visit with the person to help with reorientation (Hartjes, Meece, & Horgas, 2014). Even simulated family presence (via audio or videotape) has been shown to reduce agitation in persons with dementia in nursing homes (Zetteler, 2008). However, evidence supporting environmental control in a general palliative care population is equivocal. For example, Gagnon and colleagues (2012) examined a multimodal intervention with an environmental control component in individuals with cancer at the end of life and found no difference in treatment versus control groups in terms of incidence, severity, or duration of delirium (Gagnon, Allard, Gagnon, Mérette, & Tardif, 2012). Of note, a recent review of the impact of interprofessional education for delirium care found appropriate education and implementation of techniques such as environmental control may improve both provider and care recipient outcomes (Sockalingam et al., 2014). Though few studies address the impact environmental control may have on other common symptoms seen in palliative care, educational programs focusing on the importance of careful attention to the environment have been found to have a positive impact on sleep and mood in individuals with serious illness (Chang, Chiou, Cheng, & Lin, 2016; Papaconstantinou, Hodnett, & Stremler, 2016). These studies have included adult and pediatric individuals and address the use of educational programs both in hospital settings and in the home. Thus, the importance of environmental stimuli as well as provider education and training, should not be overlooked when working to reduce symptoms in palliative care.

Snoezelen

Snoezelen (also called Multisensory Stimulation) is an intervention designed to stimulate the senses using light, smell, sound, and taste. It often involves placing an individual in a calm, yet stimulating environment. When implemented for 18 months across various nursing homes in the Netherlands, this intervention led to improvements in apathetic behaviour, general agitation, rebellious behaviour, aggressive behaviour, and mood in patients with dementia (Van Weert, Van Dulmen, Spreeuwenberg, Ribbe, & Bensing, 2005). A recent controlled longitudinal trial of the use of Snoezelen in patients with dementia found improved daily functional behaviour and decreased verbal and physical agitation over a 16-week intervention that were maintained for eight weeks (Maseda et al., 2014). Mood was also improved in this study for some individuals, though not all, suggesting exploration of individual characteristics associated with improvement versus no change in mood may be a clinically important avenue of investigation. The above studies suggest that including individualized sensory stimulation in palliative care using the Snoezelen model may be useful in treating agitation and depression/anxiety. Although there is a dearth of research focused on individualized sensory stimulation in palliative care to date, studies examining the utility of environmental control for individuals facing serious illness are beginning to appear (e.g., Zadeh et al., 2017).

Art therapy

Art therapy is a form of psychotherapy that encourages free expression through the use of art and uses the creative process and resulting art as a way to explore and improve mental and/or physical health. In a recent study, authors report a single session of art therapy for individuals receiving palliative care with advanced cancer led to patient-reported improvements in pain, fatigue, depression, anxiety, and well-being, and also subjectively improved interpersonal relationships (Rhondali, Lasserre, & Filbet, 2013). Furthermore, Nainis and colleagues (2006) reported improvements in common palliative-specific physical symptoms (e.g., pain, nausea) and anxiety following a single art therapy session in female oncology patients (Nainis et al., 2006). Of note, evaluation of interventions such as art therapy may prove complex given the variety of intervention modalities (e.g., drawing, painting, etc.) and the difficulty in parsing out the underlying cause of benefits reported (e.g., distraction, reality testing).

Music therapy

Music therapy uses various facets of music (e.g., spiritual, physical, emotional) to help individuals improve their mental and/or physical health. Only a small number of controlled clinical trials have been conducted, though they have reported benefits on the relief of anxiety and pain in people receiving palliative care (Mansky & Wallerstedt, 2006). A 2005 review by Hilliard found that six of 11 studies supported the use of music therapy in end-of-life care to alleviate pain, fatigue, and anxiety, and to improve mood, spirituality, and quality of life. A randomized controlled trial of music therapy to treat agitation in dementia found that biweekly music therapy sessions for six weeks reduced agitation and prevented increases in medication as compared to a care-as-usual control group (Riddler, Stige, Qvale, & Gold, 2013). Even a single music therapy session incorporating therapist-guided relaxation has been found to result in lower pain ratings immediately after the session in people receiving palliative care (Gutgsell et al., 2013), though the duration of these benefits was not examined. Furthermore, music therapy was viewed positively by families of individuals who received this treatment, with family members reporting improvements in stress, mood, and quality of life, both for themselves and the individual receiving palliative care, after a single session (Gallagher al., 2017). An integrative review conducted in 2013 of 17 studies examining the use of music therapy in palliative care reported that music therapy is most often used to treat pain, anxiety, depression, and quality of life, with decreases in pain and mood symptoms, as well as improvements in reported quality of life consistently found across the majority of studies (Bowers & Wetsel, 2013).

Animal assisted therapy

Animal Assisted Therapy (AAT), or pet therapy, is an interaction involving an individual, a highly trained therapy animal, and the animal's handler, with the goal of improving physical or mental health outcomes. AAT has long been used in a variety of patient populations (including children and adults) to treat a variety of problems including chronic pain, severe mental illness, or other mental health conditions. The use of pet therapy has been shown to reduce pain, anxiety, depression, and fatigue (e.g., Marcus et al., 2012). However, examination of the effectiveness of this treatment modality in palliative care is lacking. One study by Orlandi and colleagues (2007) found that the use of AAT in patients with cancer undergoing chemotherapy was associated with decreased depressive symptoms and improved arterial oxygen saturation. Furthermore, pet therapy was found to reduce psychological distress in children with cancer and in their parents, as well as fostering adaptation to treatment processes (Gagnon et al., 2004). Engelman (2013) reported qualitative improvements in pain perception with the use of AAT in both inpatient and outpatient palliative care, and improvements in objective mood have been reported in those receiving palliative care by interacting with dogs, cats, and rabbits (Kumasaka, Masu, Kataoka, & Numao, 2012). Overall, AAT has been linked to subjective improvements in a broad range of symptoms often experienced in serious illness, with the most notable improvements reported for stress, anxiety/depression, and general mood (Marcus, Blazek-O'Neill, & Kopar, 2013). Although some concerns have been raised regarding the spread of bacteria through therapy animals, this cost-effective treatment method can be safely implemented with appropriate infection control policies and techniques (Marcus, 2012). Overall, AAT seems to be a useful option that can be tailored to specific animal preferences and has demonstrated benefit across a varied number of sessions. However, an important consideration is the possibility of selection bias in the samples in previous studies and the importance of screening for phobias, allergies, or other contraindications when considering AAT for use in individuals receiving palliative care.

Guided imagery/hypnosis/meditation/relaxation

Guided imagery is the use of words, music, directed thoughts, or suggestions used to guide individuals to a relaxed, focused state. Hypnosis is a state of consciousness often characterized by increased focus, reduced peripheral awareness, and increased responsiveness to suggestion or direction. Hypnosis, often coupled with relaxation and guided imagery, has been shown to reduce pain sensation in people receiving palliative care (Mansky & Wallerstedt, 2006). The use of hypnosis, particularly for reduction of acute procedural pain, has been shown to be effective in both pediatric (Liossi, White, & Hatira, 2006) and adult populations (Montgomery, Weltz, Seltz, & Bovbjerg, 2002). A study on the efficacy of guided imagery/hypnosis in fibromyalgia found evidence to support the use of these techniques, alone or in combination with CBT, to alleviate pain and distress in individuals experiencing chronic pain (Zech, Hansen, Bernardy, & Häuser, 2017). Hypnosis has also been shown to be effective for anticipatory nausea and vomiting, and for reducing anxiety/distress caused by invasive medical procedures (Mansky & Wallerstedt, 2006). However, the evidence overall is mixed regarding hypnosis, and the inclusion of multipart interventions makes it difficult to determine which aspect(s) are most effective.

Meditation is a broad term that generally refers to methods used to focus or gain clarity of thought, with the intent of slowing down normal activity in the mind. Similarly, relaxation refers to techniques used to calm the mind and body with the goal of alleviating anxiety and/or stress. Meditation and relaxation techniques can be helpful for dyspnea-related anxiety (Tice, 2006). In addition, diaphragmatic and/or purse-lipped breathing and air movement across the face (e.g., use of a fan) are helpful in decreasing feelings of breathlessness (LeGrand, 2002; Tice, 2006). In a 2006 review, Lafferty and colleagues examined 16 studies of the effects of meditation in individuals with cancer. They report that of two studies that measured pain, both found a reduction in pain. Ten of 12 studies examined found significant positive associations between meditation and emotion/mood. Studies have also suggested an association between meditation and other outcomes such as nausea/vomiting, relaxation, holistic comfort, sleep, quality of life, and fatigue (Lafferty et al., 2006). Overall, the evidence is promising with regard to meditation and warrants further study of its possible impact on both physical and mental health symptoms for individuals receiving palliative care.

Tai Chi/yoga/qigong

Tai Chi, yoga, and qigong are all forms of slow, focused movements usually accompanied by a breathing technique (e.g., deep breathing). Although there is only limited support for Tai Chi as a treatment for pain, this behavioural management option nevertheless may be effective in maintaining or improving mobility and mood in some individuals (Horgas et al., 2016). Yoga, which combines breath control and awareness with movement and meditation, has proven helpful in reducing stress, controlling anxiety, and improving sleep (e.g., Pascoe & Bauer, 2015). For example, yoga was found to increase self-reported quality of life and spirituality in young adults with noncurative cancer, and was seen to be an opportunity for self-care outside of traditional cancer treatment appreciated by the individuals who participated in yoga (Keats, Woodside, & Culos-Reed, 2016). In adults undergoing cancer treatment, yoga was found to be associated with decreased emotional distress, improved quality of life, improved sleep, and reduced fatigue (Danhauer, Addington, Sohl, Chaoul, & Cohen, 2017). Qigong, which combines gentle exercise and meditation, was found to improve self-reported neuropathic symptoms but not quality of life, fatigue, perceived stress, or sexual functioning in women with metastatic breast cancer (Oh et al., 2014). A treatment combining qigong and Tai Chi in men undergoing radiation therapy for prostate cancer found improvements in sleep for the treatment group, but these improvements were not durable, leading the authors to suggest the physical symptoms of their cancer and the effects of radiation therapy attenuated treatment effects (McQuade et al., 2017). Of note, as with any treatment modality that involves exercise or physical exertion, the appropriateness of the treatment for each person, especially those with cognitive impairments, severe mobility restrictions, or shortness of breath, should be carefully assessed and individualized for the patient.

Cognitive behavioural therapy/acceptance and commitment therapy

Cognitive behavioural therapy (CBT) is a type of psychotherapy in which maladaptive thought patterns are identified and challenged in order to change behaviour or treat psychological distress. Studies have found significant improvement in pain and mobility for individuals with persistent musculoskeletal pain receiving CBT from a professional therapist (Horgas et al., 2016). In addition, there is strong evidence to support the use of psychotherapy in treating depression in those facing a serious or life-limiting illness (Lorenz et al., 2008). Acceptance and commitment therapy (ACT) is an empirically based psychological intervention that incorporates acceptance, mindfulness, commitment to values, and behaviour change strategies with the goal of promoting psychological flexibility. An ACT intervention aimed at improving the quality of life of people with cancer found that increased psychological flexibility (i.e., acceptance of unpleasant thoughts and feelings) led to improvements in quality of life, distress, and mood after the intervention and at a three-month follow up (Feros, Lane, Diarrochi, & Blackledge, 2013).

Both CBT and ACT show increasing promise as effective interventions in palliative care, particularly for mood/emotional distress symptoms, though the evidence regarding their utility for common physical symptoms experienced in life-limiting illness is equivocal. For example, while some studies have found an association between behavioural methods, such as relaxation and imagery, and decreased nausea (Arakawa, 1997; Molassiotis, 2000; Van Fleet, 2000), others have found no benefit (e.g., Mundy, DuHamel, & Montgomery, 2003). Given their effectiveness at treating mood symptoms in individuals receiving palliative care, and some evidence for their utility in treating physical symptoms as well, CBT and ACT are promising methods to consider in a comprehensive approach to symptom management.

Coward and Reed (1996) highlight the idea that self-transcendence may be a goal for healing at the end of life. Self-transcendence is defined as the expansion of personal boundaries inwardly (e.g., self-awareness, introspection), outwardly (e.g., relationships with others, environment), and temporally (e.g., integration of past and future with present). Coward and Reed suggest that providers may be able to foster self-transcendence in people at the end of life by encouraging connections with similar others, promoting altruistic activities, exploring cognitive strategies to increase self-awareness and integration, and fostering spirituality and spiritual expression. Indeed, a recent study by Haugan (2014) found that positive interactions between nurses and patients in nursing homes influenced hope, life meaning, and self-transcendence. When participants felt they were being taken seriously, understood, listened to, and respected in their interactions with nursing staff, they reported higher levels of self-transcendence, which the author hypothesized may be due to increased feelings of acceptance and connectedness within oneself (Haugan, 2014). In a study of people with ALS, self-transcendence was one of many methods used to maintain hope in the face of illness and impending death (Fanos, Gelinas, Foster, Postone, & Miller, 2008). Fostering such coping strategies may be helpful in people struggling with mood symptoms related to advanced serious illness. A review of psychotherapy as an intervention in patients with cancer (Breitbart, 2002) found that, although there was overall support for the use of group psychotherapy in patients with cancer with improvements in quality of life, anxiety, depression, and physical symptoms (i.e., nausea, pain) reported, only a few of the treatment modalities focused exclusively on existential or spiritual themes such as self-transcendence (e.g., Chin-A-Loy & Fernsler, 1998; Coward, 1998; Hiatt, 1986). Coward and colleagues report a significant increase in functional performance, mood, and life satisfaction in women with breast cancer who attended a group focused on self-transcendence (Coward, 1998); however, these results did not remain at a one-year follow up, suggesting ongoing, continuous access to support resources may be needed to maintain improvements (Coward, 2003). Although there is promising evidence to date regarding the utility of self-transcendence promoting interventions, less is known about the duration of gains and applicability across a variety of patient populations, highlighting the need for further research into the utility of this specific intervention.

One caveat to the use of psychotherapeutic techniques is that the cognitive status of the patient is important, as cognitive impairment may make it difficult or impossible for an individual to engage in this treatment option. In addition, the ethical application of such techniques requires appropriate training in the underlying theories and techniques specific to the psychotherapeutic approach utilized. A final consideration may be the immediacy of an effect that can be expected from these therapeutic interventions. Given that some patients may have a prognosis of days to weeks, lengthy interventions may not be practical, and patients may be unable to achieve full benefit in the limited time they have remaining.

Spiritual/religious-based interventions

Spirituality is defined as "that which allows a person to experience transcendent meaning in life. This is often expressed as a relationship with God, but it can also be about nature, art, music, family, or community – whatever beliefs and values give a person a sense of meaning and purpose in life" (Puchalski & Romer, 2000, p. 129). In contrast, religiosity refers to activities and services focused on God or other deities, commitment to a particular faith or observance, or a personal set of beliefs or institutionalized system of religious attitudes. While a majority of individuals receiving palliative care express concerns regarding their spiritual well-being, only a minority of those individuals report having their spiritual needs addressed (Kelley & Morrison, 2015); insufficient intervention in a critical area of overall well-being is further compounded by providers' lack of comfort addressing spiritual or religious needs and scarcity of chaplains trained in palliative care (Kelley & Morrison, 2015). Spiritual concerns have been associated with lower self-reported quality of life in people with advanced cancer, and the majority of individuals surveyed felt spiritual concerns should be part of their medical care (Winkelman et al., 2011). In addition, there is evidence that individuals who receive spiritual and/or religious support as part of their treatment report higher quality of life than those who do not (Balboni et al., 2007, 2010). The integration of spiritual/religious interventions in palliative care is an important component to treating the whole person, and individual beliefs and preferences are important considerations as they may provide means of coping with illness, a resource for meaning, hope, and growth, and may influence important decisions at the end of life, such as the use of life-sustaining interventions (Phelps et al., 2009).

Summary and conclusions

Increasing evidence of symptom reduction and other positive outcomes when behavioural management strategies are used with people receiving palliative care highlights the importance of a multimodal approach to the treatment of this unique population. A variety of strategies have empirical support for their use, with many showing promise for effective management of multiple symptoms commonly experienced during serious or life-limiting illness. Acupuncture, massage, and therapeutic touch have all been examined as tools for reduction of symptoms such as pain, fatigue, and emotional distress, with acupuncture having the most consistent support in the literature. Additional behavioural management strategies include attention to environmental stimuli, as with environmental control or the use of a Snoezelen program, and the use of pleasant activities, such as AAT. Techniques that attempt to foster improved cognitive coping, processing, and resilience in patients, such as CBT, ACT, art therapy, meditation, movement therapies, self-transcendence, and spiritual/religious interventions have also shown promise in this population. An additional benefit of psychologically focused interventions is the potential generalizability to other aspects of an individual's life outside of specific illness symptomatology.

Despite the growing evidence supporting the use of behavioural management strategies in palliative care, there are several limitations in the literature base that deserve mention. First and foremost, there is a significant need for additional research into the use of these techniques, specifically in diverse patient populations receiving palliative care. Furthermore, the studies that have been conducted thus far are often limited by a small, usually homogeneous sample, highlighting the need for randomized controlled trials with more diverse samples to foster generalizability of results. Often studies are limited by the confounding impact of a multimodal treatment program, making it difficult to identify which specific aspects of treatment are responsible for which outcomes.

Overall, research supports multimodal methods of symptom management, including both pharmacological and behavioural interventions for relief of symptoms in palliative care to promote maximal comfort. It is important to consider individual preferences and abilities to participate effectively in behavioural methods when they are being used in this population. Treatment approaches should be appropriately tailored to the individual according to their wishes, abilities, and goals of care. In addition, attention to appropriate training and application of behavioural strategies will ensure ethical treatment of individuals facing serious or life-limiting illness. With an increasing amount of evidence to support the use of behavioural management of symptoms, healthcare providers will hopefully continue to develop more comprehensive, individually tailored treatment programs to ensure the highest quality, most effective symptom management in palliative care. The following case study is provided to allow readers a chance to evaluate some of the issues frequently encountered when working within palliative care. We hope it will spark conversations, provide food for thought, and encourage further research into this diverse and dynamic population.

Case example

Stella Scott is a 44-year-old woman diagnosed with Stage 3B inflammatory breast cancer with axilla lymph node involvement. She has been happily married to her husband, Blake, for 18 years and they have two daughters, ages 10 and 12. Stella was in good health prior to her diagnosis; she modelled a healthy diet for her daughters, maintained a normal weight, and enjoyed running 3–4 miles several days each week. She is a middle-school teacher at the school her daughters attend. She first noticed a change in her right breast after a run – her breast was warm and she had an itchy rash on the upper area – close to her armpit. In a whirlwind of medical interventions since her diagnosis, she received chemotherapy and Trastuzumab (Herceptin) for HER2-positive cancer prior to her bilateral mastectomy with axillary lymph node removal (she elected prophylactic mastectomy of her left breast). She was so overwhelmed with decision-making prior to her surgery that she did not elect to have breast reconstructive surgery. Following recovery from her bilateral mastectomy, she completed seven weeks of radiation therapy (treatment five days per week). Her medical team is pleased with her response to treatment and considering additional chemotherapy depending on pending test results. The treatment has left Stella with pervasive fatigue, and, in part because she has not been able to return to teaching, she is moderately depressed. She has persistent pain at the site of radiation treatment on her right chest wall. She has lost 20 pounds due to nausea and vomiting during treatment, and her appetite has been slow to return. She no longer attends her daughters' extracurricular events because of her hair loss and worries over body image and doesn't know how to talk to her children about her illness. In attempts to return to normalcy, she and Blake avoid discussions of her illness; however, due to her body image anxiety they have not had intimate relations since her surgery. Stella does not share these problems with her medical team because she does not want to complain and she wants to do everything she can to fight the cancer. She tells Blake she feels as if she has been in shock since her diagnosis and experiences terrible anxiety when she thinks about the cancer spreading. Her husband suggested she go for a run – knowing that running always improved Stella's mood. When she tried to go for a run, she had to stop because of shortness of breath and overwhelming weakness. She returned home crying.

Questions

1   Which of Stella's symptoms and concerns are amenable to palliative care interventions?
2   What behavioural interventions might help Stella?
3   What issues in the case may be contributing to the exacerbation of Stella's pain?

Resolution

During a visit from a friend, who also happens to be a nurse practitioner, Stella shares some of the troubling symptoms: anxiety, depression, fatigue, pain, occasional shortness of breath, and loss of appetite. Stella states she has pain "all over" and is not sleeping well – she has not told her oncologist about these symptoms because she doesn't want to be seen as a complainer. Her friend asks Stella if she has seen anyone from palliative care. Stella doesn't know what that is – at first, she is terrified her friend thinks she is dying. Once Stella understands that palliative care can help her with her symptoms, she agrees to ask her oncologist for a referral. During her next appointment, the physician explains that the palliative care team will partner with her medical team to help Stella and her family through her treatment. In the first appointment with palliative care, a comprehensive assessment is performed, and in addition to meeting the physician, Stella spends time with the nurse practitioner, psychologist, and social worker. The palliative care physician makes some adjustments to Stella's medications for pain and nausea/vomiting. She suggests a short course of antidepressant medication, but Stella would like to first try nonpharmacological treatment. She schedules appointments with the psychologist. Within a couple weeks of cognitive behavioural therapy and guided imagery practices Stella is sleeping better, her pain has lessened, and her nausea has decreased, which has improved her appetite. Over the next couple of months, the palliative care team makes additional recommendations to manage symptoms and improve Stella's quality of life. Seeing the psychologist on a regular basis has helped with her anxiety, body image, and depression. Stella finds it useful to share her fears with her psychologist so they do not consume her family relationships. She is using the cognitive behavioural therapy recommendations and journaling with good results. The nurse practitioner recommends that, instead of running, Stella give yoga a try and recommends that Stella enroll in a cancer survivor yoga course offered by the American Cancer Society. Through the class, Stella has made friends with other cancer survivors and her fatigue has improved – she is also sleeping better. Because she feels better rested, Stella can make her daughters' school lunches and help them with their homework. Blake, along with her daughters, has taken on dinner preparation, with a focus on small meals, including Stella's favorite foods. The social worker shared information about a summer camp for kids whose parent has cancer. Stella and Blake are scheduling weekly date nights. Due to the improvement in her body image, she and Blake are again enjoying intimate relations. With help from the palliative care team, Stella completed her advance directive and was referred for external breast prostheses while she is considering breast reconstruction. Her cancer is in remission, and she does not need additional chemotherapy at this time. Stella looks forward to returning to teaching in the next school year.

Comment: The American Society of Clinical Oncology (ASCO) has issued a consensus statement recommending palliative care concurrent with oncology care, early in the disease course, for any patient with advanced cancer and/or high symptom burden (Ferrell et al., 2016).

References

Abdulla, A., Adams, N., Bone, M., Elliott, A. M., Gaffin, J., Jones, D., . . . Schofield, P. (2013). Guidance on the management of pain in older people. *Age and Ageing, 42,* 1–57. doi:10.1093/ageing/afs200

Alders, I., Smits, C., Brand, P., & van Dulmen, S. (2017). Does patient coaching make a difference in patient-physician communication during specialist consultations? A systematic review. *Patient Education and Counseling, 100,* 882–896.

Arakawa, S. (1997). Relaxation to reduce nausea, vomiting, and anxiety induced by chemotherapy in Japanese patients. *Cancer Nursing, 20,* 342–349.

Balboni, T. A., Vanderwerker, L. C., Block, S. D., Paulk, M. E., Lathan, C. S., Peteet, J. R., & Prigerson, H. G. (2007). Religiousness and spiritual support among advanced cancer patients and associations with end-of-life treatment preferences and quality of life. *Journal of Clinical Oncology, 25*(5), 555–560. doi:10.1200/JCO.2006.07.9046

Balboni, T. A., Paulk, M. E., Balboni, M. J., Phelps, A. C., Loggers, E. T., Wright, A. A., . . . Prigerson, H. G. (2010). Provision of spiritual care to patients with advanced cancer: Associations with medical care and quality of life near death. *Journal of Clinical Oncology, 28*(3), 445–452. doi:10.1200/JCO.2009.24.8005

Bowers, T. A., & Wetsel, M. A. (2013). Utilization of music therapy in palliative and hospice care. *Journal of Hospice & Palliative Nursing, 16,* 231–239. doi:10.1097/NJH.0000000000000060

Breitbart, W. (2002). Spirituality and meaning in supportive care: Spirituality-and meaning-centered group psychotherapy interventions in advanced cancer. *Supportive Care in Cancer, 10*(4), 272–280.

Burke, T., Galvin, M., Pinto-Grau, M., Lonergan, K., Madden, C., Mays, I., . . . Pender, N. (2017). Caregivers of patients with amyotrophic lateral sclerosis: Investigating quality of life, caregiver burden, service engagement, and patient survival. *Journal of Neurology, 264*, 1–7. doi:10.1007/s00415-017-8448-5

Busolo, D., & Woodgate, R. (2015). Palliative care experiences of adult cancer patients from ethnocultural groups: A qualitative systematic review protocol. *JBI Database Systematic Reviews and Implementation Reports, 13*(1), 99–111. doi:10.11124/jbisrir-2015-1809

Chang, S. Y. (2008). Effects of aroma hand massage on pain, state anxiety and depression in hospice patients with terminal cancer. *Journal of Korean Academy of Nursing, 38*, 493–502. PMID: 18753801.

Chang, Y.-L., Chiou, A.-F., Cheng, S.-M., & Lin, K.-C. (2016). Tailored educational supportive care programme on sleep quality and psychological distress in patients with heart failure: A randomized controlled trial. *International Journal of Nursing Studies, 61*, 219–229. doi:10.1016/j.ijnurstu.2016.07.002

Chin-A-Loy, S. S., & Fernsler, J. I. (1998). Self-transcendence in older men attending a prostate cancer support group. *Cancer Nursing, 21*, 358–363. PMID: 9775486.

Coward, D. D. (1998, December). Facilitation of self-transcendence in a breast cancer support group. *Oncology Nursing Forum, 25*(1), 75–84. doi:10.1188/03.ONF.291-300

Coward, D. D. (2003). Facilitation of self-transcendence in a breast cancer support group: II. *Oncology Nursing Forum, 30*, 291–300. doi:10.1188/03.ONF.291-300

Coward, D. D., & Reed, P. G. (1996). Self-transcendence: A resource for healing at the end of life. *Issues in Mental Health Nursing, 17*, 275–288. doi:10.3109/01612849609049920

Currow, D. C., Abernethy, A. P., Fallon, M., & Portenoy, R. K. (2016). Repurposing medications for hospice/palliative care symptom control is no longer sufficient: A manifesto for change. *Journal of Pain and Symptom Management, 53*, 533–539. doi:10.1016/j.jpainsymman.2016.10.358

Danhauer, S. C., Addington, E. L., Sohl, S. J., Chaoul, A., & Cohen, L. (2017, January 7). Review of yoga therapy during cancer treatment. *Support Care Cancer*. doi:10.1007/s00520-016-3556-9

de la Cruz, M., Noguera, A., San Miguel-Arregui, M. T., Williams, J., Chisholm, G., & Bruera, E. (2015). Delirium, agitation, and symptom distress within the final seven days of life among cancer patients receiving hospice care. *Palliative and Supportive Care, 13*, 211–216. doi:10.1017/S1478951513001144

Engelman, S. R. (2013). Palliative care and use of animal-assisted therapy. *OMEGA-Journal of Death and Dying, 67*(1–2), 63–67. doi:10.2190/OM.67.1–2.g

Falkensteiner, M., Mantovan, F., Müller, I., & Them, C. (2011). The use of massage therapy for reducing pain, anxiety, and depression in oncological palliative care patients: A narrative review of the literature. *ISRN Nursing, 2011*, 1–8. doi:10.5402/2011/929868

Fanos, J. H., Gelinas, D. F., Foster, R. S., Postone, N., & Miller, R. G. (2008). Hope in palliative care: From narcissism to self-transcendence in amyotrophic lateral sclerosis. *Journal of Palliative Medicine, 11*, 470–475. doi:10.1089/jpm.2007.0098

Feros, D. L., Lane, L., Ciarrochi, H., & Blackledge, J. T. (2013). Acceptance and Commitment Therapy (ACT) for improving the lives of cancer patients: A preliminary study. *Psycho-Oncology, 22*, 459–464. doi:10.1002/pon.2083

Ferrell, B. R., Temel, J. S., Temin, S., Alesi, E. R., Balboni, T. A., Basch, E. M., . . . Stovall, E. L. (2016). Integration of palliative care into standard oncology care: American society of clinical oncology clinical practice guideline update. *Journal of Clinical Oncology, 35*, 96–114. doi:10.1200/JCO.2016.70.1474

Fine, P. G., & Kestenbaum, M. (2016). *The Hospice Companion: Best Practices for Interdisciplinary Assessment and Care of Common Problems During the Last Phase of Life*. Oxford: Oxford University Press.

FitzGerald, C., & Hurst, S. (2017). Implicit bias in healthcare professionals: A systematic review. *BMC Medical Ethics, 18*, 1–18.

FitzHenry, F., Wells, N., Slater, V., Dietrich, M. S., Wisawatapnimit, P., & Chakravarthy, A. B. (2014). A randomized placebo-controlled pilot study of the impact of healing touch on fatigue in breast cancer patients undergoing radiation therapy. *Integrative Cancer Therapies, 13*, 105–113. doi:10.1177/1534735413503545

Gagnon, P., Allard, P., Gagnon, B., Mérette, C., & Tardif, F. (2012). Delirium prevention in terminal cancer: Assessment of a multicomponent intervention. *Psycho-Oncology, 21*, 187–194. doi:10.1002/pon.1881

Gagnon, J., Bouchard, F., Landry, M., Belles-Isles, M., Fortier, M., & Fillion, L. (2004). Implementing a hospital-based animal therapy program for children with cancer: A descriptive study. *Canadian Oncology Nursing Journal/Revue canadienne de soins infirmiers en oncologie, 14*, 217–222. PMID: 15635895

Gallagher, L. M., lagman, R., Bates, D., Edsall, M., Eden, P., Janaitis, J., & Rybicki, L. (2017, January 9). Perceptions of family members of palliative medicine and hospice patients who experience music therapy. *Support Care Cancer*. doi:10.1007.s00520-017-3578-y

Gilligan, N. P. (2005). The palliation of nausea in hospice and palliative care patients with essential oils of Pimpinella anisum (aniseed), Foeniculum vulgare var. dulce (sweet fennel), Anthemis nobilis (Roman chamomile) and Mentha x piperita (peppermint). *International Journal of Aromatherapy, 15*, 163–167. doi:10.1016/j.ijat.2005.10.012

Green, E., Shaw, S. E., & Harris, T. (2016). "They shouldn't be coming to the ED, should they?" A qualitative study of why patients with palliative care needs present to the emergency department. *BMJ Supportive &Palliative Care*. doi:10.1136/bmjspcare-2015–000999

Gutgsell, K. J., Schluchter, M., Margevicius, S., DeGolia, P. A., McLaughlin, B., Harris, M., … Wiencek, C. (2013). Music therapy reduces pain in palliative care patients: A randomized controlled trial. *Journal of Pain and Symptom Management, 45*, 822–831. doi:10.1016/j.jpainsymman.2012.05.008

Hartjes, T. M., Meece, L., & Horgas, A. (2014). Implementing palliative care in the ICU: Providing patient and family centered care. *Nursing2014 Critical Care, 9*(4), 17–22. doi:10.3928/00989134–20140428–02

Haugan, G. (2014). Nurse – patient interaction is a resource for hope, meaning in life and self-transcendence in nursing home patients. *Scandinavian Journal of Caring Sciences, 28*, 74–88. doi:10.1111/scs.12028

Hendriks, S. A., Smalbrugge, M., Galindo-Garre, F., Hertogh, C., & van der Steen, J. T. (2015). From admission to death: Prevalence and course of pain, agitation, and shortness of breath, and treatment of these symptoms in nursing home residents with dementia. *Journal of the American Medical Directors Association, 16*, 475–481. doi:10/1016/j.jamda.2014.12.016

Hiatt, J. F. (1986). Spirituality, medicine, and healing. *Southern Medical Journal, 79*(6), 736–743. PMID: 3715539.

Hilliard, R. E. (2005). Music therapy in hospice and palliative care: A review of the empirical data. *Evidence-Based Complementary and Alternative Medicine, 2*, 173–178. doi:10.1093/ecam/neh076

Horgas, A. L. (2017a). Pain assessment in older adults. *Nursing Clinics of North America, 52* (3), 375–385. doi.org/10.1016/j.cnur.2017.04.006

Horgas, A. L. (2017b). Pain management in older adults. *Nursing Clinics of North America, 52* (4), e1–e7. doi:10.1016/j.cnur.2017.08.001

Horgas, A. L., Grall, M. S., & Yoon, S. L. (2016). Pain management. In M. Boltz, E. Capezuti, T. Fulmer, & D. Zwicker (Eds.), *Evidence-Based Geriatric Nursing Protocols for Best Practice* (pp. 263–281). New York, NY: Springer Publishing Company.

Hosker, C. M. G., & Bennett, M. I. (2016). Delirium and agitation at the end of life. *The BMJ 2016, 353,* i3085. doi:10.1136/bmj.i3085

IOM (Institute of Medicine). 2015. *Dying in America: Improving Quality and Honoring Individual Preferences Near the End of Life.* Washington, DC: The National Academies Press.

Keats, M., Woodside, H., & Culos-Reed, S. N. (2016). Impact of yoga on quality of life for young adult noncurative cancer patients: A pilot study. *Journal of Clinical Oncology, 34,* 249–249.

Kelley, A. S., & Morrison, R. S. (2015). Palliative care for the seriously ill. *New England Journal of Medicine, 373,* 747–755. doi:10.1056/NEJMra1404684

Kozak, L., Vig, E., Simons, C., Eugenio, E., Collinge, W., & Chapko, M. (2013). A feasibility study of caregiver-provided massage as supportive care for Veterans with cancer. *Journal of Supportive Oncology, 11,* 133–143. doi:10.12788/j.suponc.0008

Kumasaka, T., Masu, H., Kataoka, M., & Numao, A. (2012). Changes in patient mood through animal-assisted activities in a palliative care unit. *International Medical Journal, 19,* 373–377. ISSN:1341–2051

Kyle, G. (2006). Evaluating the effectiveness of aromatherapy in reducing levels of anxiety in palliative care patients: Results of a pilot study. *Complementary Therapies in Clinical Practice, 12,* 148–155. doi:10.1016/j.ctcp.2005.11.003

Lafferty, W. E., Downey, L., McCarty, R. L., Standish, L. J., & Patrick, D. L. (2006). Evaluating CAM treatment at the end of life: A review of clinical trials for massage and meditation. *Complementary Therapies in Medicine, 14,* 100–112. doi:10.1016/j.ctim.2006.01.009

Lawton, M. P., & Nahemow, L. (1973). Ecology and the aging process. In C. Eisdorfer, & M. P. Lawton (Eds.), *The Psychology of Adult Development and Aging* (pp. 619–674). Washington, DC: American Psychological Association.

LeGrand, S. B. (2002). Dyspnea: The continuing challenge of palliative management. *Current Opinion in Oncology,* 14, 394–398. doi:10.1097/00001622-200207000-00004

Liossi, C., White, P., & Hatira, P. (2006). Randomized clinical trial of local anesthetic versus a combination of local anesthetic with self-hypnosis in the management of pediatric procedure-related pain. *Health Psychology, 25,* 307–315. doi:10.1037/0278-6133.25.3.307

Lorenz, K. A., Lynn, J., Dy, S. M., Shugarman, L. R., Wilkinson, A., Mularski, R. A., … Shekelle, P. G. (2008). Evidence for improving palliative care at the end of life: A systematic review. *Annals of Internal Medicine, 148,* 147–159. doi:10.7326/0003-4819-148-2-200801150-00010

Mansky, P. J., & Wallerstedt, D. B. (2006). Complementary medicine in palliative care and cancer symptom management. *The Cancer Journal, 12,* 425–431. doi:10.1097/00130404-200609000-00011

Marcum, Z. A., Duncan, N. A., & Makris, U. E. (2016). Pharmacotherapies in geriatric chronic pain management. *Clinics in Geriatric Medicine, 32,* 705–724. doi:10.1016/j.cger.2016.06.007

Marcus, D. A. (2012). Complementary medicine in cancer care: Adding a therapy dog to the team. *Current Pain and Headache Reports, 16,* 289–291. doi:10.1007/s11916-012-0264-0

Marcus, D. A., Bernstein, C. D., Constantin, J. M., Kunkel, F. A., Breuer, P., & Hanlon, R. B. (2012). Animal-assisted therapy at an outpatient pain management clinic. *Pain Medicine, 13,* 45–57. doi:10.1016/j.jpainsymman.2012.05.008

Marcus, D. A., Blazek-O'Neill, B., & Kopar, J. L. (2013). Symptom reduction identified after offering animal-assisted activity at a cancer infusion center. *American Journal of Hospice and Palliative Medicine, 31,* 420–421. doi:10.1177/1049909113492373

Maseda, A., Sánchez, A., Marante, M. P., González-Abraldes, I., Buján, A., & Millán-Calenti, J. C. (2014). Effects of multisensory stimulation on a sample of institutionalized elderly people with dementia diagnosis: A controlled longitudinal trial. *American Journal of Alzheimer's Disease & Other Dementias, 29,* 463–473. doi:10.1177/1533317514522540

McQuade, J.L., Prinsloo, S., Chang, D. Z., Spelman, A., Wei, Q., Basen-Enqquist, K., . . . Cohen, L. (2017). Qigong/tai chi for sleep and fatigue in prostate cancer patients undergoing radiotherapy: A randomized controlled trail. *Psychooncology, 26,* 1936–1943. doi:10.1002/pon.4256

Mojapelo, T. D., Usher, K., & Mills, J. (2016). Effective pain management as part of palliative care for persons living with HIV/AIDS in a developing country: A qualitative study. *Journal of Clinical Nursing, 25*(11–12), 1598–1605. doi:10.1111/jocn.13145

Molassiotis, A. (2000). A pilot study of the use of progressive muscle relaxation training in the management of post-chemotherapy nausea and vomiting. *European Journal of Cancer Care, 9,* 230–234.

Montgomery, G. H., Weltz, C. R., Seltz, M., & Bovbjerg, D. H. (2002). Brief presurgery hypnosis reduces distress and pain in excisional breast biopsy patients. *International Journal of Clinical and Experimental Hypnosis, 50,* 17–32. doi:10.1080/00207140208410088

Mundy, E. A., DuHamel, K. N., & Montgomery, G. H. (2003). The efficacy of behavioral interventions for cancer treatment-related side effects. *Seminars in Clinical Neuropsychiatry, 8*(4), 253–275.

Nainis, N., Paice, J. A., Ratner, J., Wirth, J. H., Lai, J., & Shott, S. (2006). Relieving symptoms in cancer: Innovative use of art therapy. *Journal of Pain and Symptom Management, 31*(2), 162–169. doi:10.1016/j.jpainsymman.2005.07.006

National Healthcare Disparities Report. (2013). Retrieved from https://archive.ahrq.gov/research/findings/nhqrdr/nhdr13/index.html

Oh, B., Butow, P., Boyle, F., Costa, D. S. J., Pavlakis, N., Bell, D., . . . Clark, S. (2014). Effects of qigong on quality of life, fatigue, stress, neuropathy, and sexual function in women with metastatic breast cancer: A feasibility study. *International Journal of Physical Medicine & Rehabilitation, 2,* 1–6. doi:10.4172/2329–9096.1000217

Orlandi, M., Trangeled, K., Mambrini, A., Tagliani, M., Ferrarini, A., Zanetti, L., . . . Cantore, M. (2007). Pet therapy effects on oncological day hospital patients undergoing chemotherapy treatment. *Anticancer Research, 27,* 4301–4303. PMID: 18214035

Papaconstantinou, E. A., Hodnett, E., & Stremler, R. (2016). A behavioral-educational intervention to promote pediatric sleep during hospitalization: A pilot randomized controlled trial. *Behavioral Sleep Medicine,* 1–17. doi:10.1080/15402002.2016.1228639

Pascoe, M. C., & Bauer, I. E. (2015). A systematic review of randomised control trials on the effects of yoga on stress measures and mood. *Journal of Psychiatric Research, 68,* 270–282. doi:10.1016/j.jpsychires.2015.07.013

Phelps, A. C., Maciejewski, P. K., Nilsson, M., Balboni, T. A., Wright, A. A., Paulk, M. E., . . . Prigerson, H. G. (2009). Religious coping and use of intensive life-prolonging care near death in patients with advanced cancer. *Journal of the American Medical Association, 301*(11), 1140–1147.

Puchalski, C., & Romer, A. L. (2000). Taking a spiritual history allows clinicians to understand patients more fully. *Journal of Palliative Medicine, 3,* 129–137.

Rhondali, W., Lasserre, E., & Filbet, M. (2013). Art therapy among palliative care inpatients with advanced cancer. *Palliative Medicine, 27,* 571–572. doi:10.1177/0269216312471413

Riddler, H. M. O., Stige, B., Qvale, L. G., & Gold, C. (2013). Individual music therapy for agitation in dementia: An exploratory randomized controlled trial. *Aging & Mental Health, 17,* 667–678. doi:10.1080/13607863.2013.790926

Saria, M. G., Nyamathi, A., Phillips, L. R., Stanton, A. L., Evangelista, L., Kesari, S., & Maliski, S. (2017). The hidden morbidity of cancer: Burden in caregivers of patients with brain metastases. *Nursing Clinics of North America, 52*(1), 159–178. doi:10.1016/j.cnur.2016.10.002

Senderovich, H., Ip, M. L., Berall, A., Karuza, J., Gordon, M., Binns, M., . . . Dunal, L. (2016). Therapeutic Touch® in a geriatric Palliative Care Unit – A retrospective review. *Complementary Therapies in Clinical Practice, 24*, 134–138.

Serfaty, M., Wilkinson, S., Freeman, C., Mannix, K., & King, M. (2012). The ToT study: Helping with Touch or Talk (ToT): A pilot randomized controlled trial to examine the clinical effectiveness of aromatherapy massage versus cognitive behaviour therapy for emotional distress in patients in cancer/palliative care. *Psycho-Oncology, 21*(5), 563–569.

Shin, E., Seo, K., Lee, S., Jang, J., Jung, Y., Kim, M., & Yeon, J. (2016). Massage with or without aromatherapy for symptom relief in people with cancer. *Cochrane Database of Systematic Reviews, 6*(CD009873). doi:10.1002/14651858.CD009873.pub3

Smedbäch, J., Öhlén, J., Årestedt, K., Alvariza, A., Fürst, C., & Håkanson, C. (2017). Palliative care during the final week of life of older people in nursing homes: A register-based study. *Palliative and Supportive Care, 15*(4), 1–8. doi:10/1017/S1478951516000948

Sockalingam, S., Tan, A., Hawa, R., Pollex, H., Abbey, S., & Hodges, B. D. (2014). Interprofessional education for delirium care: A systematic review. *Journal of Interprofessional Care, 28*(4), 345–351. doi:10.3109/13561820.2014.891979

Solano, J. P., Gomes, B., & Higginson, I. J. (2006). A comparison of symptom prevalence in far advanced cancer, AIDS, heart disease, chronic obstructive pulmonary disease and renal disease. *Journal of Pain & Symptom Management, 31*, 58–69.

Suzuki, M., Muro, S., Ando, Y., Omori, T., Shiota, T., . . . Mishima, M. (2012). A randomized, placebo-controlled trial of acupuncture in patients with chronic obstructive pulmonary disease (COPD). *Archives of Internal Medicine, 172*, 878–886. doi:10.1001/archinternmed.2012.1233

Tang, S. T., Hsieh, C. H., Chiang, M. C., Chen, J. S., Chang, W. C., Chou, W. C., & Hou, M. M. (2016). Impact of high self-perceived burden to others with preferences for end-of-life care and its determinants for terminally ill cancer patients: A prospective cohort study. *Psycho-Oncology, 26*, 102–108. doi:10.1002/pon.4107

Tice, M. A. (2006). Managing breathlessness: Providing comfort at the end of life. *Home Healthcare Nurse, 24*, 207–210. doi:10.1097/00004045-200604000-00004

Van Fleet, S. (2000). Relaxation and imagery for symptom management: Improving patient assessment and individualizing treatment. *Oncology Nursing Forum, 27*, 501–510.

Van Weert, J., Van Dulmen, A. M., Spreeuwenberg, P. M., Ribbe, M. W., & Bensing, J. M. (2005). Behavioural and mood effects of Snoezelen integrated into 24-hour dementia care. *Journal of the American Geriatrics Society, 53*, 24–33.

Wilkie, D. J., & Ezenwa, M. O. (2012). Pain and symptom management in palliative care and at end of life. *Nursing Outlook, 60*(6), 357–364.

Wilkinson, S. M., Love, S. B., Westcombe, A. M., Gambles, M. A., Burgess, C. C., Cargill, A., . . . Ramirez, A. J. (2007). Effectiveness of aromatherapy massage in the management of anxiety and depression in patients with cancer: A multicenter randomized controlled trial. *Journal of Clinical Oncology, 25*, 532–539. doi:10.1200/JCO.2006.08.9987

Winkelman, W. D., Lauderdale, K., Balboni, M. J., Phelps, A. C., Peteet, J. R., Block, S. D., . . . Balboni, T. A. (2011). The relationship of spiritual concerns to the quality of life of advanced cancer patients: Preliminary findings. *Journal of Palliative Medicine, 14*, 1022–1028.

World Health Organization (WHO). *Essential Medicines in Palliative Care*. Accessed July 14, 2017. Retrieved from www.who.int/selection_medicines/committees/expert/19/appli cations/PalliativeCare_8_A_R.pdf

Zadeh, R. S., Eshelman, P., Setla, J., Kennedy, L., Hon, E., & Basara, A. (2017). Environmental design for end-of-life care: An integrative review on improving quality of life and managing symptoms for patients in institutional settings. *Journal of Pain and Symptom Management*, epub ahead of print.

Zech, N., Hansen, E., Bernardy, K., & Häuser, W. (2017). Efficacy, acceptability and safety of guided imagery/hypnosis in fibromyalgia – a systematic review and meta-analysis of randomized controlled trials. *European Journal of Pain*, *21*, 217–227. doi:10/1002/ejp.933

Zetteler, J. (2008). Effectiveness of simulated presence therapy for individuals with dementia: A systematic review and meta-analysis. *Aging and Mental Health*, *12*(6), 779–785. doi:10.1080/13607860802380631

Meaning-Centered Psychotherapy for cancer patients with advanced and terminal illness

Melissa Masterson, Barry Rosenfeld, and William Breitbart

Introduction

Facing a diagnosis of advanced cancer is challenging for even the most resilient individuals. Distress associated with this diagnosis can manifest in many ways including physical symptoms, psychological symptoms, and spiritual/existential symptoms. Although physical symptoms are indeed difficult for patients with advanced disease, it is clear that symptoms related to psychological distress and existential concerns may be even more prevalent, and are often more distressing, than pain and other physical symptoms (Portenoy et al., 1994). Existential concerns are a major issue among those with advanced cancer, as thoughts and feelings regarding one's mortality are brought to the forefront. As we continue to develop our understanding of the psychosocial needs of palliative care patients, it has become apparent that models of adequate palliative care must extend their focus beyond pain and physical symptom control, to include psychiatric, psychosocial, existential and spiritual domains of end-of-life care (Breitbart, Bruera, Chochinov, & Lynch,1995; Breitbart, Chochinov, Passik, 1998; Chochinov & Breitbart, 2000; Puchalski & Romer, 2000; Rousseau, 2000).

Defining spirituality as a construct of meaning and/or faith

The Consensus Conference on Improving Spiritual Care as a Dimension of Palliative Care defined spirituality as "the aspect of humanity that refers to the way individuals seek and express meaning and purpose and the way they experience their connectedness to the moment, to self, to others, to nature, and to the significant or sacred" (Puchalski et al., 2009). Others have defined spirituality as a construct that involves concepts of both meaning and religious faith (Brady, Peterman, Fitchett, Mo, & Cella, 1999; Karasu, 1999). Meaning, or having a sense that one's life has purpose, involves the conviction that one is fulfilling a unique role and purpose in life. Many believe that life comes with a responsibility to live to one's full potential as a human being. In striving to fulfill this responsibility, one is able to achieve a sense of peace, contentment, or even transcendence, through connectedness with something greater than one's self (Frankl, 1992). Faith is differentiated from meaning as a belief in a higher transcendent power, though not necessarily identified as God, and not necessarily through participation in the rituals or beliefs of a specific organized religion. However, the faith component of spirituality is most often associated with religion and religious belief, whereas the meaning component of spirituality is a more universal concept that can exist in both religious and non-religiously identified individuals.

Spiritual well-being/meaning and its impact on psychosocial outcomes in advanced cancer

There has been great interest among palliative care professionals regarding the role of faith and religious beliefs on health outcomes (Baider et al., 1999; Carl Pieper, Meador, & Sheip, 1992; Koenig, George, & Peterson, 1998; McCullough & Larson, 1999; Sloan, Bagiella, & Powell, 1999). Recent studies have found that religion and spirituality generally play a positive role in helping patients cope with illnesses such as cancer and HIV (Baider et al., 1999; Brady et al., 1999; Nelson, Rosenfeld, Breitbart, & Galietta, 2002). The link between religion and health is weaker and less consistent than that between spirituality/meaning and health outcomes (McCullough & Larson, 1999; Sloan et al., 1999). Importantly, researchers theorize that religious beliefs may serve to help patients construct meaning through the suffering inherent to illness, which may in turn facilitate acceptance of their situation (Koenig et al., 1998).

There is extensive evidence that demonstrates the significance of spiritual well-being for patients at the end of life. For example, in a qualitative study, Singer and colleagues found that "achieving a sense of spiritual peace" was a domain of end-of-life care that patients found to be the most important (Singer, Martin, & Kelner, 1999). Moadel and colleagues (1999) surveyed 248 cancer patients and asked them to identify their most important needs. Among the most commonly cited needs were help overcoming fears (51%), finding peace of mind (43%), finding hope (41%), finding meaning in life (40%), and finding spiritual resources (39%) (Moadel et al., 1999). Similarly, in a sample of 162 Japanese hospice inpatients, psychological distress was associated with meaninglessness and hopelessness in 37% of the participants, and with loss of social role and feeling irrelevant in 28% of participants (Morita, Tsunoda, Inoue, & Chihara, 2000). In a survey conducted by Meier and colleagues of the reasons why patients requested assisted suicide, physicians cited "loss of meaning in life" in 47% of the requests (Meier et al., 1998). Clearly, from patient and physician perspectives alike, issues related to spirituality (broadly defined) are essential elements of quality end-of-life care.

Several published studies highlight the importance of spirituality and meaning in end-of-life care. Brady and colleagues found that cancer patients who reported a high degree of meaning in their lives reported higher satisfaction with their quality of life and were able to tolerate severe physical symptoms better than patients who reported lower levels of meaning and peace (1999). Our research group (Breitbart et al., 2000) has also demonstrated a central role for spiritual well-being (i.e., sense of meaning and peace), protecting against depression, hopelessness, and desire for hastened death among terminally ill cancer patients. McClain and colleagues found that spiritual well-being mediated the effects of depression on end-of-life despair (as defined by hopelessness, desire for hastened death and suicidal ideation) (McClain, Rosenfeld, & Breitbart, 2003). Yanez and colleagues (2009) similarly found that for breast cancer survivors, increases in meaning and peace significantly predicted better mental health and lower distress, whereas increases in faith did not.

This research highlighting the role of meaning as a buffer against psychological distress is particularly significant in the face of what is known about the consequences of depression and hopelessness in cancer patients. Depression, hopelessness, and loss of meaning are associated with poorer survival (Watson, Haviland, Greer, Davidson, & Bliss, 1999) and higher rates of suicide, suicidal ideation, and desire for hastened death (Breitbart et al., 2000; Breitbart & Rosenfeld, 1999; Chochinov, Wilson, Enns, & Lander, 1994; Chochinov, Wilson, Enns, & Mowchun, 1995; Kissane et al., 1997). Additionally, hopelessness and loss of meaning have been shown to be independent of depression as predictors of desire for death, and are as influential (if not more so) in fueling desire for death as depression (Breitbart et al., 2000). Therefore, there is a critical need for the development of psychosocial interventions for the terminally ill that address loss of meaning, as a mechanism for improving psychosocial outcomes (e.g., quality of life, depression, and end-of-life despair). Given the mounting research highlighting unmet existential needs and the theoretical background provided by Viktor Frankl's Logotherapy, we began to develop a meaning-centered approach to caring for patients approaching the end of life.

Theoretical background

Nearly two decades ago, our research group at Memorial Sloan Kettering Cancer Center began to understand that a meaning-centered approach to psychosocial care was a critical element in alleviating distress in patients with advanced cancer. For patients who are facing death, the development and/or the preservation of meaning is not only clinically, spiritually, and existentially important, but is central to therapeutic intervention. Meaning-Centered Psychotherapy (MCP) was conceived at the intersection of a baffling clinical problem and growing research evidence highlighting the inadequacies of existing explanations. Clinically, we witnessed despair and hopelessness take hold of patients and, for many, give rise to a desire for hastened death. What we found most surprising was that although 45% of patients expressing a desire for hastened death met criteria for clinically significant depression, and many report significant pain or other distressing physical symptoms, the majority of these patients were not clinically depressed or responding to physical symptom distress, but rather facing an existential crisis, often encompassing a loss of meaning, value, purpose, and hope (Breitbart, 2002).

As the research published by our group as well as others (Chochinov et al., 1994; Chochinov et al., 1995; Watson et al., 1999; Yanez et al., 2009) began to demonstrate the central role that meaning plays in diminishing psychosocial distress and buffering against despair at the end of life, we recognized the need to develop a clinical intervention grounded in meaning and spirituality. This effort led us to the work of Viktor Frankl, his pioneering work with Logotherapy (Frankl, 1986, 1988, 1992), and seminal writings in existential philosophy and psychiatry such as the work of Irvin Yalom (1980). We found Frankl's concepts of meaning and spirituality to be particularly powerful tools that could be utilized in our psychotherapeutic work with advanced cancer patients facing existential issues at the end of life. One of Frankl's main contributions was focusing on the spiritual component of human experience, and the central importance of meaning (or the will to meaning) as a motivating force in human psychology. Frankl's basic concepts include (1986, 1988, 1992):

1) *Meaning of life*: Life has meaning and never ceases to have meaning even up to the last moment of life, and while meaning may change in the context of impending death, it never ceases to exist.
2) *Will to meaning*: The desire to find meaning in human existence is a primary instinct and a basic motivation for human behavior.
3) *Freedom of will*: People have the freedom to find meaning in existence and to choose their attitude toward suffering.
4) *Sources of meaning*: The main sources of meaning in life are derived from creativity (work and deeds), experience (art, nature, humor, love, relationships, and roles), attitude (the attitude one takes toward suffering and existential problems), and history (legacy).

Meaning-focused coping

Another central influence on the development of MCP was Park and Folkman's (1997) conceptual model of meaning as a means of coping with traumatic events. Park and Folkman's concept of "Meaning-Focused Coping" focuses on reevaluating an event as having positive elements (rather than being seen as entirely negative), answering the question of why an event occurred (i.e., "Why me?"), enumerating ways in which one's life has changed because of an event, and assessing the extent to which one has "made sense of" or "found meaning" in an event (Andrykowski & Hunt, 1993; Frankl, 1986, 1988, 1992; Folkman, 1997; Park & Folkman, 1997; Taylor, 1983). Unlike Frankl, who viewed meaning as a state, Park and Folkman conceptualized meaning as having two components: global and situational meaning. They also posited that individuals can move from feeling demoralized, as if their lives hold no value, to recognizing their personal sense of meaning and purpose, allowing them to place even more value on the time they have remaining. Importantly, conceptualizing meaning as a state subject to change suggests its potential responsiveness to intervention. Frankl also viewed suffering as a potential springboard, both for having a need for meaning and for finding it (Frankl, 1986, 1992). Hence, while the diagnosis of a terminal illness may be seen as a crisis in the fullest sense of the word – an experience of distress or even despair – it may also offer an opportunity for personal growth and meaning-making. Whereas the loss of one's sense of meaning and purpose in life may lead to despair, a sustained or even heightened sense of meaning, purpose, and peace can allow one to place even more value on the time remaining and positively appraise events.

Meaning-Centered Psychotherapy (MCP)

We initially developed Meaning-Centered Psychotherapy (MCP) as a group-based intervention (Meaning-Centered Group Psychotherapy, or MCGP), with the first trials of this intervention occurring more than 15 years ago (Greenstein, 2000; Greenstein & Breitbart, 2000). A primary goal of the first few treatment groups was to refine the content and structure of the intervention, explore the utility of didactic and experiential exercises, and gauge patient responses to the intervention. Following the refinement of this treatment approach (described in more detail below), we embarked on the first pilot study of this intervention (Breitbart et al., 2010). However, we quickly recognized the challenges imposed by a group-based intervention, particularly for patients approaching the end of life. Physical limitations, worsening symptoms, and acute medical crises frequently impacted attendance, and highlighted the importance of an individualized version of MCP.

Overview of intervention

Because the structure of MCP is similar across both group and individual formats, we describe the group-based intervention and highlight key differences when adapted to an individualized format. MCGP is an eight-session group-based intervention that utilizes didactics, discussions, and experiential exercises that focus on specific themes related to both meaning and advanced cancer. Group sessions of MCGP serve three major purposes: 1) to promote a supportive environment for cancer patients to explore personal issues and feelings surrounding their illness in a therapeutic group format; 2) to facilitate a greater understanding of possible sources of meaning both before and after a diagnosis of cancer; and 3) to aid patients in their discovery and maintenance of a sense of meaning in life during illness. The ultimate goal of MCGP is to optimize coping through the pursuit of an enhanced sense of meaning and purpose. As Frankl noted (1988), the possibility of creating or experiencing meaning exists until the last moment of life.

The intervention is intended to help broaden the scope of possible sources of meaning through a combination of: 1) didactic teaching of the philosophy of meaning on which the intervention is based, 2) session exercises and homework for each participant to complete and 3) open-ended discussion, which may include the therapist's interpretive insights and comments. However, it is important for clinicians to understand that meaning-making is an individualized process and, therefore, it is each individual member's responsibility to use these sessions to actively explore and discover the sources of meaning in their own right. In this intervention, patients are not passive recipients of the intervention, but are active participants in the process itself, bringing to the table their own experiences, beliefs, and hopes that shape their journey to enhanced meaning and purpose.

Although session topics remain the same within both individual and group formats, IMCP includes only seven sessions, as the third topic, Historical Sources of Meaning and Legacy, is covered over two sessions in the group format to ensure ample time for each group member to participate in the often lengthy discussion of one's legacy. Session goals, didactics, and experiential exercises are otherwise similar between the two variations (Table 4.1). The following is an overview of each session of MCGP, including the experiential exercises used to facilitate discussions and greater understanding of meaning. More detailed information regarding the delivery of IMCP is available elsewhere (Breitbart & Poppito, 2014b).

Session 1: concepts and sources of meaning

The initial session of MCGP involves introductions of each group member and an overall explanation of the group's goals. Patient introductions include

Table 4.1 Meaning-Centered Group Psychotherapy session topics and themes

Session topics	Themes
Session #1: Concepts and sources of meaning	Introductions and meaning
Session #2: Cancer and meaning	Identity before and after cancer diagnosis
Session #3: Historical sources of meaning	Life as a legacy that has been given
Session #4: Historical sources of meaning	Life as a legacy that one lives and will give
Session #5: Attitudinal sources of meaning	Encountering life's limitations
Session #6: Creative sources of meaning	Creativity, courage, and responsibility
Session #7: Experiential sources of meaning	Connecting with life through love, beauty, and humor
Session #8: Transitions	Final reflections and hopes for the future

biographical and demographic information, as well as their expectations, hopes, and questions relating to the group process. Given that MCGP is drastically different from many other psychotherapy approaches, it is imperative that the group leaders orient patients to the structure, logistics, and goals of the intervention. The session concludes with a discussion of what *meaning* means to each participant. The experiential exercise (described below) helps patients to discover how they find a sense of meaning and purpose in general, as well as specifically in relation to having been diagnosed with cancer. As a supplement to the first group session, all patients are given a copy of Frankl's book *Man's Search for Meaning* (1992), to facilitate each patient's understanding of the main themes of the intervention. The experiential exercise for the first session explores meaningful moments identified by the patient from his or her own life (see Box 4.1). During completion of this exercise, the therapist begins to develop a deeper understanding of what each patient finds to be meaningful and begins to build rapport with the group as a whole.

Box 4.1   Session I experiential exercise: meaningful moments

List one or two experiences or moments when life has felt particularly meaningful to you – whether it sounds powerful or mundane. For example, it could be something that helped get you through a difficult day, or a time when you felt most alive. And say something about it.

Session 2: cancer and meaning

Session 2 is a continuation of sharing meaningful experiences, as well as a detailed explanation of what or who made these experiences particularly meaningful to the patient. The main goal is to explore the topic of *Cancer and Meaning* in light of the guiding theme: *Identity – Before and After Diagnosis.* Each patient is asked to impart something about their identity by answering the question "Who am I?" This exercise provides the opportunity to discuss how cancer has affected each patient's identity, as well as how cancer has affected what they consider to be meaningful in their lives. This session helps to reveal the patient's authentic sense of identity, and what made his or her personal experiences meaningful. The experiential exercise for Session 2 explores what makes this individual who they are and how cancer has impacted their identity (see Box 4.2). What the patient is likely to discover through this exercise is that the core aspects of his or her identity after cancer are strikingly similar to their identity prior to cancer. Furthermore, it is the role of the clinician to attend to these themes and identify characteristics that have persevered despite a life-altering diagnosis of advanced illness (Breitbart & Poppito, 2014a).

Box 4.2 Session 2 experiential exercise: identity and cancer

1 Write down four answers to the question, "Who am I?" These can be positive or negative, and include personality characteristics, body image, beliefs, things you do, people you know, etc. . . . For example, answers might start with, "I am someone who _____," or "I am a _____" . . .

2 How has cancer affected your answers? How has it affected the things that are most meaningful to you?

Sessions 3 and 4: historical sources of meaning

Sessions 3 and 4 focus on giving each patient a chance to share their life story with the group, which helps them to better appreciate past accomplishments while still elucidating future goals. The main goal for these sessions is to introduce and explore the topic of *Historical Sources of Meaning* and the guiding theme: *Life as a Living Legacy*. The idea of legacy is presented through three temporal elements: 1) the legacy that has been given from the past; 2) the legacy that one lives in the present; and 3) the legacy one will give in the future. The experiential exercise for Session 3 allows the patient the opportunity to explore and express meaningful past experiences in order to uncover the historical context of his/her living legacy (see Box 4.3). For some patients, discussion of the "legacy given" will be a pleasant trip down memory lane, whereas for others it may include difficult experiences related to unmet needs, losses, or disappointments. Whether memories are positive or negative, it is undeniable that this legacy is a part of who the patient is. The role of the therapist is to bear witness to the patient's story; the experience of telling the story may be comforting and transformative for a patient who is struggling physically and emotionally (Breitbart & Poppito, 2014b).

Box 4.3 Session 3 experiential exercise: life as a legacy that has been given

1 When you look back on your life and upbringing, what are the most significant memories, relationships, traditions, etc., that have made the greatest impact on who you are today?

For example: Identify specific memories of how you were raised that have made a lasting impression on your life (e.g. your relationship with parents, siblings, friends, teachers, etc.). What is the origin of your name? What are some past events that have meaningfully touched your life?

Session 4 focuses on "Life as a legacy that one lives and will give," in terms of patients' living legacy, and the legacy they hope to leave for others. The Session 3 experiential exercises help patients to understand the ways in which their pasts have shaped what they find meaningful, and the Session 4 experiential exercise fosters a discussion of future goals, no matter how small (see Box 4.4). Through this process, the patient can begin to witness his/her living legacy as a cohesive whole by integrating past memories with present accomplishments toward future contributions (Breitbart & Poppito, 2014b). The therapist should help the patient find the thread that weaves through his or her past, present, and future legacy, while simultaneously listening for themes of hardship, loss, and adversity that can be reflected upon when focusing on life's limitations in Session 5.

Box 4.4   Session 4 experiential exercise: life as a legacy that you live and will give

1   As you reflect upon who you are today, what are the meaning-ful activities, roles or accomplishments that you are most proud of? As you look toward the future, what are some of the life-lessons you have learned along the way that you would want to pass on to others?

2   What is the legacy you hope to live & give?

Session 5: attitudinal sources of meaning

This session examines each patient's confrontation with limitations in life, as well as the ultimate limitation – our mortality and the finiteness of life. The main goal for this session is to explore the topic of *Attitudinal Sources of Meaning* and the guiding theme: *Encountering Life's Limitations*. Session 5 is centered on Viktor Frankl's core theoretical belief that our last vestige of human freedom is our capacity to choose our attitude toward suffering and life's limitations in any given situation (Frankl, 1992). Thus, this session focuses on our freedom to choose our attitudes towards such limitations and find meaning in life, even in the face of death. The experiential exercise for this session allows patients to reflect on occasions when he or she has faced obstacles and limitations in the past (see Box 4.5). One role of the therapist is to point out how the patient has chosen his or her attitude in the past, and can continue to use this source of meaning in facing the challenges presented by illness (Breitbart & Poppito, 2014b).

Box 4.5   Session 5 experiential exercise: encountering life's limitations

1   What are some of the life limitations, losses, or obstacles that you have faced in the past, and how did you cope or deal with them at the time?

2   Since your diagnosis, what are the specific limitations or losses you have faced, and how are you coping or dealing with them now? Are you still able to find meaning in your daily life despite your aware-ness of the limitations and finiteness of life? [If yes, please briefly describe.]

3   What would you consider a 'good' or 'meaningful' death? How can you imagine being remembered by your loved ones? [e.g., what are some of your personal characteristics, the shared memories, or meaningful life events that have made a lasting impression on them?]

Following the experiential exercise for Session 5, the therapist invites the participant to continue to process the idea of "Life as a Living Legacy" through participation in a Legacy Project. The Legacy Project invites patients to create a project that is a reflection of the legacy that they want to give. This project is patient-driven and can take on many forms. For instance, a patient may choose to create a family photo album, write letters to family members, mend broken relationships, or work toward accomplishing a personal goal. The Legacy Pro-ject is introduced at the end of Session 5, but the therapist should inquire about the status of the project throughout the remainder of treatment, as the Legacy Project is typically presented in the final group session.

Session 6: creative sources of meaning

The main goal for Session 6 is to introduce and explore the topic of *Creative Sources of Meaning* and the guiding theme: *Actively engaging in life via creativity and responsibility*. In this session, a primary role of the clinician is to provide psycho-education regarding the relationship between creativity, courage, and responsibility. In MCP, our definition of "creativity" is not limited to artistic expressions (i.e., painting), but encompasses the modes by which an indi-vidual actively creates or shapes his/her life. As humans, our existence calls us to create, and our ability to respond to this creative calling, forms the basis for taking responsibility for our lives. Creativity and responsibility, therefore, are inextricably linked. However, the challenge of creativity is that it requires courage, tenacity and inner fortitude to take risks, particularly in the face of uncertainty and doubt (as is inevitable, when confronting advanced cancer). Patients may feel existential guilt when they ignore this creative calling and fail to respond to life. It is imperative to normalize the guilt that patients may experience, as well as to foster strength by helping patients to acknowledge the courage inherent in their day-to-day ability to engage in creative endeavors. The experiential exercise for this session allows patients to explore the concepts of creativity, courage, and responsibility in their own lives (see Box 4.6).

Box 4.6   Session 6 experiential exercise: actively engaging in life

1   Living life and being creative requires courage and commitment. Can you think of a time(s) in your life when you've been courageous, taken ownership of your life, or made a meaningful commitment to something of value to you?
2   Do you feel you've expressed what is most meaningful to you through your life's work and creative activities [e.g., job, parenting, causes]? If so, how?
3   What are your responsibilities? Who are you responsible to and for?
4   Do you have unfinished business? What tasks have you always wanted to do, but have yet to undertake? If so, what do you think is holding you back?

Session 7: experiential sources of meaning

The main goal for Session 7 is to introduce and explore the topic of *Experiential Sources of Meaning* by way of the guiding theme: *Connecting with Life*. Whereas creative and attitudinal sources of meaning require active involvement with life, experiential sources of meaning embody a more passive, even sensory engagement with life. Patients explore occasions and experiences when they have felt connected with life through love, beauty, and humor. During the experiential exercise for this, patients are invited to provide examples of ways they connect to these sources of meaning (see Box 4.7). Following this exercise, the therapist reflects on the fact that experiential sources of meaning remain accessible, despite limited physical capabilities or emotional hardship (Breitbart & Poppito, 2014b). As the illness progresses, patients may find comfort in sources of meaning that require little activity to access.

Box 4.7 Session 7 experiential exercise: connecting with life

List three ways in which you connect with life and feel alive through the experiential sources of:

a Love
b Beauty
c Humor

Session 8: transitions

The final MCGP session provides an opportunity to review patients' Legacy Projects, as well as to review individual and group themes. The experiential exercise that concludes this session focuses on answering the question "What are your hopes for the future?" This exercise facilitates a discussion of transitions and the future, and helps put closure on the group (or individual) experience (see Box 4.8).

Box 4.8 Session 8 experiential exercise: reflection and feedback

1 What has it been like for you to go through this learning experience over these last seven sessions? Have there been any changes in the way you view your life and cancer experience having been through this process?
2 Do you feel like you have a better understanding of the sources of meaning in life and are you able to use them in your daily life? If so, how?
3 What are your hopes for the future?

In response to the pragmatic concerns related to group-based interventions for seriously ill cancer patients, we developed Individual Meaning-Centered Psychotherapy (IMCP), using the same essential structure and content as the group based intervention. Subsequent trials of IMCP have focused on its efficacy, providing strong evidence for both variations of the intervention, MCPG

and IMCP (Breitbart et al., 2010, 2015, 2012). More recently, several variations of MCP have been studied (Breitbart, 2016), including a recent publication by our group examining a brief, three-session version of MCP specifically
intended for hospice patients in the last weeks of life (Rosenfeld et al., 2016).
The paragraphs below highlight the findings from our primary studies of
MCGP and IMPC, all of which utilized randomized clinical trials (RCTs) to
contrast MCP with supportive psychotherapy and other potentially relevant
comparison interventions.

Overview of evidence for efficacy

Our first randomized controlled trial of Meaning-Centered Group Psychotherapy (MCGP) (Breitbart et al., 2010) provided much needed evidence of
the efficacy of this intervention in improving spiritual well-being and a sense
of meaning, as well as in decreasing anxiety, hopelessness, and desire for death.
Ninety patients received eight sessions of either MCGP or a manualized supportive group psychotherapy (SGP) intervention. Between 2002 and 2005, 90
patients were randomized to groups of either MCGP ($n = 49$) or SGP ($n = 41$);
55 patients completed the eight-week intervention and 38 completed a follow-
up assessment two months later (attrition during the study was largely due to
patient death or physical deterioration). Outcome assessments included measures of spiritual well-being, meaning, hopelessness, desire for death, optimism/
pessimism, anxiety, depression, and overall quality of life. Results of this study
demonstrated significantly greater benefits from MCGP compared to SGP, particularly in enhancing spiritual well-being and a sense of meaning and peace
and reducing desire for hastened death. Treatment effects for MCGP appeared
even stronger two months after treatment ended, suggesting that benefits not
only persist, but may grow after treatment has been completed (Breitbart et al.,
2010). Conversely, patients who participated in SGP failed to demonstrate significant improvements on any of the study variables, either post-treatment or at
the two-month follow-up assessment (Breitbart et al., 2010).

Our second pilot study contrasted IMCP with an attention-control intervention, therapeutic massage (Breitbart et al., 2012). Between 2004 and 2006,
120 patients with advanced cancer were randomly assigned to seven sessions of
IMCP ($n = 64$) or massage therapy ($n = 56$), with 88 patients completing the
study intervention and 67 providing follow-up data two months later. Like our
pilot study of MCGP, this study demonstrated significantly stronger effects of
IMCP (compared to massage therapy) for spiritual well-being, sense of meaning
and peace, overall quality of life, and decreased physical symptom distress. Once
again, moderate to large (and statistically significant) improvements ($d = 0.38$
to 0.68) were observed for patients who received IMCP, whereas the benefits
of therapeutic massage on these study variables was typically small or nonexistent (Breitbart et al., 2012). These pilot studies provided much-needed support for the efficacy of MCGP as a novel intervention for improving spiritual

well-being, a sense of meaning, and quality of life in patients with advanced cancer. More importantly, these pilot studies supported the need for larger, more rigorous trials of MCP.

Our second trial of MCGP (2007–2012) utilized a similar methodology as the pilot study, again contrasting patients who were randomized (in groups of 8–10) to MCGP (n = 132) with those participating in SGP (n = 121) (Breitbart et al., 2015). The improved power of these analyses resulted in even more robust findings than our initial pilot study, demonstrating significantly stronger improvement on virtually all study variables, including spiritual well-being, overall quality of life, desire for hastened death, hopelessness, depression and physical symptom distress. Within group analyses again demonstrated moderate to large effect sizes for improvement (e.g., Cohen's d = .3 to .7) within the MCGP group, but little or no improvement for patients who received SGP.

Our most recent RCT (2011–2016) randomized 321 advanced cancer patients to IMCP (n = 109), an individualized supportive psychotherapy (n = 108), or enhanced usual care (n = 104). In the individualized supportive psychotherapy arm, participants received seven individual sessions with a counselor (Masters level or above). Counselors utilized client-centered and supportive psychotherapy techniques during the seven sessions. In the enhanced usual care arm, participants received referral information tailored to address physical, mental health, and practical problems (i.e., acupuncture, mental health treatment, transportation services). Preliminary findings from this study have again supported the efficacy of IMCP, as patients assigned to IMCP demonstrated significantly greater improvements on key study variables when compared to those receiving enhanced usual care and those receiving the supportive psychotherapy. Taken together, these studies provide compelling evidence for the efficacy of MCP, in both group and individual formats, for the treatment of psychological distress and end of life despair in patients with advanced and terminal cancer.

Appropriate participants for MCP

The question of who might benefit from participation in MCP is an important one, and to date, little evidence has suggested that some patients benefit more or less than others. Our research studies have demonstrated efficacy with diagnostically and demographically heterogeneous groups of cancer patients, including patients with different cancer diagnoses (i.e., breast, colon, pancreatic), varying levels of distress, and from different ethnic backgrounds. Participants have identified multiple different religious affiliations, and some report no religious affiliation at all. Likewise, race and ethnicity have varied substantially across the groups, with no evidence that the intervention is better with some subsets of patients than others. However, one limitation in our current research base is the focus on patients with advanced and terminal cancer (typically stage IV disease, though some individuals have been included with stage III disease, provided the cancer had a particularly poor prognosis – e.g., pancreatic cancer). Small pilot studies have begun to examine the utility of MCP in a range of other populations, including cancer survivors, parents of children with cancer, and oncology nursing staff, but systematic evidence to support these adaptations of MCP is not yet available. Thus, at present we feel confident in recommending MCP for patients with advanced or terminal cancer, regardless of the cancer diagnosis or patient background characteristics, but are cautious about recommending the treatment in other settings until research has supported these adaptations.

Although it appears that many (if not most) advanced cancer patients could benefit from participation in MCP, the intervention is probably best suited for individuals with moderate or severe levels of distress. In fact, our most recent RCT required at least a moderate level of psychological distress as a pre-requisite to study participation, given preliminary evidence that the intervention is somewhat more effective among those with some degree of distress prior to treatment. Although MCP might also be beneficial for patients with lower levels of distress, the potential benefit from this intervention is less tangible, whereas the gain for patients who are already experiencing some distress is more readily apparent. That said, future research should focus on the potential prophylactic benefits of MCP, as this intervention may be useful in helping patients avoid developing more severe levels of distress, particularly as they cope with a worsening or poor-prognosis illness. When the source of the patient's distress is emotional or spiritual/religious in nature, MCP may be a particularly efficacious intervention, as our research has consistently demonstrated the strongest improvements in spiritual well-being, sense of meaning and purpose, and overall quality of life.

Another important consideration is the patient's physical limitations. We initially developed MCP as an intervention delivered in an outpatient setting. This setting limits the applicability of the intervention for patients with severe physical limitations. Concerns about physical limitations, and deteriorating illness more generally, may also influence decisions about whether the group or individual format is preferable. The flexibility of an individualized delivery is perhaps obvious, as sessions can often be rescheduled to fit the patient's evolving schedule conflicts. A group-based intervention, on the other hand, cannot be rescheduled simply because one group member has a schedule conflict or develops an acute illness that precludes participation. On the other hand, a group-based intervention enables both a more efficient delivery of treatment to a larger number of individuals (e.g., 6–10 group members can attend a single 90-minute group, whereas only one patient can be seen in an individualized treatment session).

In addition to a patient's physical limitations, which may interfere with attendance at outpatient therapy sessions, further considerations for the patient's energy and aspects of cognition must continually be assessed. Due to illness and cancer treatment, it is common that patients present for sessions experiencing some degree of fatigue. It is imperative to normalize this experience and allow for sessions to end early if fatigue becomes severe. Similarly, patients undergoing chemotherapy often present with mild cognitive impairments manifesting as difficulties with attention and concentration. Repetition may be needed in order to ensure that patients digest necessary information, and again allow for the session to be discontinued in the cognitive impairment becomes too disruptive.

Key therapist techniques in the application of MCGP

Psycho-educational approach: didactics and experiential exercises to enhance learning

MCP is essentially an educational intervention, with the primary goal being to help patients understand the concept of meaning and its importance in their lives, particularly when facing a terminal illness. This educational or learning process is achieved primarily through a set of brief didactics that introduce each session, followed by an experiential exercise designed to link these abstract concepts to the patient's own emotional experiences. In the group format, patients each share the content of the experiential exercises, and the process of experiential learning is reinforced through the comments of co-facilitators and other group members, as well as through the identification of commonalities among patients' responses.

A focus on meaning and sources of meaning as resources

A second goal of MCP is to help patients learn Frankl's concepts of meaning, and to incorporate and utilize these sources of meaning when coping with cancer and disease progression. In each session, the therapist or group facilitators listen carefully for, and highlight content shared by patients that reflect sources of meaning. Identification of meaningful moments described by patients, and drawing attention to "*meaning shifts*" are also critical, to highlight when patients begin to incorporate the vocabulary and conceptual framework of meaning into the material they share. Consistent with Park and Folkman's stress process theory (1997), an emphasis is also placed on the importance of the patient's ability to shift from one source of meaning to another, as selected sources of meaning may become unavailable due to disease progression. A specific technique utilized to facilitate this process in MCP is called *Moving from Ways of Doing to Ways of Being*. This technique allows individuals who have deemed their lives to be meaningless to move from a state of demoralization to one of hope as they recognize their personal sense of meaning and the value that their time remaining holds. Often this technique highlights the passive ways in which meaning can be derived. For example, a patient who had considered himself a "good father" because he played in the backyard with his son can come to recognize that even if he can no longer do this, he remains a "good father" by sitting and talking about the son's life goals and fears and expressing affection. In MCP it is also important for therapists and group facilitators to be aware of the "Co-Creation of Meaning" between therapists and patients, as well as between group members. Therapists and patient participants are witnesses, or repositories of meaning for each other, and thus are part of a meaningful legacy created by each of the patient participants in MCP.

Incorporating basic existential concepts and themes

A central concept in MCP is that human beings create values and, most importantly, fashion our own lives. In order to live fully, human beings must create a life of meaning, identity, and direction. Important existential concepts that are utilized by therapists and group facilitators in responding to the content of the experiential exercises include freedom, responsibility, choice, creativity, identity, authenticity, engagement, existential guilt, care, transcendence, transformation, direction, being unto death, being and temporality, and existential isolation. For example, creative sources of meaning are directly related to existential concepts such as responsibility, transformation, authenticity, and existential guilt. *Detoxifying Death* through the therapeutic stance and attitude of the therapist is another important existential therapy technique utilized throughout MCP. Therapists are instructed to speak openly about death as the ultimate limitation that causes suffering and for which meaning can be derived through the attitude that one takes towards that suffering (e.g., transcendence, choice). Another technique, the *Existential Nudge*, occurs when therapists gently challenge a patient's resistance to exploring difficult existential realities, such as the ultimate limitation of death or existential guilt. Although patients may have different degrees of comfort discussing death for a wide range of reasons (i.e., cultural background, religion, prognostic unawareness), the role of the MCP therapist is not to force discussion, but to meet the patient where they are and allow for open and honest discussion, with respect to the patient's preferences.

Cultural and ethnic variations on MCP

As interest in MCP has grown, clinicians and researchers around the world have developed adaptations of MCP that incorporate unique elements of the culture (Breitbart, 2016). For example, Israeli researchers (Goldzweig et al., 2017) have expanded the MCGP format by adding four additional sessions to accommodate "patterns of self-disclosure" and enhance group cohesion. They explained that Israeli participants "tend to share a lot and show deep involvement with other participants. The participants were eager to give advice and share their own experience and homework assignments with other members of the group; they did not necessarily adhere to the time limits" (p. 149). On the other hand, a Spanish research team adhered quite closely to the original MCGP and found little need for adaptation (Gil, Fraguell, & Limonero, 2017), aside from considerations related to their particular sample (i.e., patients with very advanced illness, which resulted in an increased attrition rate).

Within the U.S., adaptations for Hispanic/Latino and Asian patients have focused generally on the need for "culturally syntonic language", as well as adaptations that are specific to the particular culture (Costos-Muniz et al., 2017; Leng et al., 2017). These research teams have identified a number of important changes to the original MCGP manual, beginning with a reframing of the concept of "meaning" to be more easily understood by individuals who are less familiar with the overarching concept. For Hispanic/Latino participants, completing homework assignments within session was also recommended "to facilitate engagement and decrease difficulty related to literacy"; p. 141), as well as incorporation of family members into one of the sessions. Among Chinese patients, a focus on "stigma and shame around cancer and psychotherapy" (p. 128) was seen as a critical focus of the intervention, along with integration of the family. These authors differentiated the "family-centered" model of care from the traditional "Westernized, 'patient-autonomy' model" (p. 129), and suggested that treatment providers carefully consider the extent to which terminal illness – or even the cancer diagnosis – is directly addressed, given that many Asian family members are less forthcoming about diagnosis and prognosis. Although systematic research evaluating these adaptations is just beginning to accumulate, this literature highlights the importance of culture in adapting any psychotherapy approach to a novel culture or subgroup.

Group process skills and techniques

In the context of MCGP, a number of basic tenets of group process and dynamics are also important. Group facilitators must be cognizant of group etiquette, including working together as co-facilitators, attending to and promoting group cohesion, and facilitating an atmosphere that is conducive to productive exchanges between patients. Although MCGP is not intended to be primarily a supportive group intervention, elements of support are inevitable and important, albeit arising naturally rather than being directly promoted or specifically fostered, as would be the case in a more traditional supportive therapy.

As evident from the preceding paragraphs, many elements of MCP will be quite natural for experienced therapists who are familiar with the issues that arise in treating patients with advanced cancer. However, other techniques are more specialized, and require careful study and, ideally, supervised training opportunities. Because MCP is intended to follow a prescribed format and sequence, and our published research has adhered closely to this format, we encourage interested clinicians to learn and follow the MCP treatment manuals (Breitbart & Poppito, 2014a, 2014b), rather than incorporating selective elements into a more eclectic treatment approach (the utility of which is unknown).

Case example

Allen is a 56-year-old gay man who has worked in the advertising field for 30 years. His work is fast paced, taxing, and consuming at times. He reported that, while he enjoyed his work, he had begun to think of doing other things in recent years that may be more fulfilling. However, such feelings where usually overtaken by fears of what he would do with his life and what identity he would subsequently have. He has had a long and satisfying relationship with his partner of many years, a relationship in which Allen finds great solace and comfort.

His initial battle with cancer began 16 years ago, when he was diagnosed with thyroid cancer. The subsequent surgeries for this cancer left him with significant scarring of his neck, which significantly impacted his self-image and sense of self. He stated, "I felt like a fish that had been filleted." Despite this, he related that he felt he had overcome cancer and that the "battle was won." However, a routine examination nine months ago revealed advanced prostate cancer. Allen stated that this discovery "completely overwhelmed me. I felt crushed." He began to experience significant anxiety and depression, and to question the value of fighting this battle once again. He also reported that his current life felt empty and meaningless in the face of his new cancer, and that he felt alone and "singled out" by having to face this challenge again. Allen began seeing a psychiatrist to help with his mood symptoms, and that psychiatrist referred him for MCGP to complement the pharmacological intervention he was already receiving.

Allen reported that after the first session he felt "overwhelmed by all these other people with cancer." He considered terminating his participation in the group, but discussed this with his psychiatrist and decided to continue. He was relieved when other group members began to share similar feelings, and he began to feel more connected to them. He no longer felt as alone and now felt that he had people other than his psychiatrist who understood the unique experience of facing cancer and possible death. Allen felt increasingly connected with the other group members as each person shared the legacies that were given to them. Allen described sharing details about his childhood, particularly the financial struggles that his family experienced and the resentment that he harbored toward his father due to his lack of ability to provide for the family. Sharing these personal memories and experiences made Allen feel even more connected to the other group members. He was also able to draw connections between the legacy that he was given and the legacy that he was currently living.

As the group progressed, Allen began to alter his worldview significantly. He began to view the pressures of work, which had seemed so compelling and all-consuming, as being secondary to his own needs and his quality of life more generally. His longstanding desire to leave his work began to take on a new intensity. Session 6, which focuses on patients' feelings of responsibility to themselves and others, as well as any unfinished business, was an important turning point for Allen. He recalled "I used to be so afraid of what I would do and who I would be. But I've battled cancer twice! If I can fight these kinds of fights, those fears really seem to pale. My work was important for me. But it's the 'me' that counts here. Me and my partner count so much more."

For his "Legacy Project," Allen resolved to accomplish two goals. The first was to terminate his employment and put his available resources into his relationship. The second was to begin the process of renovating his home, something he and his partner had wanted to do but his illness had prevented. Allen recalled that he used to think, "I'm dying. Why bother?" His new outlook on life and his illness allowed him to view his remaining time as precious and worthy of investment. In addition, he came to the realization that, despite the anxiety and pain his illness caused, he was still alive and therefore he should carry on living to the end. "Until I go, I'm still here. Why should I stop experiencing the simple joy of still existing? I won't let it rob me of that."

At the conclusion of the group, Allen characterized the experience as having been of great value. He stated, "I would not have seen the purpose or even the possibility of making these changes without this group and all of you." At the two-month follow-up interview, Allen had indeed carried out the twin goals of his "Legacy Project." He felt an enhanced sense of meaning in his life, and was finding it easier to cope with his illness.

Questions

1   What are some of the most prominent existential dilemmas that Allen faced when entering the group?
2   List several ways in which Allen chose his attitude and took ownership for his life throughout the course of treatment.
3   What are some of the connections that you imagine Allen was able to make between the legacy he was given and the one that he was

currently living? Do you think any of these connections impacted the legacy he desired to give?

4   Why do you think Allen's psychiatrist referred him to MCGP? What about him made him a good candidate for the intervention?

References

Andrykowski, M. A., & Hunt, J. W. (1993). Positive psychosocial adjustment in potential bone marrow transplant recipients: Cancer as a psychosocial transition. *PsychoOncology*, *2*(4), 261–276.

Baider, L., Russak, S. M., Perry, S., Kash, K., Gronert, M., Fox, B., . . . Kaplan-Denour, A. (1999). The role of religious and spiritual beliefs in coping with malignant melanoma: An Israeli sample. *Psycho-Oncology*, *8*(1), 27–35.

Brady, M. J., Peterman, A. H., Fitchett, G., Mo, M., & Cella, D. (1999). A case for including spirituality in quality of life measurement in oncology. *Psycho Oncology*, *8*(5), 417–428.

Breitbart, W. (2002). Spirituality and meaning in supportive care: Spirituality-and meaning-centered group psychotherapy interventions in advanced cancer. *Supportive Care in Cancer*, *10*(4), 272–280.

Breitbart, W., Bruera, E., Chochinov, H., & Lynch, M. (1995). Neuropsychiatric syndromes and psychological symptoms in patients with advanced cancer. *Journal of Pain and Symptom Management*, *10*(2), 131–141.

Breitbart, W., Chochinov, H. M., & Passik, S. D. (1998). Psychiatric aspects of palliative care. In D. Doyle, G. W. Hanks, & N. MacDonald (Eds.), *Oxford Textbook of Palliative Medicine*, Second edition. New York, NY: Oxford University Press.

Breitbart, W., & Poppito, M. (2014a). *Meaning-Centered Group Psychotherapy for Patients With Advanced Cancer: A Treatment Manual*. New York, NY: Oxford University Press.

Breitbart, W., & Poppito, M. (2014b). *Individual Meaning-Centered Psychotherapy for Patients With Advanced Cancer: A Treatment Manual*. New York, NY: Oxford University Press.

Breitbart, W., Poppito, S., Rosenfeld, B., Vickers, A. J., Li, Y., Abbey, J., . . . Cassileth, B. R. (2012). Pilot randomized controlled trial of individual Meaning-Centered Psychotherapy for patients with advanced cancer. *Journal of Clinical Oncology*, *30*(12), 1304–1309.

Breitbart, W., & Rosenfeld, B. D. (1999). Physician-assisted suicide: The influence of psychosocial issues. *Cancer Control*, *6*, 146–161.

Breitbart, W., Rosenfeld, B., Pessin, H., Applebaum, A., Kulikowski, J., & Lichtenthal, W. G. (2015). Meaning-centered group psychotherapy: An effective intervention for improving psychological well-being in patients with advanced cancer. *Journal of Clinical Oncology*, *33*(7), 749–754.

Breitbart, W., Rosenfeld, B., Pessin, H., Kaim, M., Funesti-Esch, J., Galietta, M., . . . Brescia, R. (2000). Depression, hopelessness, and desire for hastened death in terminally ill patients with cancer. *JAMA*, *284*(22), 2907–2911.

Breitbart, W., Rosenfeld, B., Gibson, C., Pessin, H., Poppito, S., Nelson, C., . . . Sorger, B. (2010). Meaning-centered group psychotherapy for patients with advanced cancer: A pilot randomized controlled trial. *Psycho-Oncology*, *19*(1), 21–28.

Breitbart, W. S. (Ed.). (2016). *Meaning-Centered Psychotherapy in the Cancer Setting: Finding Meaning and Hope in the Face of Suffering*. Oxford: Oxford University Press.

Carl Pieper, D. P. H., Meador, K. G., & Sheip, F. (1992). Religious coping and depression among elderly, hospitalized medically ill men. *The American Journal of Psychiatry, 1*(49), 1–2.

Chochinov, H. M., & Breitbart, W. (2000). *The Handbook of Psychiatry in Palliative Medicine.* New York, NY: Oxford University Press.

Chochinov, H. M., Wilson, K. G., Enns, M., & Lander, S. (1994). Prevalence of depression in the terminally ill: Effects of diagnostic criteria and symptom threshold judgments. *The American Journal of Psychiatry, 151*(4), 537.

Chochinov, H. M., Wilson, K. G., Enns, M., & Mowchun, N. (1995). Desire for death in the terminally ill. *The American Journal of Psychiatry, 152*(8), 1185.

Costos-Muniz, R., Garduno-Ortega, O., Gonzalez, C. J., Rocha-Cadman, Z., Breitbart, W., & Gany, F. (2017). Cultural and linguistic adaptation of Meaning-Centered Psychotherapy for Spanish-speaking Latino cancer patients. In W. Breitbart (Ed.), *Meaning-Centered Psychotherapy in the Cancer Setting* (pp. 134–144). New York, NY: Oxford Press.

Folkman, S. (1997). Positive psychological states and coping with severe stress. *Social Science & Medicine, 45*(8), 1207–1221.

Frankl, V. F. (1955/1986). *The Doctor and the Soul.* New York, NY: Random House.

Frankl, V. F. (1959/1992). *Man's Search for Meaning,* Fourth Edition. Boston, MA: Beacon Press.

Frankl, V. F. (1969/1988). *The Will to Meaning: Foundations and Applications of Logotherapy,* Expanded Edition. New York, NY: Penguin Books.

Gil, F., Fraguell, C., & Limonero, J. T. (2017). Replication study of meaning-centered group psychotherapy in Spain: Cultural and linguistic challenges. In W. Breitbart (Ed.), *Meaning-Centered Psychotherapy in the Cancer Setting* (pp. 157–167). New York, NY: Oxford Press.

Goldzweig, G., Hasson-Ohayon, I., Elinger, G., Laronne, A., Wertheim, R., & Pizem, N. (2017). Adaptation of meaning-centered group psychotherapy in the Israeli context: The process of importing an intervention and preliminary results. In W. Breitbart (Ed.), *Meaning-Centered Psychotherapy in the Cancer Setting* (pp. 145–156). New York, NY: Oxford Press.

Greenstein, M. (2000). The house that's on fire: Meaning-Centered Psychotherapy pilot group for cancer patients. *American Journal of Psychotherapy, 54*(4).

Greenstein, M., & Breitbart, W. (2000). Cancer and the experience of meaning: A group psychotherapy program for people with cancer. *American Journal of Psychotherapy, 54*(4), 486.

Karasu, T. B. (1999). Spiritual psychotherapy. *American Journal of Psychotherapy, 53*(2), 143.

Kissane, D. W., Bloch, S., Miach, P., Smith, G. C., Seddon, A., & Keks, N. (1997). Cognitive-existential group therapy for patients with primary breast cancer-techniques and themes. *Psycho-Oncology, 6*(1), 25–33.

Koenig, H. G., George, L. K., & Peterson, B. L. (1998). Religiosity and remission of depression in medically ill older patients. *American Journal of Psychiatry, 155*(4), 536–542.

Leng, J., Lui, F., Chen, A., Huang, X., Breitbart, W., & Gany, F. (2017). Cultural and linguistic adaptation of Meaning-Centered Psychotherapy for Chinese cancer patients. In W. Breitbart (Ed.), *Meaning-Centered Psychotherapy in the Cancer Setting* (pp. 122–133). New York, NY: Oxford Press.

McClain, C. S., Rosenfeld, B., & Breitbart, W. (2003). Effect of spiritual well-being on end-of-life despair in terminally-ill cancer patients. *The Lancet, 361*(9369), 1603–1607.

McCullough, M. E., & Larson, D. B. (1999). Religion and depression: A review of the literature. *Twin Research, 2*(02), 126–136.

Meier, D. E., Emmons, C. A., Wallenstein, S., Quill, T., Morrison, R. S., & Cassel, C. K. (1998). A national survey of physician-assisted suicide and euthanasia in the United States. *New England Journal of Medicine, 338*(17), 1193–1201.

Moadel, A., Morgan, C., Fatone, A., Grennan, J., Carter, J., Laruffa, G., . . . Dutcher, J. (1999). Seeking meaning and hope: Self-reported spiritual and existential needs among an ethnically-diverse cancer patient population. *Psycho-Oncology*, *8*(5), 378–385.

Morita, T., Tsunoda, J., Inoue, S., & Chihara, S. (2000). An exploratory factor analysis of existential suffering in Japanese terminally ill cancer patients. *Psycho-Oncology*, *9*(2), 164–168.

Nelson, C. J., Rosenfeld, B., Breitbart, W., & Galietta, M. (2002). Spirituality, religion, and depression in the terminally ill. *Psychosomatics*, *43*(3), 213–220.

Park, C. L., & Folkman, S. (1997). Meaning in the context of stress and coping. *Review of General Psychology*, *1*(2), 115.

Portenoy, R. K., Thaler, H. T., Kornblith, A. B., Lepore, J. M., Friedlander-Klar, H., Kiyasu, E., . . . Scher, H. (1994). The memorial symptom assessment scale: An instrument for the evaluation of symptom prevalence, characteristics and distress. *European Journal of Cancer*, *30*(9), 1326–1336.

Puchalski, C., Ferrell, B., Virani, R., Otis-Green, S., Baird, P., Bull, J., . . . Pugliese, K. (2009). Improving the quality of spiritual care as a dimension of palliative care: The report of the Consensus Conference. *Journal of Palliative Medicine*, *12*(10), 885–904.

Puchalski, C., & Romer, A. L. (2000). Taking a spiritual history allows clinicians to understand patients more fully. *Journal of Palliative Medicine*, *3*(1), 129–137.

Rosenfeld, B., Saracino, R., Tobias, K., Masterson, M., Pessin, H., Applebaum, A., . . . Breitbart, W. (2016). Adapting Meaning-Centered Psychotherapy for the palliative care setting: Results of a pilot study. *Palliative Medicine*, doi:10.1177/0269216316651570.

Rousseau, P. (2000). Spirituality and the dying patient. *Journal of Clinical Oncology*, *18*(9), 2000–2002.

Singer, P. A., Martin, D. K., & Kelner, M. (1999). Quality end-of-life care: Patients' perspectives. *JAMA*, *281*(2), 163–168.

Sloan, R. P., Bagiella, E., & Powell, T. (1999). Religion, spirituality, and medicine. *The Lancet*, *353*(9153), 664.

Taylor, S. E. (1983). Adjustment to threatening events: A theory of cognitive adaptation. *American Psychologist*, *38*(11), 1161.

Watson, M., Haviland, J. S., Greer, S., Davidson, J., & Bliss, J. M. (1999). Influence of psychological response on survival in breast cancer: A population-based cohort study. *The Lancet*, *354*(9187), 1331–1336.

Yalom, I. D. (1980). *Existential Psychotherapy*. New York, NY: Basic Books.

Yanez, B., Edmondson, D., Stanton, A. L., Park, C. L., Kwan, L., Ganz, P. A., & Blank, T. O. (2009). Facets of spirituality as predictors of adjustment to cancer: Relative contributions of having faith and finding meaning. *Journal of Consulting and Clinical Psychology*, *77*(4), 730.

Chapter 5

Dignity Therapy

Gary Annable, Harvey Max Chochinov, Susan McClement, and Genevieve Thompson

Introduction

Heathcare providers have many effective ways of treating pain and other forms of physical suffering seen towards the end of life. Pharmacological approaches are sometimes used to mitigate psychological, spiritual, and existential distress, by way of making patients less aware of their suffering until it subsides or death ensues. In comparison, there are relatively few non-pharmacologic interventions that attempt to relieve patient suffering by directly addressing the *underlying sources* of psychological, spiritual, and existential distress (Breitbart et al., 2010; Jaiswal, Alici, & Breitbart, 2014; Lo et al., 2016).

Dignity Therapy is a short individual psychotherapy that can enhance end-of-life experience for people with terminal and chronic illnesses, as well as their families. It was designed to do so by addressing factors associated with psychological, existential, and spiritual distress, often associated with life-threatening or life-limiting illnesses (Chochinov, 2012). In a guided conversation with a trained therapist, patients reflect on their lives and identify the things that matter most to them and/or that they would most want remembered. The end result is a legacy-preserving generativity document comprised of cherished memories, life lessons, hopes, and dreams for loved ones, which they can bequeath to members of their family and others whom they deem important.

Dignity Therapy was developed as one component of a dignity-conserving approach to palliative care (Chochinov, 2002). It is based on an extensive body of empirical research regarding factors associated with the preservation or erosion of dignity reported by patients at the end of their lives. Since 2001, it has been used and studied around the world, including Canada, the United States, Australia, China, Japan, Scotland, England, Denmark, Spain, Portugal, and Italy.

Theoretical foundation

Loss of dignity is often cited as a motivation for patients who are seeking a hastened death or express a desire for early death (Ganzini et al., 2000; Ganzini, Dobscha, Heintz, & Press, 2003; Quill, 1994; Sullivan, Hedberg, & Fleming,

2000; Van Der Maas, Van Delden, Pijnenborg, & Looman, 1991). We therefore sought to discover how patients understand or conceive of the notion of dignity and whether it was possible to preserve and strengthen dignity, hence improving the quality of life for individuals approaching death.

We initially asked terminally ill cancer patients receiving palliative care (*n* = 213) to rate their sense of dignity and included measures of pain, distress, quality of life, desire for death, anxiety, hopelessness, will to live, and burden to others (Chochinov, Hack, Hassard, et al., 2002). Surprisingly, most patients rated their sense of dignity as strong or intact, suggesting that dignity is resilient and able to withstand various physical and psychological challenges at end of life. We also speculated that the quality of the palliative care these patients were receiving effectively maintained their dignity. The more striking finding, however, was that the sub-group of patients who experienced moderate to strong loss of dignity reported significantly higher depression, anxiety, desire for death, hopelessness, feelings of being a burden, and poorer quality of life relative to those whose dignity was intact.

Palliative care patients with terminal cancer (*n* = 50) were then asked how they understood and defined dignity, and what factors supported or undermined their own sense of dignity (Chochinov, Hack, McClement, Kristjanson, & Harlos, 2002). Qualitative analysis yielded an empirically derived theoretical model of dignity in the terminally ill. This model (see Figure 5.1) is comprised of

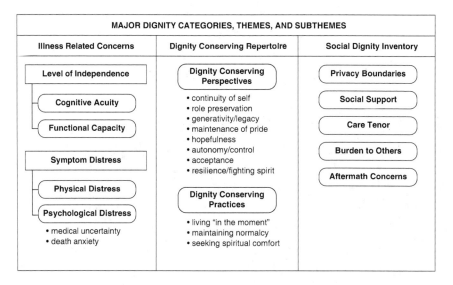

Figure 5.1 Major dignity categories, themes, and subthemes

Chochinov H. M, Hack T. McClement S., Kristjanson L., Harlos M. (2002). Dignity in the terminally ill: a developing empirical model. *Social Science and Medicine*, 54(3):433–443.

three broad categories encompassing the full range of physical, psychological, social, spiritual, and existential dimensions of the end-of-life experience:

- Illness-Related Concerns – independence/dependency (cognitive and functional capacity), physical distress, psychological distress.
- The Dignity-Conserving Repertoire – the psychological and spiritual factors, perspectives, and coping strategies embedded within a person's psychological makeup, personal background, and accumulated life experiences that influence their sense of dignity.
- The Social Dignity Inventory – social factors and relationship dynamics that enhance or detract from a person's sense of dignity.

This model extends beyond the management of pain and other physical symptoms, and can be used to inform strategies and interventions broadly addressing the physical, psychological, social, spiritual, and existential aspects of the end-of-life experience. This overarching framework, which we coined Dignity-Conserving Care (Chochinov, 2002), can help guide clinicians, patients, and families towards defining objectives, and making therapeutic choices, which will mitigate physical, psychological, social, spiritual, and existential suffering.

Every aspect of Dignity Therapy – including its format, content, and tone – are based on the model of dignity in the terminally ill. The overall *format* is shaped by the generativity subtheme of Dignity Conserving Perspectives. The generativity subtheme is derived from Erik Erikson's eight stages of psychosocial development (Erikson, 1950), which argues that the key developmental challenge of middle adulthood is the creation of a legacy that will serve to guide future generations. For many people, generativity is achieved by investing in those who will outlive them, but generativity can also be attained by other things that make a lasting imprint.

Generativity often becomes a key existential challenge for people facing life-limiting illness, as the proximity of death brings about heightened awareness of questions, such as "What difference will my life have made?" Dignity Therapy supports generativity by helping patients identify the most meaningful aspects of their lives and preserving those responses in a permanent document that will survive beyond death. Patients are then able to give this document to those whom they select.

The *content* of Dignity Therapy – that is, the question framework therapists use to guide patients through the interview (see Box 5.1) – is informed by subthemes within the Dignity Conserving Perspectives as well as the Aftermath Concerns subtheme of the Social Dignity Inventory, the latter referring to apprehensions regarding how family will manage in the wake of the patient's death. These themes, subthemes, and corresponding questions address a range of psychological and existential issues that are crucial to the preservation of dignity.

Beyond the questions themselves, the overall *tone* of Dignity Therapy must convey respect and affirmation of patient personhood. This principle is informed by the care tenor subtheme of the Social Dignity Inventory, which implies the many ways – verbal and non-verbal – clinicians can affirm the dignity of their patients.

Dignity Therapy described

In Dignity Therapy, a trained therapist uses a framework of open-ended questions as a means of guiding patients through a discussion to identify matters that are most important to them and that they would most want others to know or remember. The questions (see Box 5.1), which are meant to provide a framework of inquiry, probe for memories of important moments or events, relationships, accomplishments, roles, lessons learned, as well as the patient's hopes, dreams, advice, and instructions for loved ones. The question framework is not a structured interview guide and is meant to be highly responsive to patients' needs and preferences regarding the content of their generativity document. This means that some questions may be salient, while others will not be and thus are not included within the interview. The patient may also have other issues they wish to address or include in the service of fulfilling their generativity needs. At all times, the general principle of flexibility and responsiveness to patient needs should guide clinicians undertaking this therapeutic approach.

Box 5.1   Dignity Therapy question protocol

- "Tell me a little about your life history, particularly the parts that you either remember most, or think are the most important. When did you feel most alive?"
- "Are there specific things that you would want your family to know about you, and are there particular things you would want them to remember?"
- "What are the most important roles you have played in life (family roles, vocational roles, community service roles, etc.)? Why were they so important to you, and what do you think you accomplished in those roles?"
- "What are your most important accomplishments, and what do you feel most proud of?"
- "Are there particular things that you feel still need to be said to your loved ones, or things that you would want to take the time to say once again?"

- "What are your hopes and dreams for your loved ones?"
- "What have you learned about life that you would want to pass along to others? What advice or words of guidance would you wish to pass along to your (son, daughter, husband, wife, parents, others)?"
- "Are there words or perhaps even instructions you would like to offer your family to help prepare them for the future?"
- "In creating this permanent record, are there other things that you would like included?"

In most cases, Dignity Therapy involves three or four meetings between the therapist and patient over 7–10 days. At a brief introductory meeting, the therapist meets with the patient to describe the process, answer any questions the patient may have, provide a copy of the question framework, and collect basic demographic information. As part of this framing interview, patients are also asked who the generativity document is intended for, and what they are hoping to achieve by undertaking Dignity Therapy. At a second meeting, the therapist uses the question framework to guide the patient in a 30–60 minute discussion about their life and the things that matter most to them. The content of this interview is meant to be highly malleable and responsive to the patient's wishes and needs. Therapists also need to be mindful of the influence some disclosures may have on the recipient(s) of a generativity document, and help patients navigate those disclosures that could be harmful. This requires exquisite communication skills (Chochinov et al., 2013) and an ethical appreciation that therapists have a duty to care, both for the patient and those individuals for whom the generativity document is intended.

The therapist audio-records the discussion and the recording is transcribed verbatim. The therapist edits the transcript to transform the conversation into a carefully constructed and highly readable generativity document. The therapist then meets with the patient a third time to review the document by way of reading it to them in its entirety. If the patient is satisfied with the document, they are then provided with the finalized document. However, the patient may ask the therapist to make revisions (e.g., to correct errors, omit passages the patient does not want included or add additional content). Once Dignity Therapy is completed, the therapist presents the document to the patient, who in turn gives it to individuals of their choosing.

The content of generativity documents varies according to what each patient regards as the most important or meaningful aspects of their life. These may include poignant expressions of love and fond wishes for family members; difficult stories of deep regrets or long-standing conflicts or estrangements; acknowledging and taking responsibility for shortcomings or even seeking forgiveness. Some patients have given permission to their spouses to remarry and to continue to seek out happiness in the years ahead.

By allowing patients to narrate their own stories, and, through a supported process of legacy making, preserve those stories in a form that will outlive them, Dignity Therapy affirms the patient's sense of meaning, purpose, and dignity. It shares some similarities with other therapies, including life review, reminiscence therapy, Logotherapy, and existential psychotherapy, but differs from these other therapies in fundamental ways. Dignity Therapy does not attempt to record a complete life history; instead, it is a recounting of thoughts, ideas, and experiences that are particularly relevant and meaningful to patients, which they wish to recount and pass on to others. Dignity Therapy is comparatively brief and was primarily designed for people who are nearing end of life. It can usually be offered in three sessions totaling a few hours over the space of 7–10 days. Perhaps its most distinct characteristic, however, is that it is based on an empirical model of dignity in the terminally ill, which informs its basic structure (underscoring the importance of generativity), content, and tone. As such, Dignity Therapy aims to reduce distress, preserve dignity, and improve quality of life, while enhancing a sense of meaning and purpose, for patients approaching the end of their lives. The protocol was first published in 2005 (Chochinov et al., 2005). *Dignity Therapy: Final Words for Final Days* was published by Oxford University Press in 2012 (Chochinov, 2012) and has subsequently been translated into Japanese, Hungarian, Italian, German, Chinese, Spanish, and Taiwanese.

Applications

Dignity Therapy was developed and first studied in terminal cancer patients in hospital and community palliative care settings (Chochinov et al., 2005, 2011), but has subsequently been applied to and studied in many other patient populations. These include people with ALS and other neurodegenerative disorders (Aoun, Chochinov, & Kristjanson, 2015; Bentley, O'Connor, Breen, & Kane, 2014), end-stage renal disease (Sardoo, Abbaszade, Rafiei, Sardoo, & Borhani, 2015), dementia (Johnston et al., 2016), frail older adults (Chochinov et al., 2012; Hall, Goddard, Opio, Speck, & Higginson, 2012), as well as adolescents (Rodriguez, 2012), people with mental illness (Avery & Baez, 2012) and substance abuse disorders (Lubarsky & Avery, 2016). An urban health authority in Canada has been offering Dignity Therapy to terminally ill patients seeking medical assistance in dying.

Dignity Therapy was first piloted in Canada, the U.S., and Australia (Chochinov et al., 2005; Chochinov et al., 2011), but is now also available in many other countries, particularly in Europe and Asia. It is typically delivered by psychosocial clinicians (e.g., psychiatrists, psychologists, social workers, spiritual counselors), but also by physicians and nurses. In most cases it appears that Dignity Therapy has been delivered according to the standard protocol (Chochinov,

2012), but there have been some interesting adaptations. These include delivery via telemedicine (Passik et al., 2004) and the web (Bernat et al., 2015). Some studies, including one of our own, have included family members as proxies on behalf of patients with cognitive impairments (Chochinov et al., 2012). Some therapists have included photographs, recipes, and lists of favorite songs or poems within the patients' generativity documents (Johns, 2013).

Training workshops attracting attendees from around the world have been offered annually in Winnipeg, Canada since 2010. These two-and-one-half-day workshops are a mix of lectures, panel discussions, demonstrations, and small-group experiential learning exercises. These small group exercises give participants an opportunity to conduct a portion of a Dignity Therapy interview with a simulated patient, and edit an excerpt of an interview transcript, all under the supervision of a team of experienced therapists. Training sessions have also been provided in the United States, Denmark, United Kingdom, Portugal, Spain, Italy, China, Japan, Singapore, and Australia.

Evidence

Over 100 peer-reviewed papers have been published on Dignity Therapy, including at least 30 that report the results of primary data analyses. Findings from six randomized controlled trials (RCT) have been published and at least three additional RCTs are in progress. Dignity Therapy has also been the subject of two systematic reviews (Fitchett, Emanuel, Handzo, Boyken, & Wilkie, 2015; Martinez et al., 2016).

Dignity Therapy performed well in its first single group feasibility study conducted in Canada and Australia from 2001 to 2003. In a sample of 100 terminally ill patients receiving palliative care, there were significant improvements in suffering and depressive symptoms after patients received Dignity Therapy. Most patients (76%) also reported heightened sense of dignity and increased sense of purpose (68%), and almost half (47%) reported increased will to live. Patients who reported higher levels of baseline distress were more likely to benefit from Dignity Therapy. Overall, almost all patients (91%) were satisfied or highly satisfied with the intervention; patients who reported higher levels of baseline distress reported the greatest satisfaction (Chochinov et al., 2005). A sample of patients' family members ($n = 60$) interviewed 9–12 months after the patients' deaths felt Dignity Therapy had helped the patients (95%), increased patients' sense of dignity (78%) and purpose (72%), and helped patients prepare for death (65%). Most family members also reported the generativity document was helpful during their time of grief (78%) and would continue to be a source of future comfort (77%) (McClement et al., 2007).

The first randomized controlled trial was conducted in Canada, Australia, and the U.S. from 2005 to 2008 (Chochinov et al., 2011). In this three-arm study, 411 terminally ill palliative care patients were randomized to Dignity Therapy, standard palliative care, or client-centered care (a therapy focused on *here and now* issues rather than generativity, meaning, and purpose). Outcome measure data were collected at baseline and immediately after completion of Dignity Therapy (7–10 days after baseline for the standard palliative care and client-centered care groups). For the 326 patients who completed the study, patients in the Dignity Therapy group were significantly more likely than people in the other arms to report that the treatment improved their quality of life, sense of dignity, and spiritual well-being. Dignity Therapy patients also reported greater reductions in sadness and depression than the standard palliative care group and were significantly more likely to report that the treatment changed how their families saw and appreciated them, and that the therapy would be of help to their families.

In a U.K. trial conducted from 2008 to 2009, 60 older residents of care homes who were not necessarily facing life-limiting illness were randomized to receive Dignity Therapy or standard psychological care (Hall et al., 2012). Forty-nine residents remained at one-week follow-up, and 36 at eight weeks. Dignity Therapy patients were more likely to report that the study made their lives more meaningful and helped, or would help, their families. The same U.K. researchers conducted a trial of patients with advanced cancer from 2009–2010. Forty-five patients were randomized to Dignity Therapy plus standard palliative care, or standard palliative care only, with 27 remaining at one-week follow-up and 20 at four weeks. Dignity Therapy patients were significantly more likely to report that the study had made them more hopeful (Hall et al., 2011).

None of the first three RCT's found significant differences between Dignity Therapy and the trials' other arms on primary outcomes (i.e., various measures of psychosocial distress, including anxiety and depression). There were, however, low levels of baseline distress in the patient samples of all three trials (e.g. initial Hospital Anxiety and Depression Scale [HADS] scores of < 12) and, as a result, limited potential for reductions on these measures. Additionally, the two U.K. trials began with small samples ($n = 60; 45$) and experienced substantial loss to follow-up (40% and 56%, respectively, of the original samples), which limited their power to detect statistically significant differences between the study arms.

Given the low levels of baseline psychosocial distress in the previous trials, and the attendant challenges in demonstrating post-intervention improvements, a 2010–2013 Portuguese trial was noteworthy for recruiting a sample of patients with high levels of baseline distress (HADS > 22). The trial enrolled 80 terminally ill cancer patients randomized to Dignity Therapy or standard palliative care. Sixty-eight remained at four days post-intervention, 50 at 15 days, and 36 at 30 days. Despite the ensuing reduction in statistical power, the study found that the Dignity Therapy group demonstrated statistically significant reductions in the primary outcome measures (depression and anxiety), while the standard palliative care group exhibited *increased* distress (Juliao, Oliveira, Nunes, Carneiro, & Barbosa, 2014). The Dignity Therapy group also had significantly greater improvements on secondary outcome measures of demoralization, desire for death, and dignity (Julião, Oliveira, Nunes, Carneiro, & Barbosa, 2017). This trial was also the first to find that Dignity Therapy patients had a statistically significant survival advantage over patients receiving standard palliative care (Juliao, Nunes, & Barbosa, 2015).

In a Spanish trial conducted in 2013, 75 palliative care patients from a hospital's home care unit were assigned to Dignity Therapy or a counseling therapy (Rudilla, Galiana, Oliver, & Barreto, 2016). The sample declined to 70 at the unidentified post-intervention follow-up data collection point. Many of this study's findings and conclusions are puzzling. Between baseline and post-intervention measurements, dignity improved in both groups but anxiety and depression *increased*. Nevertheless, the authors concluded that both Dignity Therapy and counseling are effective in improving the psychosocial well-being of palliative home care patients, but their conclusion favored counseling over Dignity Therapy, including that counseling achieved "particularly good results" for depression, resilience, and anxiety (p. 326). However, in the analyses comparing the two interventions, the small differences between the two groups on depression and resilience were non-significant ($p = 0.543$ for depression, $p = 0.476$ for resilience), suggesting that the two arms may have performed equally well in terms of these patient outcomes.

The most recent systematic review of Dignity Therapy ranked this study as the methodologically weakest RCT conducted to date (Martinez et al., 2016). Randomization was less rigorous than for other trials. The authors provide little information about the protocols used to deliver the two interventions, and the description of the intervention used in the counseling arm is particularly vague. Additionally, a single psychologist delivered both interventions, which could have introduced an intervention bias if the psychologist had a preference for one intervention over the other (Juliao, 2016). Additionally, the psychologist's delivery of Dignity Therapy seems to have been based on the brief protocol description in the original feasibility study (Chochinov et al., 2005), rather than from attending a Dignity Therapy training workshop or using the detailed protocol described in *Dignity Therapy: Final Words for Final Days* (Chochinov, 2012). The article also does not mention any measures that were undertaken to ensure protocol fidelity.

A three-arm Australian trial conducted from 2012–2015 randomized 70 patients with advanced terminal cancer ($n = 56$ at follow-up) to Dignity Therapy, Life Review (a psychotherapy similar to Dignity Therapy but without generating a legacy document), or a waitlist control group (Vuksanovic, Green, Dyck, & Morrissey, 2017). The Dignity Therapy group demonstrated significantly greater increases in generativity and ego-integrity scores than the Life Review and control groups. There were no significant differences between the three groups on the study's primary outcome measures (dignity-related distress and physical, social, emotional, and functional well-being), but baseline distress was relatively low, and the small sample had inadequate power to detect differences between three arms.

Evidence discussion

While most trials have found overwhelmingly positive self-reported patient satisfaction, significant primary outcomes have been reported in only one RCT that had higher baseline rates of distress (Juliao et al., 2014). All of these Dignity Therapy trials, like many RCTs of other psychosocial interventions, faced a host of practical and methodological challenges (Nekolaichuk, 2011). Trials require large samples to be able to detect small to moderate changes in outcome measures, and large trials are costly. Because many palliative care patients are in precarious health, it is also difficult to recruit and retain large patient samples (Bakitas, Lyons, Dixon, & Ahles, 2006). We assessed 1513 patients for eligibility to yield 441 at randomization; after withdrawals and deaths, 326 completed the study. Additionally, we have found that general samples of palliative care patients in most countries where Dignity Therapy has been studied have relatively low levels of baseline psychosocial distress. This creates a floor effect, making it difficult to detect small reductions in measures that are already scored relatively low.

There is also the issue of protocol fidelity to consider. Some authors acknowledge attending a Dignity Therapy intensive training workshop (Hall et al., 2011, 2012; Juliao et al., 2014; Vuksanovic et al., 2017), and/or have sought our supervision of their initial efforts to practice Dignity Therapy. Others (Akechi et al., 2012; Rudilla et al., 2016), however, appear to have provided Dignity Therapy guided only by their reading of the brief description of the protocol in our first publication on the intervention (Chochinov et al., 2005). One would expect that the more rigor therapists have put into training, the greater likelihood of positive outcomes and mitigation of potential harms.

Finally, identifying and measuring the most appropriate outcomes of Dignity Therapy has been challenging. It is difficult to measure quantitatively the many poignant and clinically relevant qualitative outcomes of Dignity Therapy. For example, some Dignity Therapy participants have said this process helped them achieve a sense of peace while nearing death; others have given their spouses permission to find new life partners after they die.

> I don't want him to be alone because he doesn't deserve that. He needs to enjoy his life. He loves to be with people and do things. He likes to have a partner with him and I wish that for him. . . . I want him to meet the right person that he can enjoy. I know he will never forget me.
>
> (Joan)

One patient sought her daughter's forgiveness for not having revealed the identity of her father, until it was well too late. Another daughter told us that the only time her father ever indicated that he loved her and was proud of her was in his Dignity Therapy document. (Chochinov, 2012, p. 183)

There are currently three ongoing RCTs testing the efficacy of Dignity Therapy. The largest is a five-year U.S. trial led by Diana Wilkie (University of Florida) that is studying the outcomes of Dignity Therapy when provided by nurses compared to chaplains. In this three-arm trial, 560 older cancer patients at six sites will be randomized to nurse-led Dignity Therapy plus usual care, chaplain-led Dignity Therapy plus usual care, or usual care. The participation of chaplains is being framed in terms of Dignity Therapy being conceived of as a spiritual intervention. This study began in 2016 and is expected to be complete by 2021. All therapists will be provided Dignity Therapy training, and ongoing monitoring and supervision of their engagement with patients in applying this novel legacy generating approach. The latter will assure protocol adherence and concurrent treatment fidelity.

A Swiss trial led by Josef Jenewein (University of Zurich) is testing whether the inclusion of a patient's partner or other family member in Dignity Therapy helps to mitigate anxiety and depression in patients and/or their partners or family members. A total of 160 patients with advanced cancer were randomized to Dignity Therapy with partner/family member, patient-only Dignity Therapy, or standard palliative care. The primary outcome measure is psychological distress as measured by the HADS. The expected completion date of this study is April 2018.

A third current trial led by Lori Montross-Thomas (University of California – San Diego) (Montross-Thomas et al., 2015) is studying Dignity Therapy's ability to increase positive outcomes rather than decrease negative outcomes (e.g., depression, anxiety, desire for death), which have been the dominant outcome measures in previous trials. Ninety U.S. cancer patients receiving hospice or palliative care were randomized to Dignity Therapy or supportive attention (a counseling approach focused on attention, compassionate presence, and here-and-now concerns). The primary outcome measures are positive affect and contentment, and secondary measures are hope, life satisfaction, gratitude, and resilience. This study is expected to be complete by 2018.

Practice implications

Most studies of Dignity Therapy have found high patient acceptability and satisfaction. From a resources perspective, it requires time for the therapist to meet with the patient, funds to have the audio recording of the interview transcribed, and time for the therapist to edit the transcript to craft a lucid generativity document. In our experience, the total cost of providing Dignity Therapy to a patient is typically about 500 to 600 Canadian dollars, some of which may be covered in jurisdictions with universal healthcare. Some practitioners have reduced costs by up to 200 Canadian dollars per patient by using volunteer transcriptionists or the medical transcription services available through their healthcare facility). Considering its influence on patient and family experience, along with the potential for multigenerational impact, this would seem highly cost effective.

Cultural and diversity issues

Dignity Therapy was primarily developed in Canada and the U.S. The protocol was first described in an article published in English in 2005 (Chochinov et al., 2005). Most studies have been conducted in Canada, the U.S., Australia, and the UK. None of those reported any cultural incompatibilities, although its original title (Dignity Psychotherapy) was shortened when the leader of the Australian portion of our RCT (Chochinov et al., 2011) indicated that "psychotherapy" would dissuade many Australian men from considering the intervention. Gender distribution of participants to date is about equal, with 51% women in Chochinov and colleagues' RCT (Chochinov et al., 2011). In the experience of these authors, the age of the Dignity Therapy participant has not influenced ability to engage in the process; rather, "existential readiness" appears to be the basic element essential for full participation.

Studies conducted in Portugal (Juliao et al., 2014, 2015, 2017) and Spain (Rudilla et al., 2016) did not report any cultural incompatibilities. Studies conducted in Denmark, Taiwan, and Japan, however, have suggested that some components of the protocol may need to be adjusted to be culturally sensitive. A Danish study found that healthcare providers (HCPs) ($n = 10$) who had no previous exposure to Dignity Therapy identified six concerns about a Danish translation of the question protocol they felt might require modification for the Danish culture. For example, questions they felt alluded to the patient's impending death were deemed "too existentially confronting," and that Danish patients would be culturally averse to speaking about pride and achievement. Because these HCPs had not used or ever been exposed to Dignity Therapy before being interviewed for the study, the researchers asked 20 Danish patients who had participated in Dignity Therapy to verify the HCPs' concerns. The patients had far fewer concerns about the questions than the HCPs, but notable exceptions concerned inquiry regarding pride/accomplishments and providing guidance for the future, for fear of being intrusive or proscriptive, which were identified both by the patients and HCPs. The authors concluded that Dignity Therapy, with minor adaptations to the question protocol, was suitable for Danish patients (Houmann, Rydahl-Hansen, Chochinov, Kristjanson, & Groenvold, 2010), and subsequently conducted a single arm trial with generally positive results (Houmann, Chochinov, Kristjanson, Petersen, & Groenvold, 2014).

To assess the appropriateness of Dignity Therapy in Taiwan, a preliminary study explored how nine terminally ill patients and ten HCPs conceptualized dignity (Li, Richardson, Speck, & Armes, 2014). In general, the study's findings supported the Dignity Model's themes of Illness-Related Concerns and the Social Dignity Inventory, but there were several notable divergences concerning the Dignity Conserving Repertoire. In particular, the authors found no evidence that maintenance of pride and generativity/legacy are important in the Taiwanese context. They also found that living a moral life and acquiescing to God – elements not included in the model – were identified by Taiwanese patients as factors in the preservation or destruction of their dignity. The authors conclude that Dignity Therapy could potentially improve the dignity of palliative care patients in Taiwan if the protocol was modified appropriately.

A Japanese feasibility study reported problems recruiting patients in one part of the two-part study (Akechi et al., 2012). In the initial phase of this study, cancer patients were consecutively recruited in a hospice/palliative care setting. Recruitment was discontinued after 19 (86%) of 22 eligible patients refused to participate. The second part of the study was conducted in a regional cancer center and/or general hospital. Patients were recruited by trained psychiatrists who sampled a subset ($n = 8$) of patients who were expected to benefit from Dignity Therapy. There were no recruiting problems reported in this part of the study.

The authors speculated that the high rate of refusal in the first part of the study may have been due to incompatibilities between the Dignity Therapy protocol and Japanese culture, particularly that denial of death may be greater in Japan than in Western countries. With no enrollment problems in the second part of the study, this inference raises several questions. The authors do not describe how they introduced Dignity Therapy to potential participants. They do, however, indicate that their study procedure was based on our first (2005) publication on Dignity Therapy, which devoted a single page to the Dignity Therapy protocol, and did not describe how to introduce the intervention to patients. (A detailed description of how to navigate this existentially nuanced moment was subsequently incorporated in our training workshops and the book, *Dignity Therapy: Final Words for Final Days*). This leads us to wonder if the persons who introduced Dignity Therapy to potential participants in the first part of the study may have given inordinate emphasis to patients' impending deaths, rather than emphasizing the affirmation of life and legacy that is at the core of Dignity Therapy. Words like *death*, *dying*, and *terminal* should be used only if the therapist believes they resonate with the patient's level of insight and awareness of having a life limiting condition. Additionally, as was done in the second part of the Japanese study, Dignity Therapy should be offered only to people who have come to a time in their lives when they feel they might benefit from a reflective conversation about who they are and what is important to them. This suggests that the successful clinical application of Dignity Therapy must take into account what is felt to be in the best interest of patients; and using language that is sensitive and mindful of where patients are in terms of their own end-of-life illness experience.

Conclusion

Dignity Therapy's ability to mitigate various forms of end-of-life distress has been empirically established in studies of patients with high baseline distress

(Juliao et al., 2015, 2014, 2017). Most other studies of patients with lower levels of baseline distress have found overwhelmingly positive patient satisfaction, as well as family member satisfaction, when assessed. Despite barriers to recruiting and retaining large samples of palliative care patients, and difficulties measuring small-to-moderate improvements in patients with low baseline distress, we believe that Dignity Therapy has much to offer to patients nearing death as an evidence-based non-pharmacologic intervention for psychosocial end-of-life distress.

The following case example typifies many of the issues and themes that arise in the course of providing Dignity Therapy. Joan was interviewed during a Dignity Therapy training workshop. She clearly explains her motivations for selecting Dignity Therapy, which also included an element of altruism, knowing that attendees would benefit from witnessing her therapeutic encounter with Dr. Chochinov.

Case example

At the time of her Dignity Therapy interview, Joan was a 52-year-old Caucasian woman, who described herself as a wife, mother, and grandmother living with metastatic breast cancer. She first heard about Dignity Therapy while attending a group for women with advanced breast cancer. She knew immediately that Dignity Therapy was something she "felt ready to do, that no one knows when their last day will be." Prior to starting her interview she said that "Dignity Therapy will give me 'peace of mind." She also stated "this is something quite incredible. I am going to get a chance to put something down on paper for my family, my legacy of how important they were to me and how I hope I left them some good behaviors. That is not the right word to use but you know what I mean." "I need to say things to my children, to my grandchildren (they wouldn't remember right now) and to the rest of my family. You don't say it in their presence." She had tried on many occasions to write down her thoughts, but quickly found herself overwhelmed and unable to do so. As such, she saw Dignity Therapy as her chance to create something she was incapable of making on her own.

Over the course of her therapy, she conveyed various messages to specific people in her life. For instance, she told her mother that she had instilled "tremendous heart and warmth. Our family would not be what it is; she is the heart of our family; she is what keeps us all together and has shown us how we all want to be together." She told her husband that, "he needs to know that he has been so incredibly wonderful. He is such a patient, funny, generous person . . . he would give you anything that you need. His time, his thoughts, he would give you anything. He would give up anything for anyone of us . . . not just me – my brother, my sisters, my mother."

She told her son and daughter to not "live their lives in fear. I want them to make sure that they are always healthy. Try to look after themselves that way. I don't want them to live their lives in sorrow either. I don't think they will. I think they are strong enough that they know we have all had these unpredictable things in our lives and we need to carry on. And we have to do it as the good person that we are today. And they will never stop being as loving and caring as they are. I just know that. They couldn't stop that if they tried. I want them to carry that through and make sure they do. Always stay connected with family."

At the conclusion of the therapy, Joan said, "these are the things you need to address when you know you are going to die." As difficult as the discussion sometimes was, she reiterated that "these are things I desperately wanted to say, I want to leave for my family . . . how wonderful they are." She concluded by saying, "because of this, I'll have said my goodbyes, I'll have said things I need to say, and I'll have told my family to have strength."

Questions

1   How do you think the process of undergoing Dignity Therapy allowed Joan to articulate thoughts and messages for her loved ones she had been unable to articulate on her own?

2   Earlier in the chapter, an excerpt from Joan's Dignity Therapy interview transcript was quoted as an example of a person who gave their spouse/partner permission to seek a new partner in the future. Imagining that you are the partner of a person with a terminal illness, how do you think you would feel receiving this information?

3   The content of Dignity Therapy interviews varies according to each participant's character, experiences, and preferences. Do you think any of Joan's responses are specific to her demographic characteristics (e.g., woman, middle-aged, Caucasian, Canadian). Do any of her responses seem foreign to your own demographic or cultural contexts?

References

Akechi, T., Akazawa, T., Komori, Y., Morita, T., Otani, H., Shinjo, T., . . . Kobayashi, M. (2012). Dignity therapy: Preliminary cross-cultural findings regarding implementation among Japanese advanced cancer patients. *Palliative Medicine, 26*(5), 768–769. Retrieved from https://doi.org/10.1177/0269216312437214

Aoun, S. M., Chochinov, H. M., & Kristjanson, L. J. (2015). Dignity therapy for people with motor neuron disease and their family caregivers: A feasibility study. *Journal of Palliative Medicine, 18*(1), 31–37. Retrieved from https://doi.org/10.1089/jpm.2014.0213

Avery, J. D., & Baez, M. A. (2012). Dignity therapy for major depressive disorder: A case report. *Journal of Palliative Medicine, 15*(5), 509. Retrieved from https://doi.org/10.1089/jpm.2011.0522

Bakitas, M. A., Lyons, K. D., Dixon, J., & Ahles, T. A. (2006). Palliative care program effectiveness research: Developing rigor in sampling design, conduct, and reporting. *Journal of Pain and Symptom Management, 31*(3), 270–284. Retrieved from https://doi.org/10.1016/j.jpainsymman.2005.07.011

Bentley, B., O'Connor, M., Breen, L. J., & Kane, R. (2014). Feasibility, acceptability and potential effectiveness of dignity therapy for family carers of people with motor neurone disease. *BMC Palliative Care, 13*(1), 12–684X-13-12. Retrieved from https://doi.org/10.1186/1472-684X-13-12

Bernat, J. K., Helft, P. R., Wilhelm, L. R., Hook, N. E., Brown, L. F., Althouse, S. K., & Johns, S. A. (2015). Piloting an abbreviated dignity therapy intervention using a legacy-building web portal for adults with terminal cancer: A feasibility and acceptability study. *Psycho-Oncology, 24*(12), 1823–1825. Retrieved from https://doi.org/10.1002/pon.3790

Breitbart, W., Rosenfeld, B., Gibson, C., Pessin, H., Poppito, S., Nelson, C., . . . Olden, M. (2010). Meaning-centered group psychotherapy for patients with advanced cancer: A pilot randomized controlled trial. *Psycho-Oncology, 19*(1), 21. Retrieved from https://doi.org/10.1002/pon.1556

Chochinov, H. M. (2002). Dignity-conserving care – a new model for palliative care: Helping the patient feel valued. *JAMA, 287*(17), 2253–2260.

Chochinov, H. M. (2012). *Dignity Therapy: Final Words for Final Days.* New York, NY: Oxford University Press.

Chochinov, H. M., Cann, B., Cullihall, K., Kristjanson, L., Harlos, M., McClement, S. E., . . . Hassard, T. (2012). Dignity therapy: A feasibility study of elders in long-term care. *Palliative & Supportive Care, 10*(1), 3–15. Retrieved from https://doi.org/10.1017/S1478951511000538; 10.1017/S1478951511000538

Chochinov, H. M., Hack, T., Hassard, T., Kristjanson, L. J., McClement, S., & Harlos, M. (2002). Dignity in the terminally ill: A cross-sectional, cohort study. *Lancet (London, England), 360*(9350), 2026–2030. Retrieved from https://doi.org/10.1016/S0140-6736(02)12022-8

Chochinov, H. M., Hack, T., Hassard, T., Kristjanson, L. J., McClement, S., & Harlos, M. (2005). Dignity therapy: A novel psychotherapeutic intervention for patients near the end of life. *Journal of Clinical Oncology : Official Journal of the American Society of Clinical Oncology, 23*(24), 5520–5525. Retrieved from https://doi.org/23/24/5520 [pii]; 10.1200/JCO.2005.08.391

Chochinov, H. M., Hack, T., McClement, S., Kristjanson, L., & Harlos, M. (2002). Dignity in the terminally ill: A developing empirical model. *Social Science & Medicine (1982), 54*(3), 433–443.

Chochinov, H. M., Kristjanson, L. J., Breitbart, W., McClement, S., Hack, T. F., Hassard, T., & Harlos, M. (2011). Effect of dignity therapy on distress and end-of-life experience in terminally ill patients: A randomised controlled trial. *The Lancet Oncology, 12*(8), 753–762. Retrieved from https://doi.org/10.1016/S1470-2045(11)70153-X

Chochinov, H. M., McClement, S. E., Hack, T. F., McKeen, N. A., Rach, A. M., Gagnon, P., . . . Taylor-Brown, J. (2013). Health care provider communication: An empirical model of therapeutic effectiveness. *Cancer, 119*(9), 1706–1713. Retrieved from https://doi.org/10.1002/cncr.27949

Erikson, E. H. (1950). *Childhood and Society*. New York, NY: Norton.

Fitchett, G., Emanuel, L., Handzo, G., Boyken, L., & Wilkie, D. J. (2015). Care of the human spirit and the role of dignity therapy: A systematic review of dignity therapy research. *BMC Palliative Care, 14*(8), 1–12. Retrieved from https://doi.org/10.1186/s12904-015-0007-1; 10.1186/s12904-015-0007-1

Ganzini, L., Dobscha, S., Heintz, R., & Press, N. (2003). Oregon physicians' perceptions of patients who request assisted suicide and their families. *Journal of Palliative Medicine, 6*(3), 381–390. Retrieved from https://doi.org/10.1089/109662103322144691

Ganzini, L., Nelson, H. D., Schmidt, T. A., Kraemer, D. F., Delorit, M. A., & Lee, M. A. (2000). Physicians' experiences with the Oregon death with dignity act. *The New England Journal of Medicine, 342*(8), 557–563. Retrieved from https://doi.org/10.1056/NEJM200002243420806

Hall, S., Goddard, C., Opio, D., Speck, P., & Higginson, I. J. (2012). Feasibility, acceptability and potential effectiveness of dignity therapy for older people in care homes: A phase II randomized controlled trial of a brief palliative care psychotherapy. *Palliative Medicine, 26*(5), 703–712. Retrieved from https://doi.org/10.1177/0269216311418145; 10.1177/0269216311418145

Hall, S., Goddard, C., Opio, D., Speck, P. W., Martin, P., & Higginson, I. J. (2011). A novel approach to enhancing hope in patients with advanced cancer: A randomised phase II trial of dignity therapy. *BMJ Supportive & Palliative Care, 1*(3), 315–321. Retrieved from https://doi.org/10.1136/bmjspcare-2011-000054 [doi]

Houmann, L. J., Rydahl-Hansen, S., Chochinov, H. M., Kristjanson, L. J., & Groenvold, M. (2010). Testing the feasibility of the dignity therapy interview: Adaptation for the Danish culture. *BMC Palliative Care, 9*, 1–11. Retrieved from https://doi.org/10.1186/1472-684X-9-21

Houmann, L. J., Chochinov, H. M., Kristjanson, L. J., Petersen, M. A., & Groenvold, M. (2014). A prospective evaluation of dignity therapy in advanced cancer patients admitted to palliative care. *Palliative Medicine, 28*(5), 448–458. Retrieved from https://doi.org/10.1177/0269216313514883 [doi]

Jaiswal, R., Alici, Y., & Breitbart, W. (2014). A comprehensive review of palliative care in patients with cancer. *International Review of Psychiatry (Abingdon, England), 26*(1), 87–101. Retrieved from https://doi.org/10.3109/09540261.2013.868788

Johns, S. A. (2013). Translating dignity therapy into practice: Effects and lessons learned. *Omega, 67*(1–2), 135–145.

Johnston, B., Lawton, S., McCaw, C., Law, E., Murray, J., Gibb, J., . . . Rodriguez, C. (2016). Living well with dementia: Enhancing dignity and quality of life, using a novel intervention, dignity therapy. *International Journal of Older People Nursing, 11*(2), 107–120. Retrieved from https://doi.org/10.1111/opn.12103

Juliao, M. (2016). Counseling versus dignity therapy: Comments on previously published research. *Palliative & Supportive Care, 14*(5), 455. Retrieved from https://doi.org/S1478951516000201

Juliao, M., Nunes, B., & Barbosa, A. (2015). Dignity therapy and its effect on the survival of terminally ill Portuguese patients. *Psychotherapy and Psychosomatics, 84*(1), 57–58. Retrieved from https://doi.org/10.1159/000366207

Juliao, M., Oliveira, F., Nunes, B., Carneiro, A. V., & Barbosa, A. (2014). Efficacy of dignity therapy on depression and anxiety in Portuguese terminally ill patients: A phase II randomized controlled trial. *Journal of Palliative Medicine, 17*(6), 688–695. Retrieved from https://doi.org/10.1089/jpm.2013.0567

Juliao, M., Oliveira, F., Nunes, B., Carneiro, A. V., & Barbosa, A. (2017). Effect of dignity therapy on end-of-life psychological distress in terminally ill Portuguese patients: A randomized controlled trial. *Palliative & Supportive Care*, 1–10. Retrieved from https://doi.org/10.1017/S1478951516001140

Li, H. C., Richardson, A., Speck, P., & Armes, J. (2014). Conceptualizations of dignity at the end of life: Exploring theoretical and cultural congruence with dignity therapy. *Journal of Advanced Nursing, 70*(12), 2920–2931. Retrieved from https://doi.org/10.1111/jan.12455; 10.1111/jan.12455

Lo, C., Hales, S., Chiu, A., Panday, T., Malfitano, C., Jung, J., . . . Rodin, G. (2016). Managing cancer and living meaningfully (CALM): Randomised feasibility trial in patients with advanced cancer. *BMJ Supportive & Palliative Care*. Retrieved from https://doi.org/10.1136/bmjspcare-2015-000866

Lubarsky, K. E., & Avery, J. D. (2016). Dignity therapy for alcohol use disorder. *The American Journal of Psychiatry, 173*(1), 90. Retrieved from https://doi.org/10.1176/appi.ajp.2015.15070851 [doi]

Martinez, M., Arantzamendi, M., Belar, A., Carrasco, J. M., Carvajal, A., Rullan, M., & Centeno, C. (2016). "Dignity therapy", a promising intervention in palliative care: A comprehensive systematic literature review. *Palliative Medicine*. Retrieved from https://doi.org/0269216316665562 [pii]

McClement, S., Chochinov, H. M., Hack, T., Hassard, T., Kristjanson, L. J., & Harlos, M. (2007). Dignity therapy: Family member perspectives. *Journal of Palliative Medicine, 10*(5), 1076–1082. Retrieved from https://doi.org/10.1089/jpm.2007.0002

Montross-Thomas, L. P., Irwin, S. A., Meier, E. A., Gallegos, J. V., Golshan, S., Roeland, E., . . . Rodseth, L. (2015). Enhancing legacy in palliative care: Study protocol for a randomized controlled trial of dignity therapy focused on positive outcomes. *BMC Palliative Care, 14*, 44. doi:10.1186/s12904-015-0041-z. Retrieved from https://doi.org/10.1186/s12904-015-0041-z [doi]

Nekolaichuk, C. L. (2011). Dignity therapy for patients who are terminally ill. *The Lancet Oncology, 12*(8), 712–713. Retrieved from https://doi.org/10.1016/S1470-2045(11)70185-1 [doi]

Passik, S. D., Kirsh, K. L., Leibee, S., Kaplan, L. S., Love, C., Napier, E., . . . Sprang, R. (2004). A feasibility study of dignity psychotherapy delivered via telemedicine. *Palliative & Supportive Care, 2*(2), 149–155.

Quill, T. E. (1994). Physician-assisted death: Progress or peril? *Suicide & Life-Threatening Behavior, 24*(4), 315–325.

Rodriguez, A. (2012). Assessing the Benefit of Dignity Therapy for Adolescents with Advanced Cancer: A Prospective Explorative Mixed-method Study. Presented at the 7th World Research Congress of the European Association for Palliative Care, Trondheim, Norway. Retrieved from https://core.ac.uk/display/20495431

Rudilla, D., Galiana, L., Oliver, A., & Barreto, P. (2016). Comparing counseling and dignity therapies in home care patients: A pilot study. *Palliative & Supportive Care, 14*(4), 321–329. Retrieved from https://doi.org/10.1017/S1478951515001182 [doi]

Sardoo, A. M., Abbaszade, A., Rafiei, H., Sardoo, H. M., & Borhani, F. (2015). Effect of dignity therapy model on stress, anxiety and depression of hemodialysis patients. *International Journal of Healthcare, 1*(1), 28–31.

Sullivan, A. D., Hedberg, K., & Fleming, D. W. (2000). Legalized physician-assisted suicide in Oregon – the second year. *The New England Journal of Medicine, 342*(8), 598–604. Retrieved from https://doi.org/10.1056/NEJM200002243420822

Van Der Maas, P. J., Van Delden, J. J., Pijnenborg, L., & Looman, C. W. (1991). Euthanasia and other medical decisions concerning the end of life. *Lancet (London, England), 338*(8768), 669–674.

Vuksanovic, D., Green, H. J., Dyck, M., & Morrissey, S. A. (2017). Dignity therapy and life review for palliative care patients: A randomized controlled trial. *Journal of Pain and Symptom Management, 53*(2), 162–170.e1. Retrieved from https://doi.org/10.1016/j.jpainsymman.2016.09.005

Chapter 6

Cultural diversity and intersectionality in the end-of-life experience

Keisha D. Carden, Kaleb Murry, Lee H. Matthews, and Rebecca S. Allen

Cultural diversity and intersectionality in the end-of-life experience

Palliative care is defined by the World Health Organization as meeting the physical, psychosocial, and religious/spiritual needs of patients with life-limiting, terminal, or advanced chronic or progressive illness, as well as the needs of their families and caregivers, through an interprofessional team. The primary goal is to facilitate comfort and maximize quality of life (World Health Organization, 2002). Barriers to accessing quality end-of-life care stem from the intersection of many social, cultural, and economic determinants that further compound and exacerbate the experience of coping with serious illness. The swiftly changing demographics and increasing diversity of many countries, including the United States, necessitate greater knowledge of what interventions work best for various cultural groups (Allen, Noh, Beck, & Smith, 2016; Center to Advance Palliative Care, 2008; Johnson, 2013; Kelley & Morrison, 2015). They also highlight the importance of attending to notions of intersectionality of identities and patient-centered care. Providers helping familial caregivers or care partners and patients near the end of life would benefit from practicing in a culturally competent manner that emphasizes person-centeredness and avoids making assumptions about the relationship of the care partner and patient or the end-of-life care preferences of those involved.

Although families often fulfill long-term caregiving roles, providing as much as 90% of in-home long-term care (Adelman, Tmanova, Delgado, Dion, & Lachs, 2014; Institute of Medicine, 2014; National Alliance for Caregiving and AARP, 2009), families will be challenged to meet the coming demands accompanying demographic trends in long-term care (e.g., Harper, 2014). This can be attributed to a number of variables including the rapid increase in elderly dependency ratios (EDR)[1] and decrease in the working age population. Furthermore, the decrease in mortality in conjunction with delayed life transitions (e.g., increased age at first marriage/long-term cohabitation, increased age at first childbirth) and changes in fertility and size of family unit, leave larger intergenerational gaps and fewer persons per family unit to provide traditional care. At an individual level, these trends also increase the allostatic load for current familial caregivers and care partners (Juster, McEwen, & Lupien, 2010; Seeman, Singer, Rowe, Horowitz, & McEwean, 1997), as they are more often caring for both children and parents while trying to maintain stable income.

In addition to significant and rapid changes in age demographics, the racial and ethnic makeup, as well as what qualitatively or operationally constitutes a "family" in the U.S. and globally, is evolving (e.g., Settles & Steinmetz, 2013). Definitions of family vary considerably among scientists, practitioners, and the general public. Historically in the United States, a traditional nuclear family consisted of two heterosexual cisgender[2] married adults and their biological children; however, family forms have changed considerably over the last 50 years (Kowaleski-Jones & Dunifon, 2004; Miller, 2016). As examples, heterosexual couples are increasingly choosing to forgo or postpone marriage, the U.S. recently granted marriage equality for same-sex couples, and familism and fictive kinship have become increasingly popular topics of conversation when discussing families of choice (Holtzman, 2011; Kowaleski-Jones & Dunifon, 2004; Miller, 2016). The composition, functionality, and influence of a "family" near the end of life are not uniform within or across groups. With these demographic transitions and various functions of the family, a comprehensive understanding of what facilitates quality end-of-life care is needed to prepare a workforce to match the demographic demands and bolster and support ongoing care provided *by* families and *for* families.

This chapter has five aims: 1) explore various intersections of cultural factors that influence end-of-life care access and preferences, 2) highlight how these cultural factors contribute or relate to differences and disparities in receipt and provision of end-of-life care, 3) discuss variability in the role of "family" in palliative caregiving, 4) emphasize ethical practice implications, and 5) summarize interventions currently aimed at understanding and reducing disparities in palliative caregiving across diverse groups. Finally, this chapter presents case examples as well as critical thinking questions so readers may elaborate on, consolidate, and solidify knowledge gained regarding culturally competent care in this area. Although this chapter often cites the effects of singular cultural variables, it also strives to emphasize the importance of the intersectionality and the consequences of group membership across multiple categories (e.g., age, race/ethnicity, sexual orientation, gender identity, religious beliefs, social class). Individuals often experience disparities, prejudice, and oppression relating to a constellation of these factors (e.g., Cole, 2009). Moreover, any self-identified group contains great variability within its members. Therefore, intersectionality and within-group variability underscore the necessity for further research to understand these relationships more accurately and translate them into culturally competent person-centered interventions.

Cultural diversity and stress processes

While caregiving for someone with an advanced chronic illness or near the end of life can be a positive and empowering experience (Balducci et al., 2008; Hilgeman, Allen, DeCoster, & Burgio, 2007), it is also associated with a multitude of negative psychological and physiological outcomes (Thomas, Hudson, Trauer, Remedios, & Clarke, 2014; Vitaliano, Zhang, & Scanlan, 2003). The caregiver experience has historically been conceptualized by both general and disease-specific stress process models (e.g., Folkman, 1997; Lawton, Moss, Kleban, Glicksman, & Rovine, 1991; Lazarus & Folkman, 1984; Pearlin, Mullan, Semple, & Skaff, 1990) that predict important caregiver outcomes such as depression, quality of life, and overall health and well-being. Other stress process models have incorporated additional cultural factors in the stress and coping process among caregivers often stratified by race/ethnicity or geographical region (e.g., Aranda & Knight, 1997). In other words, the caregiving stress process for one caregiver may operate and function much differently for another, and this may be moderated by a number of factors such as race/ethnicity (e.g., Crawley, 2005; Hilgeman et al., 2009) or sexual/gender minority status (e.g., Meyer, 2003).

Additionally, other cultural factors such as spirituality/religion, perceptions of death, and attitudes about the healthcare system, influence patient and family perceptions of and willingness to talk about or make medical and end-of-life decisions (Crawley, Payne, Bolden, Payne, & Washington, 2000; Dilworth-Anderson, Goodwin, & Williams, 2004; Pinquart & Sörensen, 2005). The updated common core sociocultural stress process model (Knight & Sayegh, 2009) proposes that differences among various cultural groups in caregiving share a commonality – the appraisal of burden associated with caregiving. Differences in care experiences are attributed to differences in familism, obligation, family solidarity, and support; however, much of the variability in experience may also be explained by intersections of identities. While these stress process models theoretically acknowledge the influence of cultural factors, they have not been translated into culturally sensitive interventions or wholly integrated into the research evaluating the acceptability of such interventions. Moreover, these models do not specifically address stress and coping within the context of socially disadvantaged groups and families that experience discrimination or marginalization, advanced chronic illness, and palliative or end-of-life care.

Experiences of discrimination and marginalization throughout the life course, such as overt discrimination, prejudiced policies/laws and, in many cases, rejection from family have lasting effects (Fredriksen-Goldsen & Ellis, 2007). Additionally, the stress process is intertwined with unique social and historical contexts where age intersects with sexuality, gender, and race/ethnicity. For many Western cultures, recent years have seen several political and social shifts toward acceptance of sexual and gender minorities and increased attention on racial/ethnic disparities; therefore, it is important to consider a life-course perspective to understand the effects that individual and environmental stressors have had throughout the lives of older adults. Many of these individuals developed within a historical context that had serious adverse consequences (e.g., D'Augelli & Grossman, 2001). For example, internalized stigma exists when a gay cisgender man holds negative attitudes and beliefs about his own sexual identity and the gay community, subsequently projecting those attitudes inward on the self. This internalized stigma can have negative implications for one's mental health, including self-concept, use of social support, and ability to envision a future life course (Hoy-Ellis & Fredriksen-Goldsen, 2016; Meyer, 2003). While the internalization of negative societal attitudes can be a critical stressor for many individuals of all ages, and a significant barrier to healthcare access, it likely functions differently depending on historical cohort membership. This has implications for how one navigates the healthcare system and engages in end-of-life decision-making (e.g., can contribute to poor planning and lack of knowledge regarding palliative and hospice care among LGBT older adults; Acquaviva, 2017; Choi & Meyer, 2016). For the LGBT community specifically, internalized stigma has also been associated with a greater likelihood to conceal one's sexual or gender identity or expression from healthcare professionals which can present unique challenges and barriers to effective communication (Buckey & Browning, 2013).

The minority stress model (Meyer, 1995, 2001, 2003) can be used to identify these specific external and internal risk factors that are unique to the experience of socially disadvantaged groups. For example, stigma manifests in various forms for a number of socially disadvantaged individuals and can include overt hate or aggression (e.g., assault or verbal attacks), everyday discrimination and prejudice (e.g., receiving poorer service), internalized stigma, and negative perceptions of social and healthcare-related services (e.g., Hendricks & Testa, 2012; Meyer, 2003). The minority stress model provides a theoretical foundation for how these stress processes may influence disparities in access and utilization of palliative and end-of-life healthcare services. We have used the aforementioned models to frame specific variables that intersect to influence end-of-life care.

End-of-life care preferences

Despite the rapid increase in racial/ethnic minorities in the United States, racial and ethnic disparities are consistently documented in healthcare generally, and in end-of-life care specifically (Burgio et al., 2016; Crawley, 2005; Johnson, 2013; Kim, Ford, Chiriboga, & Sorkin, 2012; National Healthcare Quality and Disparities Report, 2016; Roth, Dilworth-Anderson, Huang, Gross, & Gitlin, 2015; White, Haas, & Williams, 2012). These disparities have been linked to a number of structural barriers including a lower likelihood to possess adequate health insurance (Allen et al., 2016; National Center for Health Statistics, 2016; Reese, Melton, & Ciaravino, 2004), lower income or inadequate income (Allen et al., 2016; Berdahl, Friedman, McCormick, & Simpson, 2013; LaVeist, 2005;

Williams, 1999), place[3] (White et al., 2012), and lack of knowledge about end-of-life care and overall health literacy compounded by language barriers (Bennett, Chen, Soroui, & White, 2009; Born, Greiner, Sylvia, Butler, & Ahluwalia, 2004; Carpenter, Zoller, Balsis, Otilingam, & Gatz, 2011; Porensky, & Carpenter, 2008).

Many cultural factors influence end-of-life care preferences among minority groups including religious and spiritual beliefs, kinship ties, perceived racism, and distrust in the healthcare system (Barnato, Anthony, Skinner, Gallagher, & Fisher, 2009; Harris, Allen, Dunn, & Parmelee, 2013; Hilgeman et al., 2009; Hopp & Duffy, 2000). Generally, research suggests minority groups prefer end-of-life care that emphasizes spirituality and family consensus or familism (e.g., Born et al., 2004). For example, fatalism, or the belief in fate or a religious deity (e.g., Allah, God), often influences preferences because fate determines life or death (Allen et al., 2016; Damron-Rodriguez, Wallace, & Kingston, 1995; Institute of Medicine, 2003). As a result, religiosity/spirituality may lend itself to a less supportive opinion of life-shortening end-of-life care interventions such as physician-assisted death and life-sustaining treatment removal (Bayer, Mallinger, Krishnan, Shields, 2006). This may be because pain and suffering are often viewed as spiritual or religious commitments to be embraced and may be preferred over death among some groups (Allen et al., 2016; Hallenbeck, Goldstein, & Mebane, 1996; Harris et al., 2013). As another example, racial/ethnic minorities often negatively appraise and perceive hospice as merely a "place to die" (e.g., Noh, 2012). This perception may be related to cultural and spiritual beliefs, interacting with a lack of effective education and communication by healthcare providers and hospice admissions staff (Renzaho, Romios, Crock, & Sønderlund, 2013). Disparities in referrals to hospice care are also well-documented (e.g., Crawley, 2005; Crawley et al., 2000; Reese et al., 2004; Winston, Leshner, Kramer, & Allen, 2005). These disparities are further compounded by racial/ethnic differences in preferences that should be considered (but are often not inquired about) when offering and educating patients and their families about quality end-of-life care options. Overall, there is a paucity of research clearly outlining or describing differences and disparities in end-of-life care across diverse groups, and thus, ad hoc assumptions should be avoided pending comprehensive and reliable evidence (Pinquart & Sörensen, 2005).

Additional unique issues are evident within the LGBT community. It is important that LGBT individuals are able to utilize the legal options available to them to facilitate informed end-of-life decision-making, particularly for those with chronic health conditions in need of palliative or hospice care. Knowledge and utilization of these services in this population have been reported to be lower than the general population. However, this disparity varies significantly considering the extensive diversity and additional identity intersections within the LGBT community (Fredriksen-Goldsen, Hoy-Ellis, Goldsen, Emlet, & Hooyman, 2014, 2015; Fredriksen-Goldsen, & Muraco, 2010). For example, Hughes and Cartwright (2015) reported that transgender and lesbian individuals were most likely to report preferences for their partner to be their alternative decision-maker at the end-of-life. However, the same study also reported that transgender individuals were the least likely to have made formal advance directives. Overall, the evidence regarding end-of-life care preferences within the LGBT community is mixed, and this may be an artifact of not being offered the same services legally or at an individual level. For example, Medicaid, the largest payer of long-term care in the U.S., offers spousal impoverishment protections to prevent a healthy spouse from giving up retirement savings or their home. While married LGBT individuals now have access to these protections, unmarried but partnered LGBT couples often do not because this access varies by state. This situation poses unique and stressful challenges for family-of-choice caregivers and unmarried same-sex partners. Relatedly, most family caregiving interventions have failed to address intersectionality. For example, many interventions do not incorporate large numbers of LGBT older adults, thus severely limiting our knowledge of their unique experiences.

The role of "family" in end-of-life care

The effects of familism on end-of-life care has a great impact on family-centered decision-making (Allen & Shuster, 2002; Schmid, Allen, Haley, & DeCoster, 2009). Familism is an important, culture-dependent variable to consider in palliative decision-making that often uniquely intersects with age, race/ethnicity, sexuality, and gender. For example, while racial/ethnic minority groups' decision-making processes vary considerably, they are often more family-centered than Western, non-Hispanic White families (Allen et al., 2016). Scharlach and colleagues (2006) conducted focus groups in which participants from various groups who were providing care illustrated this concept. For example, an African American participant said, "Minority groups have more cultural emphasis on caring for their own people . . . as part of the community, part of the culture'" (p. 140). A Chinese participant said, "There is a sense of tradition to take care of your parents" (p. 140). Native American and Russian participants emphasized the importance of caring for family to serve as an example to the rising generation and to pass on their cultural traditions and values. Chinese and Vietnamese participants emphasized the role of tradition and the family unit. The function of the family unit varies, even among those who emphasize a family-centered culture of care. For example, among many minority subgroups and various countries, the family will request that a terminal illness diagnosis be disclosed to the family only, and not the patient, to avoid distress; the family is then responsible for all subsequent treatment decisions (Searight & Gafford, 2005).

Familism also influences family-centered caregiving (Allen et al., 2016; Haley et al., 2002). Expectations concerning who provides care in old age and at the end of life vary greatly. In the United States, this is more common among Asian American, Hispanic, and African American caregivers than it is among non-Hispanic White caregivers (e.g., Pinquart & Sörensen, 2005). Receiving formal care from outside of the family may be perceived negatively – as a lack of ability – and this brings feelings of embarrassment upon the family (Gelfand, Balcazar, Parzuchowski, & Lenox, 2001). Previous research comparing minority groups to non-Hispanic Whites suggests that minority caregivers are more reluctant to share information related to such personal matters as death and dying, and they prioritize privacy (Winston et al., 2005). They are also more likely to engage fictive kin and congregational support networks or "church family" (Taylor, Chatters, Woodward, & Brown, 2013). Both fictive kin and members of congregational support networks are expected to assume responsibilities as extended family members. For example, compared to non-Hispanic Whites, African Americans are more likely to be providing care for a sibling, a relative other than their spouse, or a friend, and they report a more diverse informal support network (see Dilworth-Anderson, Williams, & Gibson, 2002 for a review). This is likely due to the differences in who is considered kin. Although these family structures are often strong, willing, and present to provide end-of-life care, providers should be mindful and open to hearing individuals talk about their needs regarding support as their emphasis on family-centered care does not necessarily mean they reject or lack a desire for formal care options (Pinquart & Sörensen, 2005).

The caregiving experience and definition of family can also be very different for many LGBT individuals, compared to cisgender heterosexuals. While informal caregiving for older adults is typically done by a spouse or child, LGBT individuals are less likely to have access to these family members for support and typically have fewer options for receiving informal caregiving (Croghan, Moone, & Olson, 2014). For some LGBT individuals, issues of sexual/gender identity disclosure or acceptance may also affect the informal caregiving process. Lack of acceptance of one's sexual or gender identity from family members often precipitates estranged relationships for some individuals, thereby creating additional barriers (Muraco & Fredriksen-Goldsen, 2011). Thus, many LGBT-identified individuals have varying definitions for family, which has important implications for the type of care they receive.

As a generational cohort, many LGBT older adults have spent most of their lives concealing their sexual or gender identity from work relationships, family members, and care providers for various reasons. For example, one report estimates approximately 1/5 (21%) of LGBT older adults conceal their sexual or gender identity/expression from their primary care physician (Fredriksen-Goldsen, et al., 2011) These individuals may also have concerns about the role of biological family members in end-of-life decision-making. For these individuals approaching the end of life, "families of choice" are often relied upon to assume the responsibilities of care and support typically provided by biological family members (Barker, 2002; Muraco & Fredriksen-Goldsen, 2011). The caregiving received from families of choice can be critical for maintaining the well-being of LGBT individuals. For example, many gay and lesbian older adults reported that they would turn to their partners to help with caregiving needs, while most of those without partners said that they would rely on friends (Muraco & Fredriksen-Goldsen, 2011). However, these essential relationships often do not provide the same legal benefits of typical biological families, unless a power of attorney agreement has been executed. Moreover, individuals who utilize formal care providers and those who reside in acute/residential care settings may experience bias or discrimination at an institutional level (e.g., Di Napoli, Breland, & Allen, 2013). Interventions that utilize informal family-of-choice social support networks in addition to biological and professional caregivers may enhance the broad range of care that can be received.

Historical context, distrust, and prejudices

While it is well documented that medical decision-making can be influenced by familism and religious or spiritual factors, any individual's care preferences interact with other variables, such as verbal and nonverbal language barriers and implicit as well as explicit biases (see FitzGerald & Hurst, 2017 for a review). These biases often facilitate distrust in the healthcare system or compromise the patient-caregiver or patient-caregiver-healthcare provider relationship (Renzaho, et al., 2013). Historical and systemic medical racism (Corbie-Smith, Thomas, & George, 2002; Freimuth et al., 2001; Hoberman, 2012) and general perceived racism are contextual factors to consider, as they dictate levels of trust and many decision-making processes in healthcare among racial/ethnic minority groups (Adegbembo, Tomar, & Logan, 2006; Arnett, Thorpe, Gaskin, Bowie, & LaVeist; 2016; Eliacin et al., 2016; Paradies, Truong, & Priest, 2014). Many researchers argue that the historical impact of deeply rooted medical racism has facilitated a general distrust in mainstream healthcare and may be closely associated with disparities in African Americans' engagement in end-of-life care discussions (e.g., Bullock, 2006; Pullis, 2011) and completion rates of advance directives (Braun, Onaka, & Horiuchi, 2001; Burgio et al., 2016; Johnson, Kuchibhatla, & Tulsky, 2008).

This distrust may further influence other decisions regarding medical care. For example, Bullock (2006) conducted a study in which advance directives were promoted among African Americans using a faith-based model, and 75% of participants refused to complete one. One African American participant said, "As a black man, I am subject to receive less care and attention than a white man." Researchers have argued that racial/ethnic minority families and caregivers who support hospice and palliative care are troubled by the lack of diversity among providers and lack of staff knowledge regarding cultural diversity, competency, humility, and implicit biases (Fitzgerald & Hurst, 2017; Hasnain, Connell, Menon, & Tranmer, 2011; Jæger & Jensen, 2009; Renzaho, et al., 2013). For example, research has suggested that the implicit biases of non-Black physicians play a larger role in predicting Black patients' reactions than explicit biases, and interactions were rated as less positive for providers scoring high in implicit biases (Chapman, Kaatz, & Carnes, 2013; Green et al., 2007; Penner et al., 2010). This may be for a few reasons. Individuals are often not aware of their implicit biases, and the expression of such biases is often perceived as more subtle and insidious whereas explicit biases are more overt. Additionally, there has been a significant downward trend in explicit acts of racism, whereas there has been no such trend regarding implicit biases. This has created a divide in how individuals of different races perceive the effects of prejudice, and it further perpetuates disparities in quality healthcare provision. Implicit biases regarding other variables such as socioeconomic status, weight, age, and gender also influence the quality of healthcare (see Fitzgerald & Hurst, 2017).

Similar to racial/ethnic minorities, the effects of medical discrimination can also have an impact on the interactions between LGBT patients and healthcare professionals, playing a major role in end-of-life experiences and perpetuating social, legal, and financial barriers to advance care planning (e.g., Harding, Epiphaniou, & Chidgey-Clark, 2012). This historical pervasive discrimination further contributes to and compounds concealment behaviors previously discussed, further limiting the type of services offered and eliminating opportunities for connecting with LGBT specialized services. While concealment of one's sexual or gender identity is often used as a coping mechanism to prevent discrimination, it is not always an option, especially for some transgender individuals (Meyer, 2003). Therefore, transgender and gender-nonconforming individuals may be more susceptible to medical discrimination and are less likely to utilize health services when needed (Cook-Daniels, 2015).

While the barriers associated with marriage rights for LGBT couples have undergone dynamic changes in recent years, legal specifications regarding estate planning and other family considerations continue to be a significant challenge for many (Crozier, 2008). For example, in the United States, the Supreme Court's historic ruling in *Obergefell v. Hodges* (2015) guaranteed marriage equality nationwide, ensuring the critical federal benefits related to marriage to many LGBT older adults who could not access them before. While this was a significant advancement in eliminating barriers to healthcare and end-of-life services, some challenges may continue to affect married and unmarried LGBT individuals. For example, not all LGBT couples choose to marry due to the presence of other formal or informal arrangements (Choi & Meyer, 2016). Furthermore, the estate planning process for unmarried LGBT families still holds significant challenges. This process can be critical for many families who reside in countries where benefits are not automatically granted to the surviving partner without advance legal planning. For individuals who require long-term palliative or hospice care, lack of advance planning for end-of-life care can result in costly tax requirements and extensive processes to securing their partner's estate (Choi & Meyer, 2016; Crozier, 2008).

The historical implications of these barriers may be evidenced in LGBT older adults' lower rates of utilization of palliative and hospice care services at the end of life, when compared with heterosexuals. Research on lesbian, gay, and bisexual older adults reflects that many of these individuals may delay utilizing healthcare services out of fear of discriminatory practices from healthcare providers (Claes & Moore, 2000; Cook-Daniels, 2015; Wallace, Cochran, Durazo, & Ford, 2011). LGBT individuals may also have perceptions that end-of-life care services and organizations do not have antidiscrimination policies and that sexual or gender identity would need to be concealed from residents and staff while living in a residential care facility. Patients might also experience discrimination from administration, staff, and other residents (e.g., Johnson, Jackson, Arnette, & Koffman, 2005). These trends have been observed globally as well (Brotman, Ryan, & Cormier, 2003; Choi & Meyer, 2016; Stein, Beckerman, & Sherman, 2010).

International perspectives

The numerous factors that may affect disparities and preferences for end-of-life care among diverse patients and their families, both within and outside of the United States, are complex and interconnected. The current literature highlights many parallels regarding healthcare disparities between the United States and the rest of the world. Historical contexts, changing demographic trends, shifts in policy and social justice efforts, language barriers, and biases all play an important role in end-of-life care worldwide. Internationally, rapid shifts in the demographics of developed countries have had several impacts on the demand for culturally competent professional caregivers. As people live longer, these populations have seen a rising proportion of older adults in need of formal or informal care (Lievesley, 2010; Pinquart & Sörensen, 2005). There is evidence that suggests that racial/ethnic and sexual minority patients and caregivers are less likely to utilize formal services, not only in the United States, but also internationally, which can have negative implications for health and quality of life (Greenwood, Habibi, Smith, & Manthorpe, 2015). However, the unique preferences and barriers to end-of-life care faced by racial/ethnic and sexual minorities in countries outside of the U.S. have not been well documented.

In a systematic review of research from the United Kingdom, several important factors were found to contribute to the prominent disparities in utilization and satisfaction with formal end-of-life care services for ethnic minority groups (Evans et al., 2012). These factors included low referral rates, language and communication barriers, and a lack of cultural competency training for healthcare professionals. For example, Karim, Bailey, and Tunna (2000) found that Black Caribbean and South Asian individuals in the UK were less likely than non-Hispanic Whites to be referred by a physician to palliative care services. Additionally, many international studies have attributed language and communication barriers to the low use and negative perceptions of palliative care services (Ahmed et al., 2004; Evans et al., 2012). Moreover, in different regions, the preference for formal or informal end-of-life care varies by racial/ethnic group and individual families.

Recent political shifts in the civil rights of the LGBT community have resulted in the formal recognition of same-sex marriages in countries such as Canada, the United States, and the United Kingdom, thus alleviating several obstacles to the accessibility of end-of-life care services for these individuals and their families. However, there are currently only 26 countries around the world that offer such recognition as of August 2017, most being located within Europe and the Americas. The number of countries with laws against sexual and gender minorities are even greater. While there is a substantial lack of research on the end-of life experiences of LGBT families who reside in countries without these rights, such as Nigeria and India, these individuals may face additional stressors and barriers to quality end-of-life care and may also be more likely to experience overt discrimination in these settings. LGBT criminalization laws may increase the likelihood for LGBT individuals to experience discrimination and limit the healthcare services available to them unless they conceal their sexual or gender identity.

Current efforts and future directions in palliative caregiving

There is a great need for interventions sensitive to the existing disparities in end-of-life care and designed to fit the needs of individuals of varying cultural backgrounds. Despite the aforementioned evidence, comparatively little is known about the efficacy of available interventions among diverse populations. For example, race/ethnicity is often included as a control variable in research on stress process models, which does not adequately or accurately explain the role or influence of race/ethnicity in the caregiving process. Among investigations and evaluations of interventions for palliative caregivers, a comprehensive analysis and understanding of potential racial/ethnic differences is difficult due to either insufficient inclusion of minority participants (e.g., Ingersoll-Dayton et al., 2013; Kunik et al., 2010) or the dichotomization of race into "White and non-White categories" (e.g., White versus Black, White versus Other) (Chan, Kasper, Black, & Rabins, 2007). For example, Allen and colleagues (2016) reviewed the existing community-based interventions aimed at reducing the burden of palliative caregiving. Ten of the 17 interventions they identified were investigated among primarily (78%–100%) non-Hispanic White participants. Five studies did not report race in the characteristics of the sample, and two studies were among primarily African American participants. Therefore, these studies yield little information about the effectiveness of these interventions among non-White individuals.

Few interventions exist that address disparities in palliative care among racially/ ethnically diverse groups, and even fewer consider sexual minorities, especially younger sexual minorities. While there has been a substantial lack of research regarding the LGBT community as a whole, research has been especially limited regarding LGBT younger adults and youths and transgender and gender noncon-forming individuals, both generally and at the end of life. Most of this research has been focused on gay and lesbian individuals, and LGBT palliative care and car-egiving literature has focused mainly on older adults at the end of life. Therefore, the amount of information on the unique experiences of bisexual, transgender, and the other numerous identities captured under the LGBT umbrella is signifi-cantly lacking. It is imperative that researchers have this information to provide LGBT individuals, both young and old, and their caregivers with the appropriate tools to enhance the quality of life at end of life. Future interventions that target this population must be developed that aim to eliminate the barriers and chal-lenges to quality care while also highlighting the diverse individual and family perspectives that may influence preferences for end-of-life care.

The few intervention studies that exist to address these shortcomings regard-ing intersectionality and cultural diversity (see Table 6.1) emphasize cultural competencies to address disparities. Primarily, they utilize culturally competent hospice educational materials (Enguidanos, Kogan, Lorenz, & Taylor, 2011), videos aimed at improving disparities in knowledge (Volandes, Ariza, Abbo, & Paasche-Orlow, 2008), employment of patient navigators (Fischer, Sauaia, & Kutner, 2007), and other peer support programs (Hanson et al., 2013). Overall, however, there is a lack of such interventions. This situation is further exacer-bated by a lack of a foundational understanding of factors contributing to the existence of such differences and disparities (Johnson, 2013). In order to begin designing and modifying current interventions to be effective among diverse groups, research is needed that 1) comprehensively evaluates and describes fac-tors contributing to differences and disparities in end-of-life and palliative care, 2) evaluates the effectiveness of current end-of-life interventions applied to diverse groups, and 3) suggests and implements appropriate and ethical modi-fications to said interventions to enhance quality end-of-life care for all. In the meantime, providers must rely on ethical standards to facilitate quality care to diverse patients and their families.

Ethical considerations and practice implications

The notion of intersectionality and cultural diversity brings about interesting ethical considerations and practice implications in end-of-life care. Although healthcare quality issues among diverse groups are garnering increasing atten-tion in the United States, this is not necessarily the case globally, and access issues that evoke the ethical principle of justice are still problematic. Sound research is needed to inform ethical healthcare and palliative care practices across diverse groups. Ethical issues and challenges vary as a function of the setting and context within which palliative care is being provided. As discussed herein, the current standards for palliative care provision are not sufficient for all diverse groups. While there is a dearth of information to inform sound ethical

Table 6.1 Research addressing disparities in end-of-life care among diverse individuals and families

Author(s) (Year)	Participant characteristics	Methods/Interventions	Design/Sample	Results	Implications
Abbott & Elliott (2016)	Thirty-nine articles reviewed	N/A	Systematic literature review	N/A	Community and home visitation interventions by nurses can provide an effective means for mitigating social determinants of health by empowering people at risk for health disparities to avoid injury, maintain health, and prevent and manage existing disease.
Darby & Ward-Smith (2016)	Twenty-four articles reviewed	Literature review and concept analysis to define attributes of communication during end-of-life for non-traditional families.	Concept analysis	Created a conceptual model for essential attributes of communication.	Understanding and clarifying the concept of communication in EOL care, specifically for individuals who are LGBT.
Durand et al. (2014)	Nineteen studies. Total N = 4,505. All participants were a part of one of the following groups: minority ethnic group, low literacy/low education group, low socioeconomic status, or medically underserved	N/A	Meta-analysis	Shared decision-making interventions increased knowledge, informed choice, participation in decision-making, decision self-efficacy, and preference for collaborative decision-making, and reduced decisional conflict among patients.	Results indicate shared decision-making interventions may be more beneficial to low literacy/socioeconomic patients than higher literacy/socioeconomic status patients.

Author (year)	Sample	Design	Analysis	Findings	Implications
Eggly et al. (2013)	(n = 19) Patients had breast cancer (n = 11), colon or rectal cancer (n = 5), or lung cancer (n = 3). All patients were African American; 15 (79 %) were female	Qualitative interview to create question prompt lists (QPLs) to improve patient-doctor communication; asked to discuss experiences and perspectives about asking questions and seeking information from oncologists during clinical interactions.	Thematic analysis (NVIVO)	Two key themes emerged from qualitative analysis: *topics* patients felt were relevant and should be asked in this context, and *barriers* to asking these questions.	Using QPLs to improve communication and treatment outcomes for patients seeking cancer care.
Gendron et al. (2013)	N = 199 staff members working with older adult populations (staff and direct-care-level): 46% Caucasian, 48% African American, 3% Asian, 1% Latino; 13% were 60+ in age. Four evaluators observed trainings at five sites	Formative Program Evaluation of a quasi-experimental nonequivalent-groups pretest posttest design. Outcomes were awareness of health-care issues that are unique to the LGBT aging population, and level of comfort caring for a member of the LGBT community.	Paired-sample t-tests, process evaluation, systematic observations, and qualitative interviews.	Increased participants' awareness of aging LGBTs' healthcare issues, and increased participants' comfort level working with an LGBT older adult.	This cultural competence training for working with LGBT aging populations can be effective in increasing staff knowledge of and awareness of aging LGBT's healthcare issues and comfort level in working with an LGBT older adult in healthcare settings.

(Continued)

Table 6.1 (Continued)

Author(s) (Year)	Participant characteristics	Methods/Interventions	Design/Sample	Results	Implications
Huang et al. (2016)	N = 30; 100% African American; mean age M = 55.43, SD = 6.71, range = 47–73	Multicomponent Advance Care Planning (ACP) intervention program that integrates motivational interviewing, evidence-based ACP facilitation program (Respecting Choices®), and health literacy adjusted advance directives (AD).	Pilot mixed method RCT. Thirty community dwelling African Americans in the Deep South were recruited from a University Medical Center and randomly assigned to receive intervention or educational materials.	ANCOVA and thematic content analysis. All participants reported high satisfaction and increased intent to complete an AD at postintervention. Significant increase in knowledge on AD at postintervention in intervention group only.	Similar programs may be an effective way to increase effective advance directives and engagement in advance care planning among racial/ethnic minorities.
Kalauokalani, et al. (2007)	N = 67; all English-speaking; 15 minorities	An education and coaching session designed to address misconceptions about pain treatment.	Secondary analysis of an RCT; English-speaking adult cancer outpatients with moderate pain over the prior two weeks were randomly assigned to an experimental or control group.	At baseline, minority patients reported more pain than non-Hispanic White counterparts. At follow-up, minorities continued to report more pain; however, disparities in the intervention group were eliminated.	Education regarding components of health may be an effective strategy to reduce disparities regarding physical conditions such as pain.

Kanekar & Petereit (2009)	American Indians/ Alaska Natives	Walking Forward is a community-based participatory research program in western South Dakota. Primary goal is to address the high cancer mortality rates among American Indians by facilitating access to innovative clinical trials, behavioral and genetic research and tailored patient navigation.	Community-based participatory research	Accrual rate of 25 percent in clinical trials. Significant reduction in the number of missed treatment days among navigated American Indian cancer patients undergoing radiation therapy. Partnerships were established with the American Indian communities.	Community-based participatory research may be an effective strategy to address barriers in underserved minority communities.
Krebs et al. (2013)	American Indians/ Alaska Natives	Collaborated with local American Indian organizations to provide cancer education through a series of 24-hour workshops.	Process analysis	N/A	Collaborating with patient navigators who are embedded within and trusted by their communities helps to bridge the gap between patients and providers, increases adherence to care recommendations, and improves quality of life and survival.

palliative care with diverse individuals, there are effective strategies to facilitate the ethical provision of care.

First, healthcare providers' assumptions of patient preferences may not always reflect reality and may operate as a function of explicit or implicit biases (Chapman et al., 2013; Fitzgerald & Hurst, 2017; Green et al., 2007; Penner et al., 2010). For example, language barriers can operate bidirectionally and lead to a lack of understanding of palliative care options and patient preferences. This can prevent these groups from having access to available resources and making informed end-of-life decisions. While cultural competency training is considered a necessary component of quality care, individual preferences should also be highlighted and considered with a focus on patient autonomy and the rights of their families. When appropriate and desired, including the patient's family in shared decision-making discussions is a valuable tool for ensuring culturally competent and ethical care practices. The importance of one's family structure has been repeatedly highlighted internationally as having a significant impact on palliative care or other end-of-life services (Brotman et al., 2003; Harding, et al., 2012).

For LGBT individuals, several social and legal impediments to nontraditional definitions of "family" affect the ethical provision of end-of-life care. In some regions, healthcare providers may attempt to change one's sexual or gender identity through institutionalization or conversion therapy, and legal protections are often absent (Amnesty International, 2001; Dworkin & Yi, 2003). Varying international attitudes towards sexual and gender minorities are an important consideration when framing the preferences and healthcare needs of these individuals and their families at the end of life. To provide quality patient-centered care, healthcare professionals should be mindful of the legal status for same-sex couples in their country and to involve the partner to the extent possible in end-of-life decision-making. Future interventions should focus on training healthcare professionals in culturally competent care so that LGBT patients and their families feel comfortable and accepted. Relevant training can allow healthcare professionals to recognize and discuss the specific needs and concerns related to the patient's sexual or gender identity, thus facilitating better communication and emphasizing an ethical patient-centered care approach (Cartwright, Hughes, & Lienert, 2012; Hughes & Cartwright, 2015).

Case examples

Vignettes are provided below to illustrate intersections of the variables discussed throughout this chapter. Each vignette is followed by a series of critical thinking questions to encourage readers to elaborate on, consolidate, and solidify knowledge gained.

Case example 1

Kiaan is a 76-year-old man suffering from advanced frontotemporal dementia, chronic obstructive pulmonary disease (COPD), congestive heart failure, as well as a fractured ankle. He has recently been placed in an inpatient hospice facility. Kiaan immigrated to the United States from Pakistan when he was in his early 20s with his wife, Lian, who passed away two years earlier. His daughter, Sara, a 31-year-old full-time graduate student and mother of two, is his primary caregiver and only living relative. Sara has noticed her father has been much more agitated than usual and has had to be sedated several times. This has been distressing for both Kiaan and Sara, so Sara started visiting her father more frequently and began to notice that each time she would arrive, her father would grab her arms and try to get out of bed to his knees. Sara knew what he needed. Although frontotemporal dementia had limited Kiaan's facial expressions and ability to speak, he always completed his prayers facing Mecca five times each day as part of his Islamic faith. Sara realized the nurses did not understand what her father was trying to do, and they had been sedating him each time he tried to get out of bed to pray.

Sara explained this to Kiaan's nurses, but they did not seem to understand why Kiaan would need to get out of bed. The nurses argued it was dangerous for Kiaan, and they said he would have to pray in bed. Sara felt discouraged and even discriminated against. She noticed how the nurses stared at her hijab with disgust and how they would barely speak to her when she had questions. In addition, her father was the only patient who did not have any roommates. All of this brought Sara a sense of shame in addition to her grief. She was unsure about how to advocate for her father in a respectful and assertive manner, and she did not feel like she could trust any of the staff enough to ask for advice or help. She knows how important it is for her father to pray each day, how much peace it brings to him, and how much it calms him. Sara is overwhelmed and distressed, and she does not know what to do.

Questions

1 How might Sara's multiple competing roles as a mother, graduate student, and primary caregiver affect the quality of care for Kiaan?
2 How might Sara effectively go about addressing this perceived discrimination in order to increase the quality of her father's care?

3   If this issue is not resolved and Kiaan continues to be sedated when he tries to engage with his faith and pray, what are the potential implications for his quality of care?

Case example 2

Joe is a 67-year-old Caucasian male currently hospitalized after being diagnosed with stage-IV lung cancer. The cancer has progressed quickly, and Joe's oncologist, Dr. Smith, reports a prognosis of about three months. Joe decides that he does not want to undergo chemotherapy due to the potentially detrimental effects on his quality of life. Dr. Smith requests that Joe discuss treatment options and other end-of-life issues with his family. However, upon further inquiry Joe reveals that he has never been married, has no children, and is currently estranged from his biological family. Joe's roommate, David, seems to be his only source of support and is listed as next of kin in his record. David visits Joe daily at the hospital and has been extremely helpful in providing details of Joe's functioning and medical history. Dr. Smith suspects that the two men are in a romantic relationship; however, despite all attempts, the two men have been reluctant to give any information about Joe's sexual identity to the medical staff.

Having spent most of his life living in a small rural community, Joe prefers to exercise caution when disclosing his sexual identity to others, particularly healthcare professionals. Joe also recalls a previous experience in which his primary care physician made several offensive comments after learning that Joe identifies as gay. Additionally, Joe and David have significant concerns over their lack of knowledge regarding appropriate end-of-life decision-making and planning, such as obtaining durable power of attorney for healthcare status and getting an estate will executed. While Joe would like to talk to Dr. Smith about navigating this process, he fears the potential discrimination that he may experience. Furthermore, Dr. Smith is uncertain how to ensure that Joe gets the information he needs to make the best decisions regarding his end-of-life care, without being offensive or making assumptions about Joe's sexual identity.

Questions

1   How might Dr. Smith go about establishing a sense of trust with Joe to ensure that he receives quality care, while also being respectful of his hesitation to discuss the topic?

2 How can healthcare professionals work to create a more inclusive and welcoming environment in which individuals like Joe feel safe to discuss details related to their sexual/gender identity with their providers?

3 While understanding how Joe's sexual identity may influence his preferences for care is important, what other cultural factors might Dr. Smith consider when approaching the discussion on Joe's end-of-life care options?

Case example 3

Dex is a 15-year-old African American transgender male (AFAB)[4] suffering from a grade IV glioblastoma (GBM) in his brain. Since his diagnosis six months ago, Dex's doctors have treated him with chemotherapy and various pharmacological interventions; however, due to the location of Dex's tumor doctors have not been able to operate, and he has not been responding well to current treatments. This has created immense stress for Dex and his parents, who have relied heavily on their faith to cope. While his parents have been a great source of social support for Dex, his church family has been coming to the hospital to pray for his salvation. They do not approve of the way he presents himself, and they often confuse his gender for his sexuality. This has created a great deal of distress for the family; Dex's parents feel they cannot fully rely on their church family for support, and the doctors feel that their church community has created so much chaos in the palliative care unit that they have suggested that Dex and his family be transferred elsewhere. Dex likes and trusts his care team, so his parents feel that staying in this unit is ideal for his care. Dex regularly asks his parents and his care team many questions about death and the afterlife, and he often asks if the things members of his church family say (e.g., he will go to hell) are true. This exacerbates the discomfort and tension among Dex's care team, as they struggle to maintain balance between Dex's well-being and the cultural preferences of his parents.

Questions

1 How can Dex's care team ensure a safe and accepting environment for him and his family while simultaneously maintaining a peaceful and professional environment that has been disturbed by their congregation?

2   Some members of Dex's care team have suggested transferring Dex because of the disruption his church family has caused, even though it is against his wishes and he has already established trust in his providers. What are relevant ethical considerations?

Notes

1 EDR: Elderly dependency ratios; the number of persons of working age [aged 15 to 64] per person aged 65.
2 Denoting an individual whose personal or gender identity corresponds with their sex assigned at birth.
3 "Place" here refers to the function of geographical clustering of the population by race/ethnicity and how this influences healthcare quality, accessibility, availability, affordability, and overall utilization.
4 AFAB indicates "Assigned Female at Birth." Synonyms include FAAB ("Female Assigned at Birth") and DFAB ("Declared Female at Birth").

References

Abbott, L. S., & Elliott, L. T. (2016). Eliminating health disparities through action on the social determinants of health: A systematic review of home visiting in the United States, 2005–2015. *Public Health Nursing, 34*(1), 2–30. doi:10.1111/j.1440-1800.2010.00500.x.

Acquaviva, K. D. (2017). *LGBTQ-Inclusive Hospice and Palliative Care: A Practical Guide to Transforming Professional Practice.* New York, NY: Columbia University Press.

Adegbembo, A. O., Tomar, S. L., & Logan, H. L. (2006). Perception of racism explains the difference between Blacks' and Whites' level of healthcare trust. *Ethnicity & Disease, 16*(4), 792–798.

Adelman, R. D., Tmanova, L. L., Delgado, D., Dion, S., & Lachs, M. S. (2014). Caregiver burden: A clinical review. *The Journal of the American Medical Association, 311*(10), 1052–1060. doi:10.1001/jama.2014.304.

Ahmed, N., Bestall, J. C., Ahmedzai, S. H., Payne, S. A., Clark, D., & Noble, B. (2004). Systematic review of the problems and issues of accessing specialist palliative care by patients, carers and health and social care professionals. *Palliative Medicine, 18*(6), 525–542. doi:10.1191/0269216304pm921oa.

Allen, R. S., Noh, H., Beck, L. N., Smith, L. J. (2016). Caring for individuals near the end of life. In L. D. Burgio, J. E. Gaugler, & M. M. Hilgeman (Eds.), *The Spectrum of Family Caregiving for Adults and Elders With Chronic Illness* (pp. 142–172). New York, NY: Oxford University Press.

Allen, R. S., & Shuster, J. L. (2002). The role of proxies in treatment decisions: Evaluating functional capacity to consent to end-of-life treatments within a family context. *Behavioral Sciences & the Law, 20*(3), 235–252. doi:10.1002/bsl.484.

Amnesty International. (2001). *Crimes of Hate, Conspiracy of Silence.* Oxford, United Kingdom: The Alden Press.

Aranda, M. P., & Knight, B. G. (1997). The influence of ethnicity and culture on the car-egiver stress and coping process: A sociocultural review and analysis. *The Gerontologist*, *37*(3), 342–354. Retrieved from https://doi.org/10.1093/geront/37.3.342.

Arnett, M. J., Thorpe, R. J., Gaskin, D. J., Bowie, J. V., & LaVeist, T. A. (2016). Race, medi-cal mistrust, and segregation in primary care as usual source of care: Findings from the exploring health disparities in integrated communities study. *Journal of Urban Health*, *93*(3), 456–467.

Balducci, C., Mnich, E., McKee, K. J., Lamura, G., Beckmann, A., Krevers, B., . . . Öberg, B. (2008). Negative impact and positive value in caregiving: Validation of the COPE index in a six-country sample of carers. *The Gerontologist*, *48*(3), 276–286. Retrieved from https://doi.org/10.1093/geront/48.3.276

Barker, J. C. (2002). Neighbors, friends, and other non-kin caregivers of community-living dependent elders. *Journal of Gerontology: Social Sciences*, *57*, 158–167. Retrieved from https://doi.org/10.1093/geronb/57.3.S158

Barnato, A. E., Anthony, D. L., Skinner, J., Gallagher, P. M., & Fisher, E. S. (2009). Racial and ethnic differences in preferences for end-of-life treatment. *Journal of General Internal Medicine*, *24*(6), 695–701. doi:10.1007/s11606-009-0952-6.

Bayer, W., Mallinger, J. B., Krishnan, A., & Shields, C. G. (2006). Attitudes toward life-sustaining interventions among ambulatory black and white patients. *Ethnicity and Disease*, *16*(4), 914–919.

Bennett, I. M., Chen, J., Soroui, J. S., & White, S. (2009). The contribution of health literacy to disparities in self-rated health status and preventive health behaviors in older adults. *The Annals of Family Medicine*, *7*(3), 204–211.

Berdahl, T. A., Friedman, B. S., McCormick, M. C., & Simpson, L. (2013). Annual report on health care for children and youth in the United States: Trends in racial/ethnic, income, and insurance disparities over time, 2002–2009. *Academic Pediatrics*, *13*(3), 191–203.

Born, W., Greiner, K. A., Sylvia, E., Butler, J., & Ahluwalia, J. S. (2004). Knowledge, attitudes, and beliefs about end-of-life care among inner-city African Americans and Latinos. *Jour-nal of Palliative Medicine*, *7*(2), 247–256. doi:10.1089/109662104773709369

Braun, K. L., Onaka, A. T., & Horiuchi, B. Y. (2001). Advance directive completion rates and end-of-life preferences in Hawaii. *Journal of the American Geriatrics Society*, *49*(12), 1708–1713. doi:10.1046/j.1532-5415.2001.49284.x.

Brotman, S., Ryan, B., & Cormier, R. (2003). The health and social service needs of gay and lesbian elders and their families in Canada. *The Gerontologist*, *43*(2), 192–202. doi:10.1093/geront/43.2.192

Buckey, J. W., & Browning, C. N. (2013). Factors affecting the LGBT population when choosing a surrogate decision maker. *Journal of Social Service Research*, *39*(2), 233–252. Retrieved from http://dx.doi.org/10.1080/01488376.2012.754205

Bullock, K. (2006). Promoting advance directives among African Americans: A faith-based model. *Journal of Palliative Medicine*, *9*(1), 183–195. doi:10.1089/jpm.2006.9.183

Burgio, K. L., Williams, B. R., Dionne-Odom, J. N., Redden, D. T., Noh, H., Goode, P. S., Kvale, E., Bakitas, M., & Bailey, F. A. (2016). Racial differences in processes of care at end of life in VA medical centers: Planned secondary analysis of data from the BEACON Trial. *Journal of Palliative Medicine*, *19*(2), 157–163. doi:10.1089/jpm.2015.0311

Carpenter, B. D., Zoller, S. M., Balsis, S., Otilingam, P. G., & Gatz, M. (2011). Demographic and contextual factors related to knowledge about Alzheimer's disease. *American Journal of Alzheimer's Disease and Other Dementias*, *26*(2), 121–126. doi:10.1177/1533317510394157

Cartwright, C., Hughes, M., & Lienert, T. (2012). End-of-life care for gay, lesbian, bisexual and transgender people. *Culture, Health & Sexuality, 14*(5), 537–548. doi:10.1080/136910 58.2012.673639

Center to Advance Palliative Care. (2008). Clinical practice guidelines for quality palliative care. In *National Consensus Project for Quality Palliative Care*. Retrieved from www.national consensusproject.org/guideline.pdf

Chan, D. C., Kasper, J. D., Black, B. S., & Rabins, P. V. (2007). Clinical diagnosis of dementia, not presence of behavioral and psychological symptoms, is associated with psychotropic use in community-dwelling elders classified as having dementia. *Journal of Geriatric Psychiatry and Neurology, 20*(1), 50–57. doi:10.1177/0891988706297088

Chapman, E. N., Kaatz, A., & Carnes, M. (2013). Physicians and implicit bias: How doctors may unwittingly perpetuate health care disparities. *Journal of General Internal Medicine, 28*(11), 1504–1510. doi:10.1007/s11606-013-2441-1

Choi, S. K., & Meyer, I. H. (2016). *LGBT Aging: A Review of Research Findings, Needs, and Policy Implications*. Retrieved from http://williamsinstitute.law.ucla.edu/wp-content/uploads/LGBT-Aging-A-Review.pdf

Claes, J. A., & Moore, W. (2000). Issues confronting lesbian and gay elders: The challenge for health and human services providers. *Journal of Health and Human Services Administration, 23*(2), 181–202. Retrieved from www.jstor.org/stable/25780946?seq=1#page_scan_tab_contents.

Cole, E. R. (2009). Intersectionality and research in psychology. *American Psychologist, 64*(3), 170. Retrieved from http://dx.doi.org/10.1037/a0014564

Cook-Daniels, L. (2015). Transgender aging: What practitioners should know. In N. A. Orel, & C. A. Fruhauf (Eds.), *The Lives of LGBT Older Adults: Understanding Challenges and Resilience* (pp. 193–215). Washington, DC: American Psychological Association.

Corbie-Smith, G., Thomas, S. B., & George, D. M. M. S. (2002). Distrust, race, and research. *Archives of Internal Medicine, 162*(21), 2458–2463. doi:10.1001/archinte.162.21.2458

Crawley, L. M. (2005). Racial, cultural, and ethnic factors influencing end-of-life care. *Journal of Palliative Medicine, 8*(1), s58–s69. doi:10.1089/jpm.2005.8.s-58./

Crawley, L., Payne, R., Bolden, J., Payne, T., & Washington, P. (2000). Palliative and end-of-life care in the African American community. *The Journal of the American Medical Association, 284*(19), 2518–2521. doi:10.1001/jama.284.19.2518.

Croghan, C. F., Moone, R. P., & Olson, A. M. (2014). Friends, family, and caregiving among midlife and older lesbian, gay, bisexual, and transgender adults. *Journal of Homosexuality, 61*(1), 79–102. doi:10.1080/00918369.2013.835238

Crozier, P. (2008). Nuts and bolts: Estate planning and family law considerations for same-sex families. *Western New England Law Review, 30*(3), 751–771.

Damron-Rodriguez, J., Wallace, S., & Kington, R. (1995). Service utilization and minority elderly: Appropriateness, accessibility and acceptability. *Gerontology & Geriatrics Education, 15*(1), 45–64. Retrieved from http://dx.doi.org/10.1300/J021v15n01_05

Darby, J. E., & Ward-Smith, P. (2016). End-of-life communication with non-traditional families and lesbian, gay, bisexual and transgender patients for nurses. *Clinical Nursing Studies, 4*(4), 40–45. Retrieved from www.sciedu.ca/journal/index.php/cns/article/view/10042

D'Augelli, A. R., & Grossman, A. H. (2001). Disclosure of sexual orientation, victimization, and mental health among lesbian, gay and bisexual older adults. *Journal of Interpersonal Violence, 16*(10), 1008–1027. doi:10.1177/088626001016010003

Di Napoli, E. A., Breland, G. L., & Allen, R. S. (2013). Staff knowledge and perceptions of sexuality and dementia of older adults in nursing homes. *Journal of Aging and Health, 25*(7), 1087–1105. doi:10.1177/0898264313494802

Dilworth-Anderson, P., Goodwin, P. Y., & Williams, S. W. (2004). Can culture help explain the physical health effects of caregiving over time among African American caregivers? *The Journals of Gerontology Series B: Psychological Sciences and Social Sciences, 59*(3), S138–S145. Retrieved from https://doi.org/10.1093/geronb/59.3.S138

Dilworth-Anderson, P., Williams, I. C., & Gibson, B. E. (2002). Issues of race, ethnicity, and culture in caregiving research a 20-year review (1980–2000). *The Gerontologist, 42*(2), 237–272. Retrieved from https://doi.org/10.1093/geront/42.2.237

Durand, M. A., Carpenter, L., Dolan, H., Bravo, P., Mann, M., Bunn, F., & Elwyn, G. (2014). Do interventions designed to support shared decision-making reduce health inequalities? A systematic review and meta-analysis. *PloS one, 9*(4), 1–13. Retrieved from http://dx.doi.org/10.1371/journal.pone.0094670

Dworkin, S. H., & Yi, H. (2003). LGBT identity, violence, and social justice: The psychological is political. *International Journal for the Advancement of Counselling, 25*(4), 269–279. doi:10.1023/B:ADCO.0000005526.87218.9f

Eggly, S., Tkatch, R., Penner, L. A., Mabunda, L., Hudson, J., Chapman, R., . . . Albrecht, T. (2013). Development of a question prompt list as a communication intervention to reduce racial disparities in cancer treatment. *Journal of Cancer Education, 28*(2), 282–289. doi:10.1007/s13187-013-0456-2

Eliacin, J., Coffing, J. M., Matthias, M. S., Burgess, D. J., Bair, M. J., & Rollins, A. L. (2016). The relationship between race, patient activation, and working alliance: Implications for patient engagement in mental health care. *Administration and Policy in Mental Health and Mental Health Services Research*, 1–7. doi:10.1007/s10488-016-0779-5

Enguidanos, S., Kogan, A. C., Lorenz, K., & Taylor, G. (2011). Use of role model stories to overcome barriers to hospice among African Americans. *Journal of Palliative Medicine, 14*(2), 161–168. doi:10.1089/jpm.2010.0380

Evans, N., Menaca, A., Andrew, E., Koffman, J., Harding, R., Higginson, I. J., . . . Gysels, M. (2012). Systematic review of the primary research on minority ethnic groups and end-of-life care from the United Kingdom. *Journal of Pain and Symptom Management, 43*(2), 261–286. doi:10.1016/j.jpainsymman.2011.04.012

Fischer, S. M., Sauaia, A., & Kutner, J. S. (2007). Patient navigation: A culturally competent strategy to address disparities in palliative care. *Journal of Palliative Medicine, 10*(5), 1023–1028. doi:10.1089/jpm.2007.0070

FitzGerald, C., & Hurst, S. (2017). Implicit bias in healthcare professionals: A systematic review. *BMC Medical Ethics, 18*(1), 19. doi:10.1186/s12910-017-0179-8

Folkman, S. (1997). Positive psychological states and coping with severe stress. *Social Science & Medicine, 45*(8), 1207–1221. doi:10.1007/978-1-4419-1005-9_215.

Fredriksen-Goldsen, K. I., & Ellis, C. (2007). Caregiving with pride: An introduction. *The Journal of Gay and Lesbian Social Services, 18*, 1–13. Retrieved from http://dx.doi.org/10.1300/J041v18n03_01

Fredriksen-Goldsen, K. I., Hoy-Ellis, C. P., Goldsen, J., Emlet, C. A., & Hooyman, N. R. (2014). Creating a vision for the future: Key competencies and strategies for culturally 43 competent practice with LGBT older adults in the health and human services. *Journal of Gerontological Social Work, 57*, 80–107. doi:10.1080/01634372.2014.890690

Fredriksen-Goldsen, K. I., Hoy-Ellis, C. P., Muraco, A., Goldsen, J., & Kim, H. (2015). The health and well-being of LGBT older adults: Disparities, risks, and resilience across the life course. In N. A. Orel, & C. A. Fruhauf (Eds.), *The Lives of LGBT Older Adults: Understanding Challenges and Resilience* (pp. 25–53). Washington, DC: American Psychological Association.

Fredriksen-Goldsen, K. I., Kim, H. J., Emlet, C. A., Muraco, A., Erosheva, E. A., Hoy-Ellis, C. P., . . . Petry, H. (2011). *The Aging and Health Report: Disparities and Resilience Among*

Lesbian, Gay, Bisexual, and Transgender Older Adults. Retrieved from www.age-pride.org/wordpress/wp-content/uploads/2011/05/Full-Report-FINAL-11-16-11.pdf

Fredriksen-Goldsen, K. I., & Muraco, A. (2010). Aging and sexual orientation: A 25-year review of literature. *Research on Aging, 32*(3), 372–413. doi:10.1177/0164027509360355

Freimuth, V. S., Quinn, S. C., Thomas, S. B., Cole, G., Zook, E., & Duncan, T. (2001). African Americans' views on research and the Tuskegee Syphilis Study. *Social Science & Medicine, 52*(5), 797–808. Retrieved from https://doi.org/10.1016/S0277-9536(00)00178-7

Gelfand, D. E., Balcazar, H., Parzuchowski, J., & Lenox, S. (2001). Mexicans and care for the terminally ill: Family, hospice, and the church. *American Journal of Hospice and Palliative Medicine, 18*(6), 391–396. doi:10.1177/104990910101800608

Gendron, T., Maddux, S., Krinsky, L., White, J., Lockeman, K., Metcalfe, Y., & Aggarwal, S. (2013). Cultural competence training for healthcare professionals working with LGBT older adults. *Educational Gerontology, 39*(6), 454–463. doi:10.1080/03601277.2012.701114

Green, A. R., Carney, D. R., Pallin, D. J., Ngo, L. H., Raymond, K. L., Iezzoni, L. I., & Banaji, M. R. (2007). Implicit bias among physicians and its prediction of thrombolysis decisions for black and white patients. *Journal of General Internal Medicine, 22*(9), 1231–1238. Retrieved from https://doi.org/10.1007/s11606-007-0258-5

Greenwood, N., Habibi, R., Smith, R., & Manthorpe, J. (2015). Barriers to access and minority ethnic carers' satisfaction with social care services in the community: A systematic review of qualitative and quantitative literature. *Health and Social Care in the Community, 23*(1), 64–78. doi:10.1111/hsc.12116

Haley, W. E., Allen, R. S., Reynolds, S., Chen, H., Burton, A., & Gallagher-Thompson, D. (2002). Family issues in end-of-life decision making and end-of-life care. *American Behavioral Scientist, 46*(2), 284–298. Retrieved from http://journals.sagepub.com/doi/abs/10.1177/000276402236680

Hallenbeck, J., Goldstein, M. K., & Mebane, E. W. (1996). Cultural considerations of death and dying in the United States. *Clinics in Geriatric Medicine, 12*(2), 393–406. Retrieved from http://europepmc.org/abstract/med/8799356

Hanson, L. C., Armstrong, T. D., Green, M. A., Hayes, M., Peacock, S., Elliot-Bynum, S., Goldmon, M. V., Corbie-Smith, G., & Earp, J. A. (2013). Circles of care: Development and initial evaluation of a peer support model for African Americans with advanced cancer. *Health Education & Behavior, 40*(5), 536–543. doi:10.1177/1090198112461252

Harding, R., Epiphaniou, E., & Chidgey-Clark, J. (2012). Needs, experiences, and preferences of sexual minorities for end-of-life care and palliative care: A systematic review. *Journal of Palliative Medicine, 15*(5), 602–611. doi:10.1089/jpm.2011.0279

Harper, S. (2014). Economic and social implications of aging societies. *Science, 346*(6209), 587–591. Retrieved from http://science.sciencemag.org/content/346/6209/587

Harris, G. M., Allen, R. S., Dunn, L., & Parmelee, P. (2013). "Trouble won't last always": Religious coping and meaning in the stress process. *Qualitative Health Research, 23*(6), 773–781. Retrieved from http://journals.sagepub.com/doi/abs/10.1177/1049732313482590

Hasnain, M., Connell, K. J., Menon, U., & Tranmer, P. A. (2011). Patient-centered care for Muslim women: Provider and patient perspectives. *Journal of Women's Health, 20*(1), 73–83. doi:10.1089/jwh.2010.2197

Hendricks, M., & Testa, R. J. (2012). A conceptual framework for clinical work with transgender and gender nonconforming clients: An adaptation of the minority stress model. *Research and Practice, 43*(5), 460–467. Retrieved from http://psycnet.apa.org/index.cfm?fa=buy.optionToBuy&id=2012-21304-001

Hilgeman, M. M., Allen, R. S., DeCoster, J., & Burgio, L. D. (2007). Positive aspects of caregiving as a moderator of treatment outcome over 12 months. *Psychology and Aging, 22*(2), 361. Retrieved from http://dx.doi.org/10.1037/0882-7974.22.2.361

Hilgeman, M. M., Durkin, D. W., Sun, F., DeCoster, J., Allen, R. S., Gallagher-Thompson, D., & Burgio, L. D. (2009). Testing a theoretical model of the stress process in Alzheimer's caregivers with race as a moderator. *The Gerontologist, 49*(2), 248–261. Retrieved from http://dx.doi.org/10.1037/0882-7974.22.2.361

Hoberman, J. (2012). *Black and Blue: The Origins and Consequences of Medical Racism.* Berkeley, CA: University of California Press.

Holtzman, M. (2011). Nonmarital unions, family definitions, and custody decision making. *Family Relations, 60*(5), 617–632. doi:10.1001/archneurol.2011.208

Hopp, F. P., & Duffy, S. A. (2000). Racial variations in end-of-life care. *Journal of the American Geriatrics Society, 48*(6), 658–663. doi:10.1111/j.1532–5415.2000.tb04724.x

Hoy-Ellis, C. P., & Fredriksen-Goldsen, K. I. (2016). Lesbian, gay, & bisexual older adults: Linking internal minority stressors, chronic health conditions, and depression. *Aging and Mental Health, 20*(11), 1119–1130. doi:10.1080/13607863.2016.1168362

Huang, C. H. S., Crowther, M., Allen, R. S., DeCoster, J., Kim, G., Azuero, C., . . . Kvale, E. (2016). A pilot feasibility intervention to increase advance care planning among African Americans in the deep south. *Journal of Palliative Medicine, 19*(2), 164–173. Retrieved from https://doi.org/10.1089/jpm.2015.0334

Hughes, M., & Cartwright, C. (2015). Lesbian, gay, bisexual and transgender people's attitudes to end-of-life decision-making and advance care planning. *Australasian Journal on Ageing, 34*(2), 39–43. doi:10.1111/ajag.12268

Ingersoll-Dayton, B., Spencer, B., Kwak, M., Scherrer, K., Allen, R. S., & Campbell, R. (2013). The couples life story approach: A dyadic intervention for dementia. *Journal of Gerontological Social Work, 56*(3), 237–254. doi:10.1080/01634372.2012.758214

Institute of Medicine. (2003). *Unequal Treatment: Confronting Racial and Ethnic Disparities in Healthcare.* Washington, DC: The National Academies Press.

Institute of Medicine. (2014). *Dying in America: Improving Quality and Honoring Preferences Near the End of Life.* Washington, DC: The National Academies Press.

Jæger, K., & Jensen, A. A. (2009). Troubling diversity? Exploring nurses' discursive construction of intercultural encounters in healthcare settings. *International Journal of Diversity in Organisations, Communities & Nations, 9*(4), 99–108.

Johnson, K. S. (2013). Racial and ethnic disparities in palliative care. *Journal of Palliative Medicine, 16*(11), 1329–1334. doi:10.1089/jpm.2013.9468

Johnson, M., Jackson, N., Arnette, J., & Koffman, S. (2005). Gay and lesbian perceptions of discrimination in retirement care facilities. *Journal of Homosexuality, 49*, 83–102. Retrieved from http://dx.doi.org/10.1300/J082v49n02_05

Johnson, K. S., Kuchibhatla, M., & Tulsky, J. A. (2008). What explains racial differences in the use of advance directives and attitudes toward hospice care? *Journal of the American Geriatrics Society, 56*(10), 1953–1958. doi:10.1111/j.1532–5415.2008.01919.x

Juster, R.-P., McEwen, B. S., & Lupien, S. J. (2010). Allostatic load biomarkers of chronic stress and impact on health and cognition. *Neuroscience and Biobehavioral Reviews, 35*(1), 2–16.

Kalauokalani, D., Franks, P., Oliver, J. W., Meyers, F. J., & Kravitz, R. L. (2007). Can patient coaching reduce racial/ethnic disparities in cancer pain control? Secondary analysis of a randomized controlled trial. *Pain Medicine, 8*(1), 17–24. doi:10.1111/j.1526-4637.2007.00170.x

Kanekar, S., & Petereit, D. (2009). Walking forward: A program designed to lower cancer mortality rates among American Indians in western South Dakota. *South Dakota Medicine:*

The Journal of the South Dakota State Medical Association, 62(4), 151. Retrieved from www. ncbi.nlm.nih.gov/pmc/articles/PMC2719825/

Karim, K., Bailey, M., & Tunna, K. (2000). Nonwhite ethnicity and the provision of specialist palliative care services: Factors affecting doctors' referral patterns. *Palliative Medicine, 14*(6), 471–478. doi:10.1191/026921600701536390

Kelley, A. S., & Morrison, R. S. (2015). Palliative care for the seriously ill. *New England Journal of Medicine, 373*(8), 747–755. Retrieved from www.nejm.org/doi/pdf/10.1056/ NEJMra1404684

Kim, G., Ford, K. L., Chiriboga, D. A., & Sorkin, D. H. (2012). Racial and ethnic disparities in healthcare use, delayed care, and management of diabetes mellitus in older adults in California. *Journal of the American Geriatrics Society, 60*(12), 2319–2325. doi:10.1111/jgs.12003

Knight, B. G., & Sayegh, P. (2009). Cultural values and caregiving: The updated sociocultural stress and coping model. *The Journals of Gerontology Series B: Psychological Sciences and Social Sciences, 65B*(1), 5–13. doi:10.1093/geronb/gbp096

Kowaleski-Jones, L., & Dunifon, R. (2004). Children's home environments: Understanding the role of family structure changes. *Journal of Family Issues, 25*(1), 3–28. Retrieved from http://journals.sagepub.com/doi/abs/10.1177/0192513X03256516

Krebs, L. U., Burhansstipanov, L., Watanabe-Galloway, S., Pingatore, N. L., Petereit, D. G., & Isham, D. (2013). Navigation as an intervention to eliminate disparities in American Indian communities. *Seminars in Oncology Nursing, 29*(2), 118–127.

Kunik, M. E., Snow, A. L., Davila, J. A., Steele, A. B., Balasubramanyam, V., Doody, R. S., Schulz, P. E., Kalavar, J. S., & Morgan, R. O. (2010). Causes of aggressive behavior in patients with dementia. *The Journal of Clinical Psychiatry, 71*(9), 1145–1152. doi:10.4088/ JCP.08m04703oli

LaVeist, T. A. (2005). Disentangling race and socioeconomic status: A key to understanding health inequalities. *Journal of Urban Health, 82*(3), iii26–iii34. Retrieved from https://doi. org/10.1093/jurban/jti061

Lawton, M. P., Moss, M., Kleban, M. H., Glicksman, A., & Rovine, M. (1991). A two-factor model of caregiving appraisal and psychological well-being. *Journal of Gerontology, 46*(4), P181–P189. Retrieved from https://doi.org/10.1093/geronj/46.4.P181

Lazarus, R. S., & Folkman, S. (1984). Coping and adaptation. *The Handbook of Behavioral Medicine*, 282–325.

Lievesley, N. (2010). *The Future Ageing of the Ethnic Minority Population of England and Wales.* London: Centre for Policy on Ageing and the Runnymede Trust.

Meyer, I. H. (1995). Minority stress and mental health in gay men. *Journal of Health and Social Behavior, 36*(1), 38–56. Retrieved from www.jstor.org/stable/2137286.

Meyer, I. H. (2001). Why lesbian, gay, bisexual, and transgender public health? *American Journal of Public Health, 91*, 856–859. Retrieved from www.ncbi.nlm.nih.gov/pmc/articles/ PMC1446455/

Meyer, I. H. (2003). Prejudice, social stress, and mental health in lesbian, gay, and bisexual populations: Conceptual issues and research evidence. *Psychological Bulletin, 129*(5), 674–697.

Miller, L. R. (2016). Definition of family. *The Wiley Blackwell Encyclopedia of Family Studies.* doi:10.1002/9781119085621.wbefs137

Muraco, A., & Fredriksen-Goldsen, K. (2011). "That's what friends do": Informal caregiving for chronically ill midlife and older lesbian, gay, and bisexual adults. *Journal of Social and Personal Relationships, 28*(8), 1073–1092. Retrieved from https://doi.org/10.1177/ 0265407511402419

National Alliance for Caregiving and AARP. (2009). *Caregiving in the United States*. Retrieved from www.caregiving.org/data/04finalreport.pdf

National Center for Health Statistics. (2016). *Health, United States, 2015: With Special Feature on Racial and Ethnic Health Disparities*. Retrieved from www.ncbi.nlm.nih.gov/pubmed/27308685

National Healthcare Quality and Disparities Report and 5th Anniversary Update on the National Quality Strategy. (2016). Rockville, MD: Agency for Healthcare Research and Quality (AHRQ). Retrieved from www.ahrq.gov/research/findings/nhqrdr/nhqdr15/index.html

Noh, H. (2012). Terminally ill black elders: Making the choice to receive hospice care. *The Gerontologist, 52*, 443–443.

Paradies, Y., Truong, M., & Priest, N. (2014). A systematic review of the extent and measurement of healthcare provider racism. *Journal of General Internal Medicine, 29*(2), 364–387. Retrieved from https://doi.org/10.1007/s11606-013-2583-1

Pearlin, L. I., Mullan, J. T., Semple, S. J., & Skaff, M. M. (1990). Caregiving and the stress process: An overview of concepts and their measures. *The Gerontologist, 30*(5), 583–594. Retrieved from https://doi.org/10.1093/geront/30.5.583

Penner, L. A., Dovidio, J. F., West, T. V., Gaertner, S. L., Albrecht, T. L., Dailey, R. K., & Markova, T. (2010). Aversive racism and medical interactions with Black patients: A field study. *Journal of Experimental Social Psychology, 46*(2), 436–440. doi:10.1016/j.jesp.2009.11.004

Pinquart, M., & Sörensen, S. (2005). Ethnic differences in stressors, resources, and psychological outcomes of family caregiving: A meta-analysis. *The Gerontologist, 45*(1), 90–106. Retrieved from https://doi.org/10.1093/geront/45.1.90

Porensky, E. K., & Carpenter, B. D. (2008). Knowledge and perceptions in advance care planning. *Journal of Aging and Health, 20*(1), 89–106. Retrieved from http://journals.sagepub.com/doi/abs/10.1177/0898264307309963

Pullis, B. (2011). Perceptions of hospice care among African Americans. *Journal of Hospice & Palliative Nursing, 13*(5), 281–287. Retrieved from http://journals.lww.com/jhpn/Abstract/2011/09000/Perceptions_of_Hospice_Care_Among_African.7.aspx

Reese, D. J., Melton, E., & Ciaravino, K. (2004). Programmatic barriers to providing culturally competent end-of-life care. *American Journal of Hospice and Palliative Medicine, 21*(5), 357–364. Retrieved from http://journals.sagepub.com/doi/abs/10.1177/104990910402100510

Renzaho, A. M. N., Romios, P., Crock, C., & Sønderlund, A. L. (2013). The effectiveness of cultural competence programs in ethnic minority patient-centered health care – A systematic review of the literature. *International Journal for Quality in Health Care, 25*(3), 261–269. Retrieved from https://doi.org/10.1093/intqhc/mzt006

Roth, D. L., Dilworth-Anderson, P., Huang, J., Gross, A. L., & Gitlin, L. N. (2015). Positive aspects of family caregiving for dementia: Differential item functioning by race. *The Journals of Gerontology Series B: Psychological Sciences and Social Sciences, 70*(6), 813–819. Retrieved from https://doi.org/10.1093/geronb/gbv034

Scharlach, A. E., Kellam, R., Ong, N., Baskin, A., Goldstein, C., & Fox, P. J. (2006). Cultural attitudes and caregiver service use: Lessons from focus groups with racially and ethnically diverse family caregivers. *Journal of Gerontological Social Work, 47*(1–2), 133–156. Retrieved from http://dx.doi.org/10.1300/J083v47n01_09

Schmid, B., Allen, R. S., Haley, P. P., & DeCoster, J. (2009). Family matters: Dyadic agreement in end-of-life medical decision making. *The Gerontologist, 50*(2), 226–237. Retrieved from https://doi.org/10.1093/geront/gnp166

Searight, H. R., & Gafford, J. (2005). Cultural diversity at the end of life: Issues and guidelines for family physicians. *American Family Physician*, *71*(3), 515–522. Retrieved from http://marianjoylibrary.org/Diversity/documents/CulturalDiversityattheEndofLifeIssuesand Guidelines.pdf

Seeman, T. E., Singer, B. H., Rowe, J. W., Horwitz, R. I., & McEwen, B. S. (1997). Price of adaptation – allostatic load and its health consequences: MacArthur studies of successful aging. *Archives of Internal Medicine*, *157*(19), 2259–2268.

Settles, B. H., & Steinmetz, S. (2013). *Concepts and Definitions of Family for the 21st Century*. New York, NY: Routledge.

Stein, G. L., Beckerman, N. L., & Sherman, P. A. (2010). Lesbian and gay elders and long-term care: Identifying the unique psychosocial perspectives and challenges. *Journal of Gerontology of Social Work*, *53*(5), 421–435. Retrieved from http://dx.doi.org/10.1080/0163 4372.2010.496478

Taylor, R. J., Chatters, L. M., Woodward, A. T., & Brown, E. (2013). Racial and ethnic differences in extended family, friendship, fictive kin, and congregational informal support networks. *Family Relations*, *62*(4), 609–624. doi:10.1111/fare.12030

Thomas, K., Hudson, P., Trauer, T., Remedios, C., & Clarke, D. (2014). Risk factors for developing prolonged grief during bereavement in family carers of cancer patients in palliative care: A longitudinal study. *Journal of Pain and Symptom Management*, *47*(3), 531–541.

Vitaliano, P. P., Zhang, J., & Scanlan, J. M. (2003). Is caregiving hazardous to one's physical health? A meta-analysis. *Psychological Bulletin*, *129*(6), 946.

Volandes, A. E., Ariza, M., Abbo, E. D., & Paasche-Orlow, M. (2008). Overcoming educational barriers for advance care planning in Latinos with video images. *Journal of Palliative Medicine*, *11*(5), 700–706.

Wallace, S., Cochran, S., Durazo, E., & Ford, C. (2011). *The Health of Aging Lesbian, Gay and Bisexual Adults in California*. Los Angeles: UCLA Center for Health Policy Research.

White, K., Haas, J. S., & Williams, D. R. (2012). Elucidating the role of place in health care disparities: The example of racial/ethnic residential segregation. *Health Services Research*, *47*(3 pt 2), 1278–1299.

Williams, D. R. (1999). Race, socioeconomic status, and health the added effects of racism and discrimination. *Annals of the New York Academy of Sciences*, *896*(1), 173–188. doi:10.1111/j.1749–6632.1999.tb08114.x

Winston, C. A., Leshner, P., Kramer, J., & Allen, G. (2005). Overcoming barriers to access and utilization of hospice and palliative care services in African-American communities. *OMEGA-Journal of Death and Dying*, *50*(2), 151–163. Retrieved from http://journals.sagepub.com/doi/abs/10.2190/QQKG-EPFA-A2FN-GHVL

World Health Organization. (2002). *The World Health Report 2002: Reducing Risks, Promoting Healthy Life*. World Health Organization. Retrieved from www.barnesandnoble.com/w/world-health-report-2002-world-health-organization/1119231978?ean=9789 241562072

Similarities and differences in behavioural interventions and impact on mental health and wellness in palliative and end-of-life care

Rebecca S. Allen, Brian D. Carpenter, Morgan K. Eichorst, and Hillary R. Dorman

Chapter 1 revisited: what is this intervention book about and why is it needed?

We state in Chapter 1 that our purpose in writing and editing this book is to offer an accessible resource for scientists, practitioners, and trainees with relevant information on behavioural mental health and wellness interventions in palliative and end-of-life care. Fundamentally, we believe that this book provides a foundation for collaborative, international and interprofessional work by offering state-of-science information on such interventions. Behavioural interventions are those that directly address psychosocial issues that arise, particularly those that reflect conflicts of cognition, emotion, and communication both within the individual and within the interpersonal and environmental care context. Our definition of behavioural mental health and wellness interventions fits within current theoretical models that drive intervention development and delivery (Carstensen, Fung, & Charles, 2003; Carstensen, Isaacowitz, & Charles, 1999; Charles, 2010; Folkman, 1997). For example, in his biopsychosocial-spiritual model, Sulmasy (2002) proposed that: 1) individuals exist as beings in relationship within physical, interpersonal, social, and transcendent contexts, and 2) healing may occur in these relationships by restoring what may be restored, even when this does not restore perfect wholeness and health. Hence, conflicts or imbalances in relationships may be addressed through behavioural interventions that promote healing in the face of immutable loss and change.

Additionally, our definition of behavioural mental health and wellness intervention is supported through theories of development and stress and coping. Specifically, the ideas that 1) a person's perspective on time left to live may motivate a deeper search for meaning and emotion regulation (Carstensen et al., 2003), and 2) meaning-based coping serves to perpetuate the coping process in the face of unchangeable outcomes (Folkman, 1997), highlight the opportunity for healing and wellness in the face of death. These ideas suggest targets and goals for intervention in seeking what others have labeled a "good death" (Byock, 1997; Gawande, 2014; Granda-Camerson & Houldin, 2012).

Recently, Meier and colleagues (2016) conducted a narrative review of 36 studies that provided a definition of a good death. Perspectives of individuals near the end of life, their family members, and their healthcare providers were compared, and the authors identified themes they termed as "successful dying." Stakeholder perspectives differed in the relative importance of themes, yet all stakeholders endorsed 11 core themes that included, but were not limited to, the following behavioural mental health and wellness targets: 1) emotional well-being, 2) life completion, 3) religiousness/spirituality, 4) dignity, 5) family, 6) quality of life, and 7) relationship with healthcare providers. These seven of 11 core themes of "successful dying" focus on frequent outcomes identified in the delivery of behavioural interventions. These may include focusing individuals' attention on lifetime accomplishments and challenges, relationships, and values. Such focus, and the cognitive and emotional processing engaged in by individuals near the end of life, may be facilitated by healthcare providers during behavioural and mental health and wellness interventions. When therapeutically effective, these interventions facilitate meaning reconstruction, reduce existential distress, and promote healing in intrapersonal, interpersonal, and transcendent relationships.

As noted in Chapter 1, the intersection of ethnicity, gender identity, socio-economic status, and geographic place of residence may expose individuals with greater combinations of low social status identities to significantly more stigma and discrimination. Therefore, providers must recognize and seek to expand their skills in the support of individuals' sense of intersectionality and, potentially, positive marginality (Mayo, 1982; Unger, 2000). Acknowledging and valuing one's thorough and integrated uniqueness may be a therapeutically effective component in healing. Chochinov and colleagues (Chochinov et al., 2013) proposed a model of therapeutic effectiveness that may be beneficial to healthcare providers in conceptualizing clinical competencies necessary for this work. This model was derived from focus groups comprised of 78 experienced psychosocial oncology clinicians throughout Canada. Three interrelated therapeutic skill domains emerged: personal growth and self-care (domain A), therapeutic approaches (domain B), and creation of a safe space (domain C). In the opinion of the editors, the most exciting and useful aspects of Chochinov's therapeutic effectiveness model are the intersections of these three primary domains: domain AB labeled *therapeutic humility*, domain BC or *therapeutic pacing*, and domain AC called *therapeutic presence*. Perhaps the most critical components of this model for practitioners are those that facilitate exploration of intersectionality. These include the skills encompassed in therapeutic humility (e.g., honouring the client as expert, modeling healthy processing of emotion, tolerating clinical ambiguity, exploring difficult topics) and therapeutic presence (e.g., being fully present and mindful of boundaries; being genuine, authentic, compassionate, nonjudgemental, and emotionally resilient).

Behavioural interventions in palliative and end-of-life care are useful tools in broadening treatment approaches to address psychosocial needs including conflicts of cognition, emotion, and communication within the individual and within the interpersonal and environmental care context. Yet the chapters included in this book demonstrate widely varying levels of evidence for the treatments described. As noted in Chapter 1, conducting research to investigate treatment efficacy and effectiveness in these settings poses many challenges. These include issues of individual consent capacity, stress on the family system, and attrition due to health decline and death. Additionally, institutional review boards seeking to protect the rights of human research subjects may be apprehensive about approving research in palliative and end-of-life care. On the one hand, individuals receiving such care are vulnerable, and caution in working with this population is needed. However, many individuals want to participate in research (Hall, Goddard, Speck, & Higginson, 2013), and many are able and willing to give consent. The cost of avoiding this population because of the hurdles inherent in conducting research in palliative and end-of-life care is ill-informed interventions or interventions that apply "one size fits all" approaches that do not honor individuality or intersectionality. Such interventions are based on assumptions that what works in other, "similar" populations will work – or work well enough – in palliative and end-of-life care. Thus, there is a strong case to be made for the inclusion of palliative and end-of-life populations in research, logistical difficulties notwithstanding, and an ethical imperative to give them a voice in the literature that informs their psychosocial treatment. In the next section we will briefly review material conveyed in these chapters and identify core themes in the evidence base.

Core themes and needs in the evidence base across chapters

Table 7.1 presents a brief review of the information provided in the chapters written by our author teams. As stated in Chapter 1, the editors asked that each of the writing groups include in their work certain material: 1) a review of behavioural interventions, 2) an evaluation of the strength of the evidence base, 3) identification of gaps within the knowledge base, 4) coverage of cultural and diversity issues, 5) consideration of ethical issues, 6) practice implications, and 7) at least one case example with questions illustrating salient issues. A few of the interventions mentioned in this book have substantial evidence of efficacy (e.g., Meaning-Centered Psychotherapy for cancer patients, Dignity Therapy); however, many of the interventions show initial promise but could stand additional evaluation. For many interventions, research suffers from lack of diversity in samples, lack of generalizability, small numbers, and the inherent challenge of high attrition within palliative and end-of-life care patients, their family members, and their healthcare providers. Moreover, research frequently considers only one or two stakeholders' perspectives, not all three (i.e., the patient, the provider, the patient and family, or the patient and provider) as would represent a "gold standard" perspective in defining a "good death" (Meier et al., 2016).

Table 7.1 Core themes in evidence base supporting behavioural interventions in palliative and end-of-life care

Chapter	Topic	Themes
2	Communication and decision-making	• Preliminary evidence that question prompt lists increase the frequency with which patients ask questions of their healthcare providers and the amount of information providers give them. When providers have a copy of the question prompt list it improves these outcomes.
		• Empowering patients and care partners to gain information for supported communication and decision-making is important, and appointment coaching is one way to do this.
		• SPIRIT intervention incorporates spirituality into the decision-making process and, thus, provides a culturally competent intervention component for many patients and families.
		• Communication tools targeting providers, such as conversational scripts and templates, also enhance the flow of information.
		• Resources to improve communication around care preferences have expanded into a variety of media and modes, but evidence for their effectiveness is limited.
		• Decision aids rely on a variety of approaches, levels of specificity, and degrees of collaboration. They appear to be effective guides for helping patients consider care options.
3	Physical and mental health symptoms	• Evidence is mixed for interventions to address these symptoms.
		• Evidence for acupuncture is most robust in the area of pain management, particularly when paired with transcutaneous electrical nerve stimulation.
		• Effects of massage not clearly established, but research is ongoing.
		• Evidence regarding therapeutic touch is mixed.
		• Use of Snoezelen with individuals who have dementia appears to have positive effects.
		• Animal assisted therapy has been supported but not in palliative care; some positive results in small trials.
		• Imagery/relaxation/meditation/hypnosis studies show usefulness in reducing pain; meditation and relaxation can reduce dyspnea-related anxiety; diaphragmatic and/or purse-lipped breathing and air movement across the face (e.g., use of a fan) are helpful in decreasing feelings of breathlessness.
		• Tai Chi/yoga/qigong improve pain and may improve mobility and mood in some patients, though sample sizes have been small.
		• Evidence for the effectiveness of CBT and ACT is good, but these treatments are not frequently used in palliative care and may need adaptation.
		• Research of music therapy suggests its value in alleviating pain, fatigue, and anxiety and in improving mood, spirituality, and quality of life.

Chapter	Topic	Themes
4	Meaning-Centered Therapy in cancer	• Evidence based efficacy but not effectiveness in improving existential concerns and reducing desire for hastened death and finding peace of mind, hope, and meaning in life. • Delivered in groups or individually. • Tested most extensively in advanced cancer, with some applicability across disease contexts.
5	Dignity Therapy	• An evidence-based and theory driven treatment, with theoretical model empirically derived. • Applied across illness contexts, including cognitive status. • Initial evidence of positive outcomes for family members. • Cross-cultural efficacy internationally. Better results following the methodology of the randomized controlled trials rather than the initial study. • No certification for providers and variability in supervision and support sought from the research group. • Evidence that some cultures may define dignity differently. • Ongoing trials test differing models of intervention delivery.
6	Diversity and intersectionality	• Diversity and intersectionality compound the challenges and stress faced by patients and care partners. • Caution and mistrust toward healthcare systems are the result of historical mistreatment and marginalization. • End-of-life care preferences are likely to vary across diverse groups, and those differences should be fully explored. • Definitions of "family" are themselves diverse and demand routine and sensitive inquiry. • Evidence for applicability of traditional assessments measures and treatments across most social identity categories is scant. • Implicit bias may influence providers' behaviour and intervention delivery.

Certain core themes are evident across chapters. First, behavioural and mental health and wellness interventions in palliative and end-of-life care strive for "patient-centredness." Certainly the case examples presented in every chapter illustrate clinical sensitivity to diversity and cultural context. Additionally, each of the authorship teams make clear and concise recommendations for practice that consider the wishes of the patient within the context of a given treatment site or illness context. A second core theme is that more and better research is needed. Specifically, scientific methodology to establish intervention efficacy and effectiveness (Glasgow, Lichtenstein, & Marcus, 2003; Nathan, Stuart, & Dolan, 2000) within these settings may need greater flexibility than is typical of the "gold standard" randomized controlled trial. Particularly in palliative and end-of-life care settings, effectiveness, or the degree to which behavioural interventions can be successfully and therapeutically applied in real-world settings, is of the utmost importance for patient-centredness. Evidence for the effectiveness of even interventions with established efficacy (see Chapters 4 and 5) is needed.

Two possibilities for flexible research approaches may fit the palliative and end-of-life care setting and facilitate patient-centred outcomes research. As discussed in Chapter 1, community-based participatory research (CBPR; Israel et al., 1998, 2010) is one such methodology. Partnerships incorporating individuals near the end of life, their families, and their healthcare providers into research design from the beginning and throughout design, refinement, and implementation of behavioural interventions will ensure that important and appropriate clinical targets are the focus of intervention. These true partnerships take time to build but result in rich and meaningful research outcomes. Biglan and colleagues (2012) describe ways in which research may be conducted in collaboration with communities to create "nurturing environments" to promote health. In seeking to foster a "good death" or "successful dying process" in palliative and end-of-life care settings (Meier et al., 2016), what might providers and scientists learn by applying approaches frequently used in preventive health and self-management of chronic illness studies? We hope our readers will be among the minds addressing this, and other important questions in the coming years.

Another methodological modification may be greater reliance on pragmatic clinical trials (MacPherson, 2004; March et al., 2005; Zwarenstein et al., 2008) rather than traditional randomized controlled trials. March and colleagues identify eight key features of pragmatic clinical trials when testing psychiatric interventions: 1) a straightforward, clinically relevant question, 2) a representative sample of patients and practice settings, 3) sufficient power to identify modest clinically relevant effects, 4) randomization to protect against bias, 5) clinical uncertainty regarding the outcome of treatment at the patient level, 6) assessment and treatment protocols that enact best clinical practices, 7) simple and clinically relevant outcomes, and 8) limited subject and investigator burden. These goals may be fostered by interprofessional collaboration that incorporates CBPR principles and partnerships to establish an evidence base that is meaningful, inclusive, and sound. Most importantly, a developmental and intersectional approach is needed in research design, implementation, analysis, and dissemination in order to provide a truly patient-centered perspective, from multiple stakeholders, on the process of successful dying and achieving a good death through behavioural mental health and wellness interventions.

Conclusions

This book and its companion text, *Palliative and End-of-Life Care: Disease, Social and Cultural Context*, highlight international perspectives on behavioural and mental health and wellness interventions in palliative and end-of-life care. Across chapters, the editors and authors underscore the importance of communication (between patients, family members, and healthcare providers), personal choice/decision-making, values, and meaning making. Furthermore, the various case examples presented throughout these books emphasize the heterogeneity of end of life and death and dying. We clearly state that our purpose in writing and editing these books is to offer an accessible resource for scientists, practitioners, and trainees that may provide a foundation for collaborative, international and interprofessional work. Defining a good death or successful dying experience entails issues that are innately behavioural and psychosocial (Meier et al., 2016). Psychologists, as well as other healthcare providers, may implement behavioural and mental health and wellness interventions with the goal of facilitating meaning reconstruction, reducing existential distress, and promoting healing in intrapersonal, interpersonal, and transcendent relationships. It is our fervent hope that the information contained in this book may assist scientists, practitioners, and trainees in this endeavor.

References

Biglan, A., Flay, B. R., Embry, D. D., & Sandler, I. N. (2012). The critical role of nurturing environments for promoting human well-being. *The American Psychologist, 67*(4), 257–271.

Byock, I. (1997). *Dying Well: The Prospect for Growth at the End of Life*. New York, NY: Riverhead Books.

Carstensen, L. L., Fung, H. H., & Charles, S. T. (2003). Socioemotional selectivity theory and the regulation of emotions in the second half of life. *Motivation and Emotion, 27*(2), 103–123.

Carstensen, L. L., Isaacowitz, D. M., & Charles, S. T. (1999). Taking time seriously: A theory of socioemotional selectivity theory. *American Psychologist, 54*(3), 165–181.

Charles, S. T. (2010). Strength and vulnerability integration: A model of emotional well-being across adulthood. *Psychological Bulletin, 136*(3), 1068–1091.

Chochinov, H. M., McClement, S. E., Hack, T. F., McKeen, N. A., Rach, A. M., Gagnon, P., . . . Taylor-Brown, J. (2013). Health care provider communication: An empirical model of therapeutic effectiveness. *Cancer, 119*(9), 1706–1713. Retrieved from https://doi.org/10.1002/cncr.27949

Folkman, S. (1997). Positive psychological states and coping with severe stress. *Social Sciences and Medicine, 45*, 1207–1221.

Gawande, A. (2014). *Being Mortal*. New York, NY: Metropolitan Books.

Glasgow, R. E., Lichtenstein, E., & Marcus, A. C. (2003). Why don't we see more translation of health promotion research to practice? Rethinking the efficacy-to-effectiveness transition. *American Journal of Public Health, 93*(8), 1261–1267.

Granda-Cameron, C., & Houldin, A. (2012). Concept analysis of good death in terminally ill patients. *American Journal of Hospice and Palliative Care, 29*, 632–639.

Hall, S., Goddard, C., Speck, P., & Higginson, I. J. (2013). "It makes me feel that I'm still relevant": A qualitative study of the views of nursing home residents on dignity therapy and taking part in a phase II randomized controlled trial of a palliative care psychotherapy. *Palliative Meidicine*, *27*(4), 358–366.

Israel, B. A, Coombe, C. M., Cheezum, R. R., Schulz, A. J., McGranaghan, R. J., Lichtenstein, R., . . . Burris, A. (2010). Community-based participatory research: A capacity-building approach for policy advocacy aimed at eliminating health disparities. *American Journal of Public Health*, *100*(11), 2094–2102. doi:10.2105/AJPH.2009.170506

Israel, B. A., Schulz, A. J., Parker, E. A., & Becker, A. B. (1998). Review of community-based research: Assessing partnership approaches to improve public health. *Annual Review of Public Health*, *19*, 173–202.

MacPherson, H. (2004). Pragmatic clinical trials. *Complementary Therapies in Medicine*, *12*(2), 136–140.

March, J. S., Silva, S. G., Compton, S., Shapiro, M., Califf, R., & Krishnan, R. (2005). The case for practical clinical trials in psychiatry. *American Journal of Psychiatry*, *162*(5), 836–846.

Mayo, C. (1982). Training for positive marginality. In L. Bickman (Ed.), *Applied Social Psychology Annual* (Vol. 3, pp. 57–73). Beverly Hills, CA: Sage.

Meier, E. A., Gallegos, J. V., Montross-Thomas, L. P., Depp, C. A., Irwin, S. A., & Jeste, D. V. (2016). Defining a good death (successful dying): Literature review and a call for research and public dialogue. *American Journal of Geriatric Psychiatry*, *24*(4), 261–271.

Nathan, P. E., Stuart, S. P., & Dolan, S. L. (2000). Research on psychotherapy efficacy and effectiveness: Between Scylla and Charybdis?. *Psychological Bulletin*, *126*(6), 964.

Sulmasy, D. P. (2002). A biopsychosocial-spiritual model for the care of patients at the end of life. *The Gerontologist*, *42*(Spec. no III), 24–33.

Unger, R. W. (2000). Outsiders inside: Positive marginality and social change. *Journal of Social Issues*, *56*(1), 163–179.

Zwarenstein, M., Treweek, S., Gagnier, J. J., Altman, D. G., Tunis, S., Haynes, B., . . . Moher, D. (2008). Improving the reporting of pragmatic trials: An extension of the CONSORT statement. *British Medical Journal*, *337*, 1–8.

Index